Delivery With Grace

Bellevue Maternity Hospital 1931-2001

Don Rittner

**New Netherland Press
Schenectady, NY**

First Edition March 2021

ISBN:9-780937-666579

Front Cover: Elmer and Grace Jorgensen
Back Cover: The Jorgensen family, founders and leaders of Bellevue. Left to right, bottom: Mary Grace Jorgensen, little Pamela, Elmer Jorgensen. Top row: Paul Jorgensen, Grace G. Jorgensen.

Copyright © 2021 Don Rittner
All Rights Reserved

No part of this publication may be reproduced, stored in a retrieval system, or transmitted in any form or by any means, electronic, mechanical, photocopying, recording, or otherwise, without prior written permission.

Dedication

Dedicated to Mary Grace Jorgensen and her daughter Grace Gertrude Jorgensen.

Two women who pioneered the best practices and medical care for expectant mothers.

Table of Contents

Dedication

Acknowledgements - Don Rittner, 1

Acknowledgements - Grace J. Jorgensen MD, 2

Preface: A Total Family Affair, 5

Introduction, 9

Schenectady and Medicine, 11

The Nordlund Family, 11

Bellevue Maternity Hospital Is Born, 14

The Berger Commission, 88

The End of an Era, 102

Appendix

Bellevue's Legal Historic Time Line by Rita Glavin, 107

Biographies of Bellevue Maternity Hospital Personnel, 125

Selected Personnel Affiliated With Bellevue Hospital, 151

Recollections of Dr. George Albright at Bellevue Hospital, by Grace Jorgensen, MD, 154

My Memories of Bellevue by Mary Elena Toms, 206

My Management Style, by Grace Jorgensen, 227

Paul Jorgensen Biography, 229

Dr. J's "Three Moms," 231

Westney, Howard J. "Doc" M.D. 1927-2012, 235

Bellevue Awards and Recognitions, 267

History of Childbirth in New York State, 277

Recruiting, by Grace Jorgensen, 342

Grace Jorgensen Resume, 343

Sources, 347

Index, 349

Acknowledgements

I am most grateful for Dr. Grace Jorgensen (Dr. J.) for letting me compose the history of Bellevue Maternity Hospital. I want to also thank Walter Grattidge, Dr. J.'s partner, for his contributions and in assisting me to all of the documents and records, and to Vicky Bohm who meticulously organized the volumes of documents.

I would also like to thank the following for their contributions: Mary Printsky, Sandforth Roth, Bill Hammond, Dominick Mele, Maria Fort, Doris Lane Wood, Cindy Lucas, Ann Morrow, Rita Glavin and Clarissa and John Westney. I also want to acknowledge the contributions of Elly Czebiniak, my superb administrative assistant, who has served me well over many years.

Don Rittner

Acknowledgements

Grace J. Jorgensen MD

My desire has been to put into print the story of Bellevue Hospital over the years from its founding by my mother in 1931 as an owner-operated facility to its conversion to a not-for-profit institution 70 years later. Many people have contributed in different ways to put together what I hope is a coherent story of what happened at Bellevue over those years. The following are mentioned by name but there are others unnamed for whom I welcomed their help and advice and therefore they deserve a blanket acknowledgement and a sincere 'Thank You.'

First, I acknowledge the patience and scholarship of my co-author. Don has not only unearthed events in Bellevue's story that were out of my experience but also as an historian he has provided a perspective of Bellevue's place in the unfolding remarkable saga of Schenectady's and the Capital District's medical history. He is also the father of three children all born at Bellevue, so he has experienced the family nature of the Bellevue environment during this period. Thank you Don.

Second, I want to acknowledge the contributions of my late husband, Howard. We met and married during our years at New York Medical College and though his upbringing had centered round

Philadelphia and Atlantic City, he took his residency in the Capital District and as a General Practice Physician established his own private practice in Latham, N.Y., and was a member of the medical staff of Bellevue. He provided great advice to me on many professional aspects of my position as medical director and was especially helpful in the design of the 1971 facility extension. Together with our children, Diana, Clarissa and John, we enjoyed a wholesome family life. Here I want to acknowledge my gratitude to them. Growing up, they had a worms-eye view of the goings-on at the Hospital and I'm happy to say that both Clarissa and John, after their respective professional educations, both became members of the professional staff of the hospital. Also, I acknowledge the contributions of my late brother Paul, who was a part of the business management side of Bellevue for many years.

Further, I acknowledge with gratitude the contributions made to this project by my current partner, Walter Grattidge. He has managed to provide coherency and logic to my mouldering memories of events long past, especially since my stroke of 2013 has left me with memory problems. There are several other persons I would like to thank for their contributions and advice to this project. To Rita Glavin and her late husband James, who were Bellevue's lawyers over the years. To the late Sanford Roth, who was the Financial Officer for Bellevue and who was particularly helpful in the period of transition to a not-for-profit institution. To Vicky Bohm, an archivist whose sharp intellect and strong organizing ability has managed to create order out of the chaotic sets of documents held in the family's personal private archives. Unfortunately, the formal hospital records and papers created over the 1931 to 2001 period of private ownership were apparently not considered important and were destroyed during the not-for-profit period. I also offer special thanks to Mary Printsky, whose commitment to Bellevue for over 50 years is well known, and who has been especially helpful in her remembrance of the nursing and professional staff during her tenure. Finally, I gratefully acknowledge Leanne Sackett Levine, whose friendship, advice and counsel over the years, greatly assisted me in a strong supporting role.

Preface

A Total Family Affair

The commitment to operating Bellevue Hospital as a total family affair has been present since its very beginning. At the Bradt St. location, the patients occupied three rooms on the ground floor and the family of Mary Grace, husband Elmer, and children Grace and Paul, resided on the second floor. At that time, patients stayed for 10 days and Mary Grace took great pains to ensure that mothers had a family type stay. The year 1931 was a time of economic depression and jobs were scarce. The women members of the Jorgensen extended family were on hand to help with the patient care and the necessary babysitting. Several of the Jorgensen men were entertainers, primarily accordion players, and active in the Danish Men's club and so at the weekend, the extended family would gather at Bradt St. for fellowship and amusement. With the move to Union St., the family moved to be next door to the hospital facility. However the family support continued, though by then the patient load required the employment of nurses and kitchen and cleaning staff beyond the extended family.

From the beginning, Mary Grace was the owner and chief care-giver, with her husband Elmer as the business manager and principal chef. In those early days Elmer oversaw the food supplies and sought out local farmers to supply fresh meat and eggs.

With the move to the mansion in 1942, things were on a much larger scale and professionals such as bookkeepers and others were hired. However, the concept of the institution as a family affair continued and with Mary Grace's passing in 1959, Dr. Grace J. Jorgensen and her children, became owners with Dr. Grace owning 51 percent of the shares.

In the cases of the many awards which were received over the years, many in her name, Dr. J was always certain to be sure that all members knew that it was the hospital as a whole that was being honored. Accordingly, there were hospital-wide celebrations held at least twice a year at which time awards were highlighted and appropriate personnel recognized, especially those with long service.

The hospital expansion of the early 1970's also involved the family. Dr. J's husband Dr. Howard Westney played a central part in the design of the building and selecting the appropriate equipment essential in each part of the facility. Others, not part of the family, certainly helped, particularly with the interior decoration of the patient related spaces, and the physicians and nurses and other professionals gave their input too. The ideas for the design started in the mid-1960's and the financing was a potential major hurdle.

The proposed financing of the expansion, some $3 million was quite an undertaking. Ed Curren, an executive with the Mohawk Carpet Company in

Amsterdam, and a loyal volunteer supporter of Bellevue, helped considerably in lining up a Troy bank, The Marine Midland, to provide the financing. Mr. Jean Rowley was Chairman of the bank's directors and he was so impressed with Dr. J and the project that he enlisted her as the first female member of the bank's Board of Directors. Her service continued when the bank was taken over by HSBC. Dr. J was the sole health representative on the board and served many years.

In 1970, during the construction phase, President Nixon signed an executive order freezing wages and prices, which prevented the start of construction on the extension. Dr. J and Rita and Jim Glavin and several others travelled to Washington to plead their case for construction to proceed. Luckily, the person responsible to provide the waiver was a Mr. Moses whose acquaintance they had made at several of the Federation of American Hospital's conferences. Bellevue was a founding member of the FAH.

Son John in 1983 graduated from Dartmouth College with a BA degree in Science, Languages, Business and Economics and joined the management staff at Bellevue. From 1983 to 2001, he served in several different roles including Information Systems and Facilities Management to support the direction of the business. He was a principal of the organization, a board member, and served as Board Chairman. Daughter Clarissa in 1987 graduated from New York Medical College as an Obstetrics and Gynecology physician and following her residency at Albany Medical Center, she joined the family practice, Women's Health Care Plus, and also became a member of the Bellevue staff.

The 1970's, 80's and 90's were the golden years for Bellevue. Its reputation became known nation-wide. It attracted highly competent staff and it expanded its services, forming a Research Foundation, particularly to pursue issues connected with in-vitro fertilization and later STD's and then HIV. With the parallel increasing influence of health insurance organizations and government programs such as Medicaid, the economic pressure on owner-operated hospitals increased severely. Local real-estate taxes became a non-competitive burden and so in 2000 steps were taken to convert Bellevue into a not-for–profit hospital. This formally occurred in 2001, and so the family ownership and management ended after 70 years. During the following five years, New York State Governor George Pataki formed the Berger Commission to investigate and analyze the condition of hospitals in the state.

Introduction

It was more than 25 years ago that I first experienced the professionalism of Dr. Grace G. Jorgensen and her staff. I was in the delivery room of Bellevue Hospital with my wife Nancy when Dr. Jorgensen delivered each of our three sons between 1991 and 1997. The care my wife received was exceptional as was the care given by every member of the staff. When Dr. J. (as she is affectionately known) asked me if I wanted to write the hospital's history, I had no reservations about bringing the story of this woman-owned institution to light for the general public.

Bellevue Hospital began in 1931 in a former church rectory in the Bellevue section of Schenectady. Mary Grace Jorgensen, a registered nurse, had given birth to her daughter Grace on a kitchen table and realized there had to be a better way for babies to be delivered. Three years later, Mary Grace and her husband Elmer, a former General Electric employee, opened Bellevue Maternity Home and made history. Throughout the book you will see how this unique institution made major advances in women's care with women at the helm throughout its history.

The success of Bellevue saw it expand several times not only as a hospital but as a research institution working on the problems associated with prenatal care and women's health and leading the way in several areas. The "Stork Club," as it was called, became the envy of many local medical institutions. Just as remarkable as the hospital's founding by a woman is that it was continually managed by a woman during its entire existence from 1931 until 2001 when Bellevue Woman's Medical Center, Inc. became non-proft and was forced to merge with Ellis hospital in 2007.

The Jorgensen-Westney family had an extraordinary ability to hire the best and brightest to be part of the Bellevue family. You could feel it in the hospital's home-like rooms and halls, and a picture of founder Mary Grace hung in the lobby to remind everyone that the sole purpose of its existence was to provide the best care possible for expectant mothers.

In 2020, actress Vanessa Kirby was watching a live birth during the filming of "Pieces of Woman," remarked that she *"saw the power and the fear in all of it. I came away…appreciating the sacredness of the feminine."* This book is about that sacredness of the feminine!

Bellevue is also an important part of the history of medicine in New York and in particular Schenectady County, the latter area that fostered many women pioneers in medical care for women over the years. The Jorgensen family and Bellevue became the best example of what Mary Grace proclaimed many years ago: *"Do the right thing and do it right."*

    — Don Rittner, Schenectady. March, 2021

Schenectady and Medicine

When Mary Grace Jorgensen started Bellevue Maternity Home in 1931, Schenectady County already had a reputation for innovation in medical care. It was the home to some of the earliest female physicians such as Doctor Elizabeth Gillette (1874-1965), who also became the first upstate women to get elected to the New York State Assembly in 1919. Others such as Janet Murray (1856-1940) and Frances E. Vosburgh (1897-1989) were pioneers in women's care during the early 20th century. Schenectady was also home to Dr. Robert M. Fuller who is considered the inventor of the medicine tablet. He is called "The Father of Tablet Triturates." So it is not surprising that the Jorgensen family would carry on this tradition by creating one of the first hospitals dedicated to women's care in Schenectady.

The Nordlund Family

When 19 year old Swedish-born Andrew Nordlund (1860/61-1930) came to America in 1880 and settled in Randolph, West Virginia, his goal was to work for fellow Swede and General Electric (GE) scientist Ernst Alexanderson in Schenectady, New York. Alexanderson was better known as the father of television and radio. Ironically it was Alexanderson who had come to America wanting to work for the famous "Little Wizard," Charles Steinmetz, the electrical genius.

By 1900 Nordlund was working in West Virginia on a job as an engineer in a saw mill and later machinist in a machine shop in 1910. In 1920 he was a laborer in the railroad shops in Braxton, WV.

Nordlund was no stranger to invention himself having invented a new type of "current motor" which he patented in 1908 while in West Virginia. He described it as *"an improvement in current motors, and is particularly directed to a means whereby the pressure generated by the current will automatically control the operation of the motor."*[1]

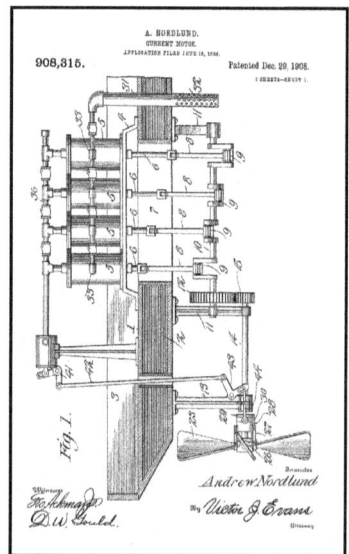 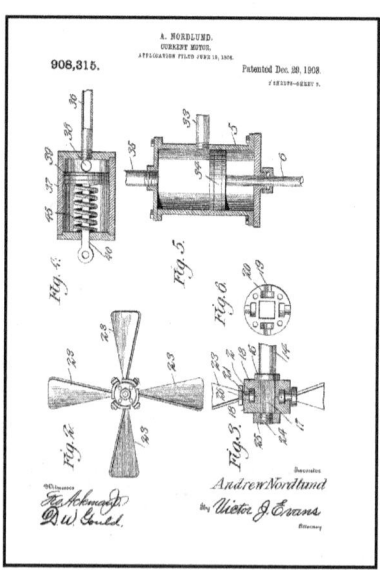

Andrew Nordlund's current motor patent of 1908.

[1] U.S. Patents, No. 908,315. Dec. 29, 1908.

The Jorgensen Farm in West Charlton, NY

While in West Virginia, Andrew met German-born Theresa Wasmer (1871-1948) who arrived in America in 1872 onboard the passenger ship *Thuringia*. They were married in 1892, although the United States Census says 1893, in Lewis, West Virginia. They had eight children: Gertrude (1894-1979), Arthur (1896-1934), Andrew (1896-1969), Anna (1899-1971), Josephine (c 1901-), Mary Grace (c 1904-1959), and Charles (1913-1970). All were born in West Virginia.

By 1925, Andrew and his family moved to a farm on Division St. in West Charlton in Saratoga County, New York. His daughter Mary Grace met Elmer Jorgensen (1903-1984) (see page 226), a General Electric worker and at age twenty-two they married. Grace attended St. Mary's Hospital nursing school in Amsterdam, New York where she graduated in 1926 specializing in obstetrics.

Mary Grace and Elmer then moved to Schenectady, N.Y. After giving birth at home to her daughter Grace Gertrude in August, 1928, on the kitchen table, she decided there had to be a better way for women to have safe births in a more comfortable and home setting. The idea for Bellevue Maternity Home was born. Both decided that personalized quality medical care for delivery was necessary and decided to do something about it.

Bellevue Maternity Home Is Born

Infant mortality during the first half of the 20th century was a subject of great importance to the medical field. According to the Center for Disease Control (CDC), at the beginning of the twentieth century for every 1000 live births some six to nine women in the United States died of pregnancy-related complications, and approximately 100 infants died before the age of one. In 1900, in some US cities, up to 30 percent of infants died before reaching their first birthday. In 1912, the Federal Children's Bureau was formed and became the primary government agency to work toward improving maternal and infant welfare until 1946, when its role in maternal and child health diminished. The bureau was eliminated in 1969.

In 1915, the journal *Medical Review of Reviews* published a report on "Infant Mortality in Maternity Hospitals." It revealed that there was a tendency to increase the number of maternity hospitals in some parts of the United States to offset the alleged pernicious activities of midwives. A study in one New York maternity hospital revealed that of 10,000 consecutive births during the first fourteen days, three percent of living births died. Some 48 percent of the total deaths occurred on the first day. Premature births were responsible for half the deaths and mortality from conditions connected to labor itself constituted twenty percent of the deaths during the first two weeks. While twenty percent of the hospital infant mortally during the first two weeks of life was connected to accidents incident to labor it was suggested that were was plenty of room for improvement in the obstetrical services in order to give safety and comfort under the careful direction of trained obstetricians.[2] While infant mortality varied from the period 1920 from 86 deaths per thousand in 1920 to 46 per thousand in 1931, Schenectady reported the highest infant

---

[2] Review of Reviews. Medical Review of Reviews, Volume 21, No. 4. April, 1915. Page 193.

Birth Rates in Schenectady City Prior to Bellevue*

DATE	SCHENECTADY	TROY	ALBANY
1920	86	102	77
1921	65	93	81
1922	81	116	80
1923	69	100	90
1924	66	92	72
1925	68	98	75
1926	71	79	61
1927	68	86	67
1928	74	70	69
1929	71	55	70
1930	47	65	60
1931	46	86	57

*Infant mortality rates equal number of deaths of infants less than one year per 1000 living births.

mortality rates of the largest cities in the country in 1936 with 145 deaths.[3]

Maternal mortality rates were highest in this century during 1900-1930. Poor obstetric education and delivery practices were the main reason for the high

---

[3] Weekly Heath Index, Dept. of Commerce, Bureau of Census. September 12, 1936, page 2.

numbers of maternal deaths, most of which were preventable.

If a mother did not have access to a maternity hospital during the Depression babies were often delivered at the mother's house in bed or even on the kitchen table. If complications set in, there was a chance that the baby, or mother, or both would not make it. Only forty percent of women in Schenectady birthed at hospitals during this time.

This was the setting in which Mary Grace and Elmer Jorgensen decided to act. Grace had graduated in 1926 from St. Mary's Hospital in Amsterdam, N.Y., and her talents were even recognized there. During her tenure at the hospital a fire broke out and Mary Grace inhaled toxic fumes that caused severe health problems to her lungs for the rest of her life. To recuperate at first, she went down to West Virginia where her family originated, and was mentored by a Dr. Cunningham where she learned about obstetrics.

Upon graduation and moving to Schenectady, Grace had developed a reputation in the Schenectady area as an expert delivery nurse and became a favorite for many area physicians and was often given the most difficult cases to deal with. Her technical knowledge was superb but she combined it with a humanistic approach. Those doctors who worked with her often said that, *"She was a most remarkable woman."*

Delivery With Grace

Elmer with children Grace and Paul.

Mary Grace met with her family doctor William F. Nealon to discuss her plans for a maternity hospital. He later would become president of the Medical Society of the County of Schenectady.

The Jorgensens purchased the old rectory of the Immaculate Conception Catholic Church at 523 Bradt St. (formerly Central St. prior to 1906) in the Bellevue section of Schenectady. Bellevue is French for "beautiful view." In 2010 the church closed for good merging with Our Lady of Assumption and creating a new parish Our Lady, Queen of Peace.

The local newspaper featured a story on the opening day of the new birthing home which the newspaper called Bellevue Maternity Hospital on July 2, 1931.

Delivery With Grace

First Bellevue Maternity Hospital, 523 Bradt St. Mary Grace Jorgensen, founder and daughter Grace G. who would later expand and direct Bellevue into the 21st century.

However the official name that Mary Grace Jorgensen used was Bellevue Maternity Home. The newspaper article went on to write:

The most modern Betz equipment (BetzCo made surgical supplies and medical equipment and was located in Hammond, Indiana-DR) *has been installed and patients will receive the close personal attention of Ms. Jorgensen. The rooms are large, sunny and airy and a home atmosphere prevails through the building. The location at 523 Bradt Street is said to be ideal for sun, air and quiet. A feature of the opening of the Bellevue Maternity Hospital is the offer of a $10 bank account at the Bellevue branch of the Citizens*

Delivery With Grace

First Bellevue Maternity Home, 523 Bradt St. Mary Grace Jorgensen with children Grace G. and Paul.

Delivery With Grace

> # Bellevue Maternity Home
>
> **Non-sectarian**
>
> ## Opening Days
> **THURSDAY, FRIDAY AND SATURDAY**
> **JULY 2nd, 3rd, and 4th.**
>
> Your inspection is invited. Through the courtesy of the Bellevue Business Men's Association the first baby born here, will receive a bank account of $10.00 at the Bellevue Branch, Citizen's Trust Company.
>
> Modern Equipment   Low Rates
>
> ### M. Grace Jorgensen R. N.
> **523 BRADT STREET.**   **DIAL 4-3623**

Newspaper advertisement announcing the opening of Bellevue for the first time.

Trust Company to the first baby born in the home. The offer is made through the courtesy of the Bellevue Business Men's Association, an organization to promote the interests of Bellevue.

Elmer and Mary Grace Jorgensen, founders of Bellevue.

The hospital had six beds with one alcove in the front and expectant mothers stayed ten days. The Jorgensens lived on the first floor. Mary Grace's own doctor William F. Nealon lived around the corner at 2126 Broadway and would be available for any emergency.

Delivery With Grace

Founder Mary Grace Jorgensen with children Grace G. and Paul at original Bellevue Maternity Home.

Delivery With Grace

The hospital located in the former rectory of the Immaculate Conception Catholic Church did not go over well with the pastor of the congregation. In fact Mary Grace was excommunicated from the church because of her falling out with the priest.

The second Bellevue Home at 1567 Union began in 1935.

Delivery With Grace

The male domination in Schenectady in the majority of professions did not approve of women doing these kinds of activities. For the next forty years, Mary Grace and later her daughter Grace G. Jorgensen would have to endure a male dominated profession but successfully overcame those obstacles. Bellevue may well be the only woman-founded and woman-run maternity hospital throughout the United States.

The first year of operation saw 94 babies born and this success forced the Jorgensens to find a larger home. In 1935 they purchased the house at 1567 Union St., the former home of Dr. Edwin J. Faber. The larger house allowed up to 24 patients and with a larger delivery room and waiting room. Fortunately, two other medical doctors lived nearby. Across the Street at 1574 Union St. was Dr. William Jameson who specialized in gynecology but was famous as a missionary once having tea with Mahatma Gandhi. The other was Dr. Clarence F. Ackerknecht at 1410 Union Street. However, even these quarters at Union Street proved too small and once again the Jorgensens needed to move to larger quarters. In 1941, they purchased the estate known as the Stone Mansion, home of General Electric engineer Charles Waterman Stone, just above the Schenectady City line in Niskayuna on Upper Union Street. In 1968, the Schenectady Gazette published an extensive piece about the property:

Delivery With Grace

LAND RECORDS OF HISTORIC NISKAYUNA TRACE OWNERSHIP OF HOSPITAL PROPERTY.

A source of fresh water for early inhabitants of historic Canistahejoene still flows through the hospital. The stream called Canistahejoene, which means stream that joins

A total cost for a delivery and stay at Union St. for mother and baby in 1938 was $72.

Built in 1920 by Charles W. Stone, Stone Mansion became the third and final location of Bellevue when it was purchased by the Jorgensen family in 1942 and adapted into a hospital.

Delivery With Grace

Niskayuna, can be seen under the rustic bridge adjacent to the hospital entrance gates. There it cuts across Rte. 7 through back yards of houses on Hickory Road and eventually joins the Lishakill to empty in the Mohawk River.

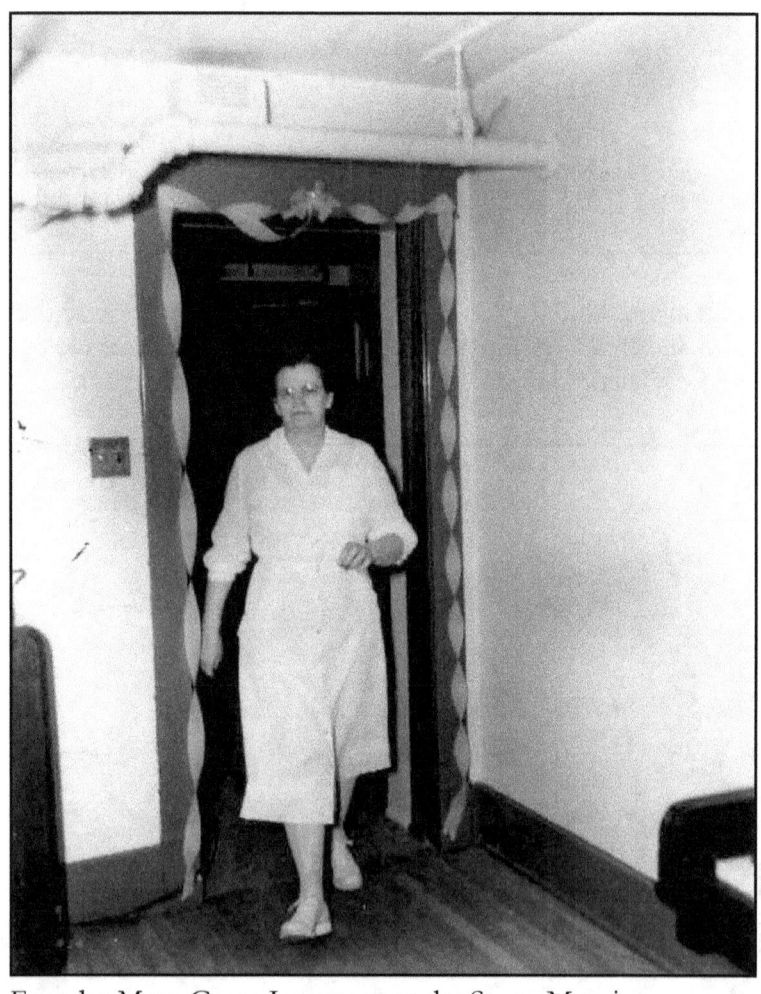

Founder Mary Grace Jorgensen at the Stone Mansion.

Delivery With Grace

Interior of the Stone Mansion.

Interior of the Stone Mansion.

Interior of the Stone Mansion.

Interior of the Stone Mansion.

Stoneridge Road

Stoneridge Road was named for C. W. Stone, an electrical engineer of some note. Son-in-law of John Westinghouse, brother of the late industrialist. Stone himself worked close with Thomas A. Edison in Edison's early Schenectady career and he was also in consulting work with RCA. His most famous scientific

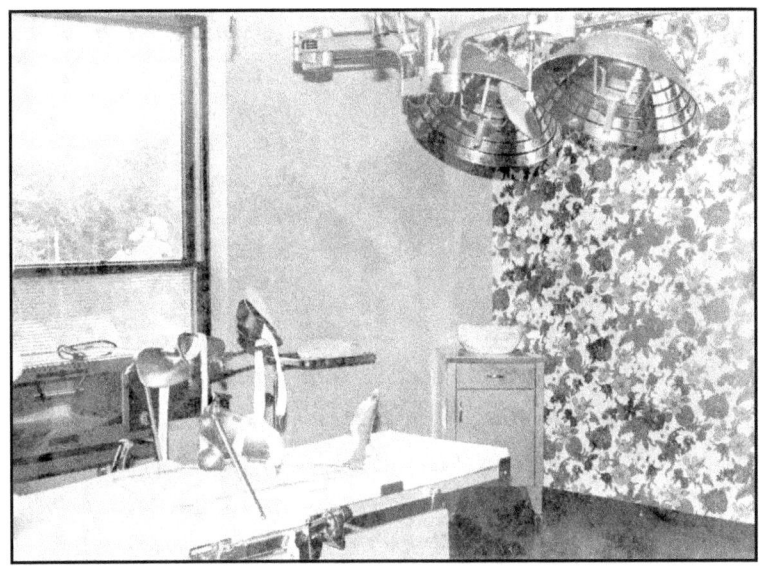

An early delivery room at Bellevue.

credit includes work on the first talkie movies although a number of other credits such as work on DC electric transmission as well. When Stone acquire the property to build a summerhouse in Niskayuna, he bought about 70 acres and developed the property well. The four-story brick building is in present used by Bellevue attests to his imaginative design. Niskayuna property originally ran from St. David's Lane and 1944 Union St (the present first Baptist church old building) where a cousin, George Westinghouse Jones had his home. Jones eventually had acquired the property from the Gebhardt gamily who in turn had purchased from the Clute's. In about 1910 or 1912 Stone negotiated with his cousin by marriage and acquired the total property which ran to the limits of the present estate and parts of Stoneridge Road and included a barn, milk house, a "play house" a water house and cistern, and a servable brown clapboard residence, which was located immediately in front of the present Bellevue building. The house was occupied until about 1920 by the Stone family and at that time was moved to its present location on the corner of Morgan Ave and St David's Lane where it still stands.

Cornerstone Laid

The cornerstone of the present building was laid in 1918 and construction started under the direction of William Mynderse, a local (Scotian) architect and under the direction of Mr. Stone himself whose engineering ideas such as vacuum cleaners built-in to the walls and a superior furnace and electrical system were greatly advanced for that day. Mrs. Stone in the meantime consulted with a gardening expert from New York City and planned imaginative gardens to enhance the buildings Georgian design.

During the winter of 1919 when the house shell and much of the inside was already finished a careless workman's cigarette caused an inside fire, which was discovered from the then-occupied brown house late on a winters night. Since the Troy Road area at that time had no public water or fire hydrants the stream Canistahejoene and the cistern system were the only sources of water, much damage was done before the blaze was brought under control. Consequently rebuilding and occupancy of the house was delayed until the late months of 1920.

Delivery With Grace

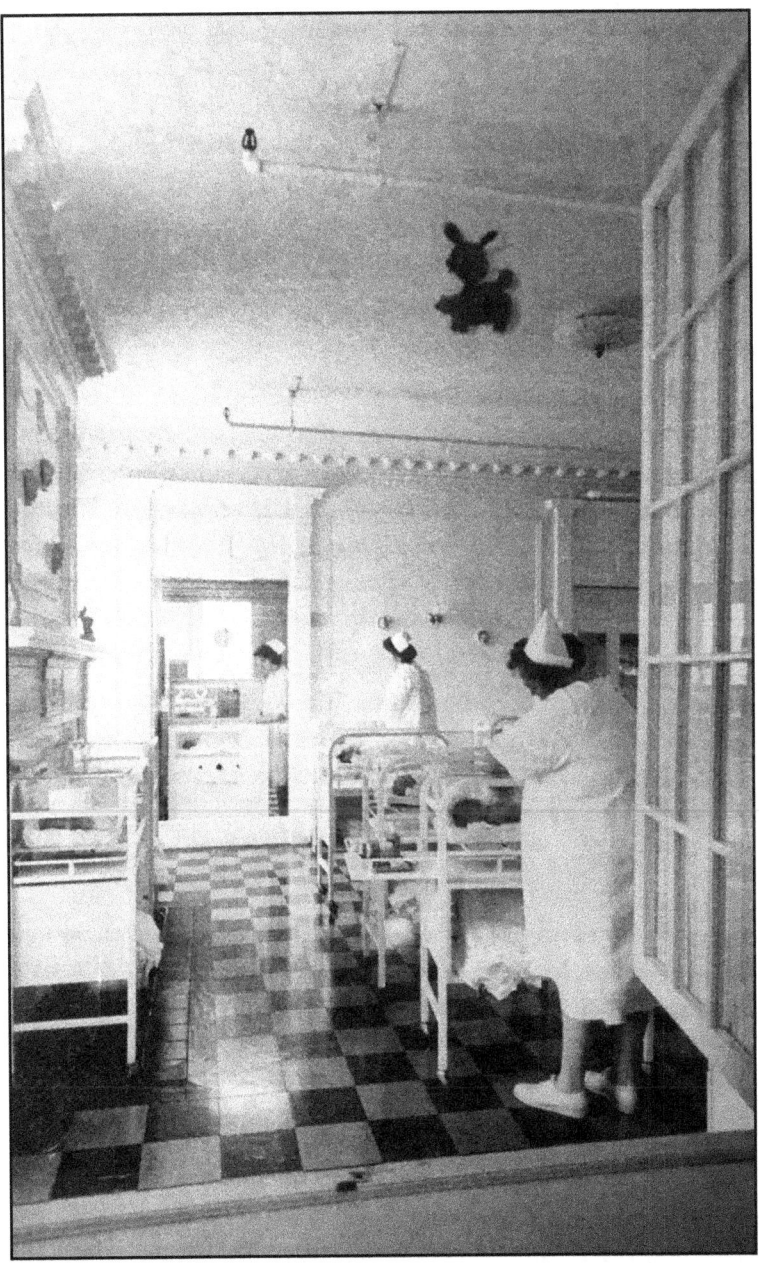

A view of the babies and nurses at Bellevue Maternity in Niskayuna, New York.

Delivery With Grace

The Interior

The interior structure of the building shows a gracious summer residence. A generous foyer and staircase on the first floors are surrounded by auxiliary rooms originally used for dining, studies, solaria, and living area. The second main floor contains generous bedroom, dressing room and bath areas. One of the charming features of the main parts of the house are its beautiful fireplaces and wood paneling. Kitchen facility, including a walk in refrigerators are located on the basement level and two top floors were used as extra bedroom areas. An elevator services all four floors. To the left facing the building is a carriage house and three-stall garage, which are themselves connected by underground tunnel. Steps leading to the former are terraced to depict beautiful garden plantings and stately trees, including white birch, pins and hemlock red maple and tamarack. The original plantings also included elms which

Exterior of the Stone Mansion.

have succumbed largely to blight and several trees were also lost during the Schenectady Tornado a few yeas ago.

Landscaping

On the other side of the building is an orchard, which still contains about a dozen bearing apple and pear trees. It is in this section of the property that Canistahejoene flows and along its banks are planted willow trees. To the back of the house is a formal garden, outlined by a brick wall and a private hedge. The garden — in contrast to being "sunken" — is raised slightly above ground level with steps leading up. In front of the private hedge is a four-foot section traditionally

Aerial view of the Stone Mansion/Bellevue Hospital before expansion in the 70s.

Delivery With Grace

planted in both perennial and annual flowers and carefully tended by the maintenance personnel.

The estate has its own private nursery to replenish winter-killed stock and also maintains storage for perennials bulbs such as gladiola, dahlias, and canna. The nursery as maintained today contains mostly evergreens, but a few deciduous trees are also grown.

Also since the property is now used as a hospital the building itself has fire escapes and other safety devices and an auxiliary generator within the carriage house takes up one entire room space.

The property has two access points leading in from Vrooman Avenue and Stoneridge Road and one on the main entrance driveway. Within the grounds several roads are maintained by the staff who regularly operate two jeeps, two tractors and one truck. Bud Schaible and Joe Ross supervise the maintenance and hold an employee service of about 14 years. During the summer months of 1968 they were assisted by teen agers Paul Jay and Scott Nelson.

The fountain

In front of the building dedicated to the memory of Mrs. M. Grace Jorgensen RN is an Italian marble fountain, giving the dates of her life, 1904-1959 and the words Humility Courage, Strength, Integrity and a simple inscription: Love, Her greatest Gift. The fountain was erected in 1960 and a lithograph of its outline has become the hospital symbol.

Delivery With Grace

Mrs. Jorgensen acquired the property, then reduced to 12 acres, in 1942 from the Stone family heirs following Mr. Stone's death in 1939. Several pieces of original furnishing were left in the present foyer and waiting room. One of these is a hand crave Walnut marble topped table now situated in the left foyer entrance the original sterling silver chandelier above the reception desk; and in the waiting room a hand carve coat rack and study sofa."

Charles Waterman Stone or C. W. Stone was born in 1874 and died on February 3, 1938. He was married to Harriet Anna Westinghouse, daughter of John Westinghouse and sister to the famed inventor George Westinghouse, Jr.

Stone was famous as an American engineer working for General Electric alongside of Charles Steinmetz and Alfred Hull. He later became president of the Pioneer Thresher Company, the former Westinghouse Threshing Company.

According to the 1984 book *Technological History of Motion Pictures and Television: An Anthology from the Pages of "The Journal of the Society of Motion Pictures and Television Engineers,"* by Raymond Fielding, Stone's work at General Electric was important:

In addition to L. T. Robinson, head of the General Engineering Laboratory, the man who played the major role in initiating and promoting a large scale project for developing talking pictures was C. W. Stone, manager of the Central

Delivery With Grace

Station Dept., who had taken great interest in all of the sound developments. His enthusiasm, confidence and influence encouraged those who were engaged in development, helped to secure the financial backing and established fruitful contacts outside the company.

Stone purchased the 70-acre Niskayuna parcel to build a summer home. There was a brown clapboard house on the property which he had moved to the corner of St. David's Lane and Morgan Avenue which still exists today. Stone began constructing his mansion in 1918 under the direction of Scotia architect William Mynderse. He introduced into the house a wall built vacuum cleaner system and furnace and electrical systems superior to others. A fire caused by a careless workman set back completion until 1920.

The first floor contained a spacious foyer and winding staircase surrounded by a large living and dining room, study area and solaria. Paneling was used along with beautiful fire places. The second floor was occupied by bedrooms, dressing room and bathrooms. The top two floors were used as extra sleeping rooms. The kitchen included a walk-in refrigerator and was located in the basement. There was a small elevator that went to all floors. Items which remained in the mansion included a hand carved coat rack (a tree climbed by small bears), a silver chandelier and hand-carved walnut table.

Stone also built a three-stall garage at the back and side of the mansion and connected by an underground tunnel. There was an orchard of apple and pear trees and weeping willows were next to the stream that flowed through the property. A formal garden was in the back of the house.

Stone worked closely with Thomas A. Edison and was a consultant for the RCA Company. He is credited with early work on the first "talkie" movies as well as DC electrical transmission.

After his death in 1939 the land surrounding the property was reduced in size. In 1942 the Jorgensens purchased eight acres and the house, and the "Stork Club," the name affectionately given to Bellevue, would now expand.

The mansion was retrofitted to serve as a maternity hospital. The first floor was the business office, waiting area and rooms for patients and a nursery. The second floor was patient rooms. The third floor contained the labor rooms, a small operating and recovery room. There was also a small elevator of 40 x 44 inches that was used to bring patients to the delivery room. Elmer Jorgensen constructed a special gurney to fit the elevator for the patients. Special stretchers were designed by Elmer Jorgensen to accommodate expecting mothers that allowed the foot section to drop so that mothers-to-be could

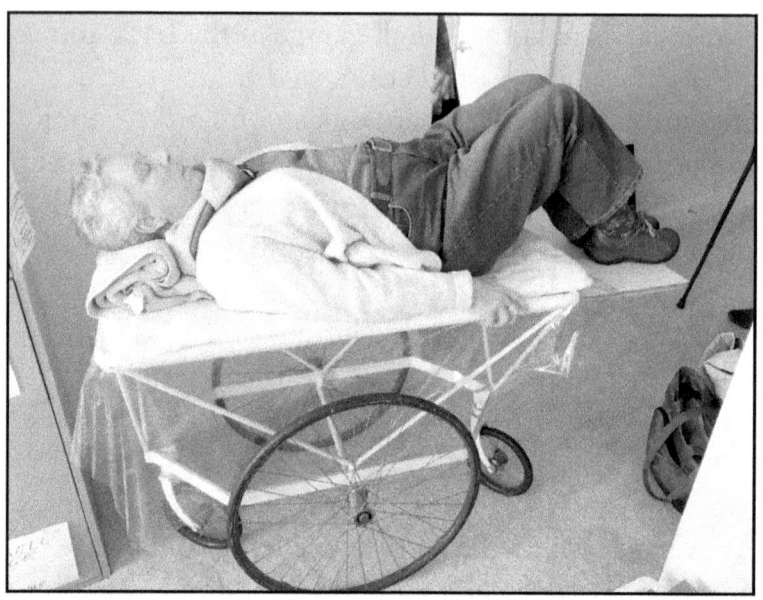

Special gurney invented by Elmer Jorgensen so that patients could fit in the small elevator. Demonstrated here by retired Bellevue nurse Mary Printsky.

hold their legs up. In addition the basement was made into the kitchen and nursery.

The first year of operations saw 896 babies born at the hospital. It earned the nickname, "The Stork Club." In all of Schenectady that same year there were 1,679 births. Breakfast was served fresh to Bellevue's patients by

Delivery With Grace

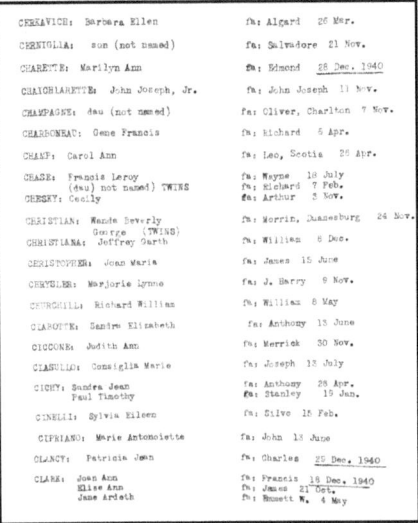

Before there were computers, all births were indexed the old fashion way — with a typewriter. A sample of births in 1941.

Elmer Jorgensen who took control of the kitchen, even squeezing oranges for fresh juice. Much of the food served was grown right on the grounds.

Shortly before opening the Mansion, Bellevue became a member of the American Hospital Association in 1941. The American Hospital Association (AHA) is the national organization that represents and serves all types of hospitals, health care networks, and their patients and communities. Today nearly 5,000 hospitals, health care systems, networks, other providers of care and 43,000 individual members form the AHA.

In 1943 ten babies were born on New Year's Day in area hospitals. Bellevue was the first in that year's "Stork Derby" contest delivering a baby girl to Mrs. Joseph Siska at 12:10 AM. Runner up was also born at Bellevue with a baby girl to Mr. and Mrs. Robert Rowe at 12:52 AM. In those days the local newspapers took great pride in announcing the first baby born on New Year's Day.

Delivery With Grace

Tragedy struck one of the hospital's pivotal mentors, Dr. Ackerknecht in 1945 during World War II. A blood drive was started by the nurses at Bellevue in honor of PFC William C. Ackerknecht, son of Dr. and Mrs. Clarence F. Ackerknecht who was killed in action in Germany in December. The Bellevue nurses also held a blood drive on February 8 in honor of PFC John McBride, Jr., who was killed in action in Luxembourg in January. It was initiated by fellow employees of GE Publicity Division Association. He was the first member of the publicity group to give his life in the war. He was overseas for only two months before being killed.

In 1946 the hospital created a new "Pacing Room" for fathers of newborns. The room was part of a $20,000 addition to the hospital. It also included a private room, the pacing or waiting room, and a new nursery. A public address

> **Two Babies Claim 1947's 'First' Title**
>
> ALBANY —(AP)— A Schenectady boy and a New York City girl appeared today to be leading contenders for the title of the first baby born in the United States in 1947.
>
> Bellevue **Maternity** Home near Schenectady said delivery of Robert Meers, son of Mr. and Mrs. Willam Meers, started at one second after midnight. He cried his arrival when the year was 10 seconds old.
>
> In New York City, Marie Antoinette, daughter of Mr. and Mrs. Victor Agostina, made her appearance at one second after the stroke of 12, Parkchester General Hospital reported.
>
> Mr. and Mrs. Raymond Weatherby, Buffalo, are the parents of a daughter born at 12:01 a.m. New Year's Day at Louise De Marillac Hospital, Buffalo.

Delivery With Grace

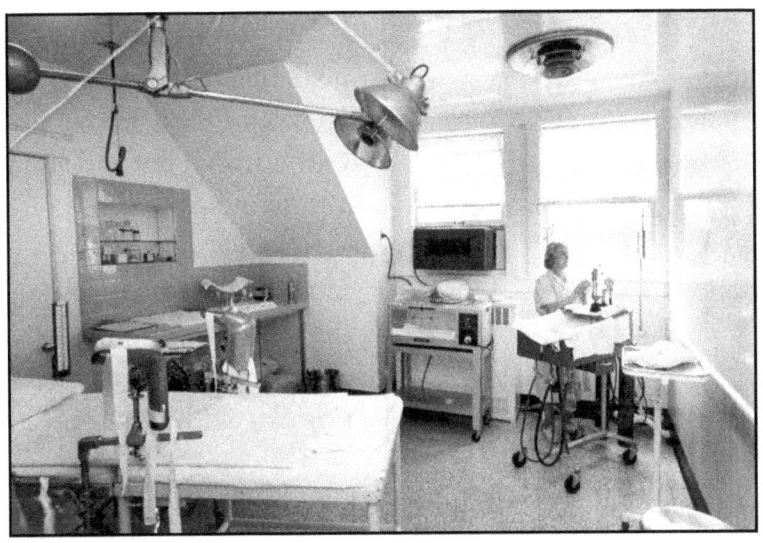

Early delivery room at Bellevue. Lena Ott standing.

system was also included to keep fathers and other interested people informed of the progress and delivery of newborns. The founder, Mary Grace Jorgensen was quoted as saying: *"We feel that the babies and their fathers deserve consideration along with the mothers."* She also added: *"...and we have tried to give Schenectady parents and their babies every possible service."*

In 1953, a few years after moving to the mansion, an in-house laboratory was created to provide a wide range of services including out-patient services such as prenatal testing and birth monitoring which improved the health of the patients and babies. With this expansion came new doctors and staff. This included the founder's daughter physicians Grace G. Jorgensen Westney and her husband Howard Westney.

Delivery With Grace

Dr. Virginia Apgar (1909-1974) was a pioneer in women's care. She introduced the use of the epidural to Dr. Grace G. Jorgensen.

Grace G. became the resident physician in 1955 and the following year studied under Dr. Virginia Apgar at Columbia who introduced the use of the caudal/epidural anesthesia that became popular with patients.

Dr. Apgar was appointed the first woman full professor at Columbia University College of Physicians and Surgeons in 1949. Apgar designed and introduced the Apgar Score, the first standardized method for evaluating a newborn's transition to life outside the womb. This score consisted of five points—heart rate, respiratory effort, muscle tone, reflex response, and color—

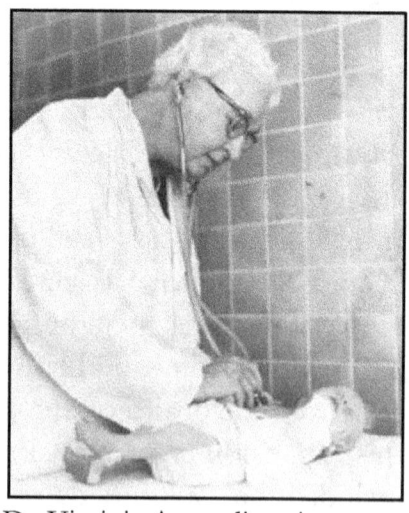

Dr. Virginia Apgar listening to a baby's heartbeat in 1966. Photo Library of Congress.

Only freshly prepared foods were served to patients and often from food grown right on the premises. Left to right: Kay Venier, Louise Borghart, Rita Venier.

Patients relaxing outside on the patio at Bellevue. Nurse Henriett Ostrander standing.

are observed and given 0, 1, or 2 points. The points are then totaled to arrive at the baby's score. The

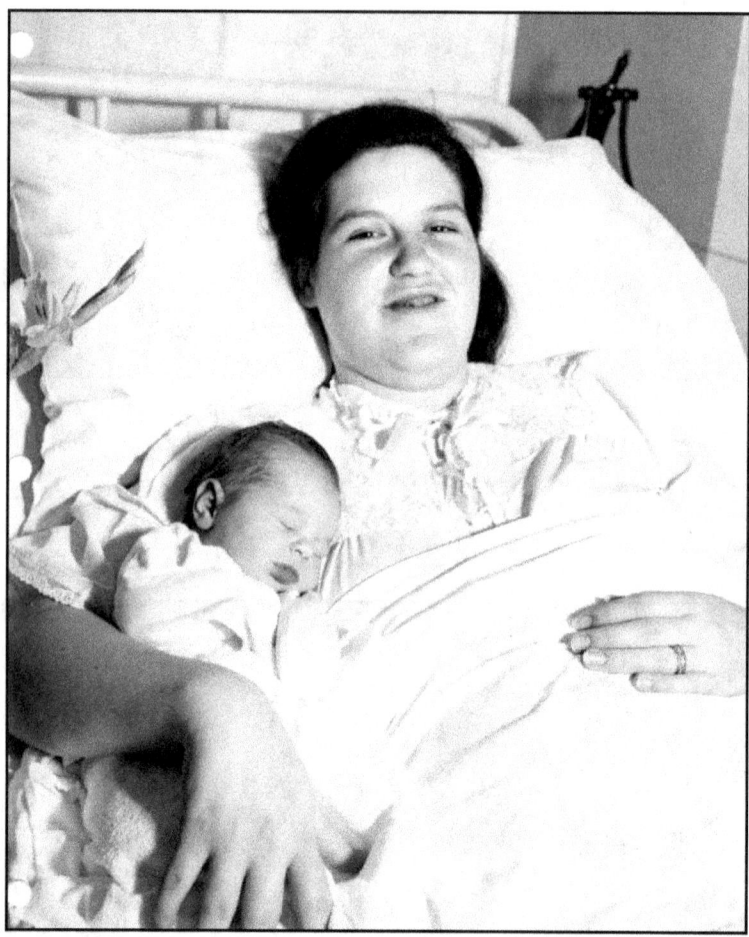

General Electric Company began giving stocks to all babies born on January 15, 1953, to parents who were GE employees as part of their 75th anniversary. Little Lynn Ann Morrissey became the first in the Capital District to receive five shares. She was born at Bellevue to Mr. and Mrs. James Morrissey who were from Rotterdam Junction. He was a drill operator with GE beginning in 1951. Mrs. Morrissey worked at GE as a file clerk.

Delivery With Grace

score was presented in 1952 at a scientific meeting, and first published in 1953. The Apgar Score is now used around the world to assess new borns.

The head of the laboratory at Bellevue was Aram A. Atashian (1924-1991). One of Atashian's major contributions to Bellevue and the community was bringing Rhogam to the region in the mid 1960s. Rhogam was an intramuscular injection, manufactured by Ortho Pharmaceuticals given to Rh negative mothers for the prevention of Rh disease in the newborn. Aram worked with representatives from Ortho's Pharmaceuticals and diagnostic divisions to bring Rhogam to the area. He set up a program at the Mohawk Golf Club to present the product to the OB/GYN physicians in the region to explain how Rhogam worked and also the testing that would need to be done to determine if a patient should be a candidate for the injection. The results of this

Dr. J. and Geronimo, a St. Bernard, that was truly one of the first "service" dogs at a hospital.

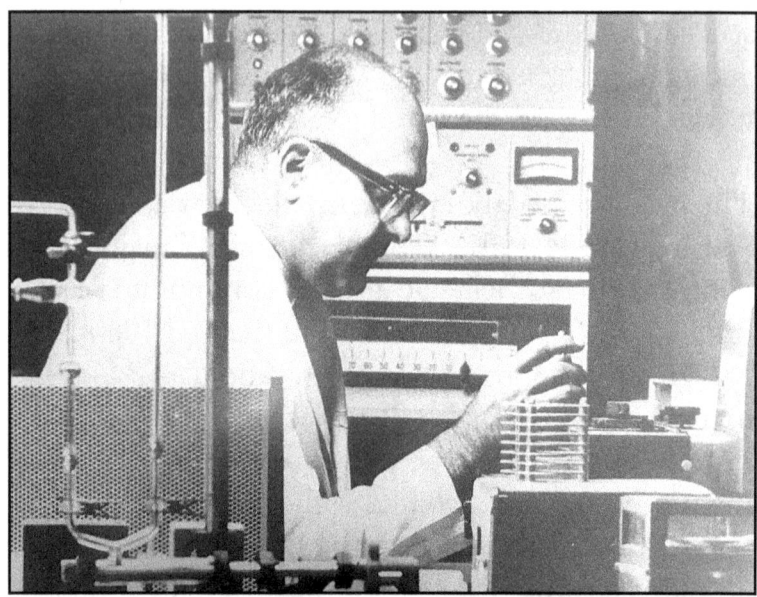

Aram Atashian, Director of the Laboratory.

Aram Atashian working in the Laboratory.

product have greatly reduced the trauma and mortality associated with Rh disease even protecting the baby before birth. In addition, Aram embraced new technology for the laboratory as it became available. Examples were modeler Hematology and Chemistry analyzers, also being the first laboratory in the area utilizing less tedious and more accurate procedures in testing for chlamydia and gonorrhea. X-Ray and radiology departments were also established at this time.

Mary Grace Jorgensen sharing a laugh with George Bernhart, a talented craftsman who made special furniture.

Later, the lab director's son Aram A. Atashian, Jr., a medical technologist also worked at the lab. He graduated from Trinity College with a BS in Biology in 1969 and became a full-time medical technologist at the hospital upon graduation. He started working there in a part-time capacity in 1962. He completed a certification course in General Medical Bacteriology at the Center of Disease Control in Atlanta, Georgia,

Model Joan Romano gave birth to a baby boy in 1954 at Bellevue. Source Pinterest.com

Delivery With Grace

in 1972. He moved on to head a veterinary laboratory.

In 1954, the $35,000 a year ($50 an hour) New York photographer's model Joan Romano gave birth to a baby boy at Bellevue but gave up the baby to an adoption service. Two years later she sued to recover the baby and it made headlines.

Romano was a secretary at the Schenectady Army Depot in 1954 when she met Donald McGaffin a Schenectady newspaperman and became pregnant. They were married in Troy, N.Y. on May 23, 1954, (and divorced in January 1956). She was 21 years old when she married McGaffin with the understanding that the baby would be given up when born.

She was working her way to becoming a fashion model and gave up the child then four-days old, to an Albany adoption agency. The baby was given to the agency on November 12, 1954, and it was adopted on November 9, 1955. Romano had said she was coerced into signing the baby away. However, she lost the case finally in 1957 and never saw the child again.

Romano went on to grace the pages and covers of many high fashion magazines in the country. At 21 she was called high fashion's "tall hipless and sophisticated" and was featured by the likes of Clifford Coffin (*Vogue*), Horst B. Horst (*Vogue*),

Delivery With Grace

Dick Rutledge (*Vogue, Glamour,* and *House & Garden*), Joseph Leombruno & Jack Bodi (*Vogue*)

Dr. Grace G. Jorgensen, daughter of the founder, became resident physician in 1955 and took over the leadership of the hospital upon the death of her mother in 1959.

Delivery With Grace

and Tom Palumbo (*Vogue, Harper's Bazaar*).

On May 10, 1959, Mary Grace Norlund Jorgensen founder of Bellevue died at her home. Her daughter Grace G. and her son Paul R. Jorgensen took over the administration of the hospital. Funeral services were held on May 12 and Dr. Clarence F. Ackerknecht, former president of the Schenectady County Medical Society and long time friend said of her:

"She demonstrated her sincerity and devotion to her work in the care of young mothers and their babies and devoted her whole life to supplying them with the best facilities available. The present hospital is a monument to the hard work and devotion Mrs. Jorgensen gave throughout her life. She will long be remembered by the thousands of women who have come under her loving care."

The medical staff of Bellevue announced the establishment of a scholarship fund in the memory of Mrs. Jorgensen to provide financial aid to a deserving girl to help defray expenses in obtaining nurses training. The scholarship at Russell Sage continues to this day.

M. GRACE JORGENSEN NURSING ACHIEVEMENT AWARD & THE BELLEVUE HOSPITAL NURSING ACHIEVEMENT AWARD.

To two third-year Russell Sage students majoring in nursing who display academic and personal excellence, who

Delivery With Grace

Russell Sage College offers the M. Grace Jorgensen Nursing Achievement Award and the Bellevue Hospital Nursing Achievement Award to two third-year Sage students majoring in nursing who display academic and personal excellence, who demonstrate interest in women's health, who show promise of making significant contributions to the health-related professions, and who show interest in working in cooperation with others rather than in competition with others. The awards are given to RSC students by Dr. Grace G. Jorgensen (daughter of founder) seated in the middle and continues each year. The 2017 winners were Caitlin Owoo (left) and Kaleigh Kennedy (right).

Delivery With Grace

The Fountain dedicated to the memory of Mary Grace Jorgensen was set up in 1961.

demonstrate interest in women's health, who show promise of making significant contributions to the health-related professions and who show interest in working in cooperation with others rather than in competition with others. These two awards are given by Dr. Jorgensen (Mary Grace Jorgensen's daughter) and need to be applied for by the students. The award applications are available in February for students who have completed NSG 323 the previous fall semester or are in NSG 323 in the spring semester. An essay is required that addresses women's health issues. Each award is substantial and applications and essays are screened by faculty.

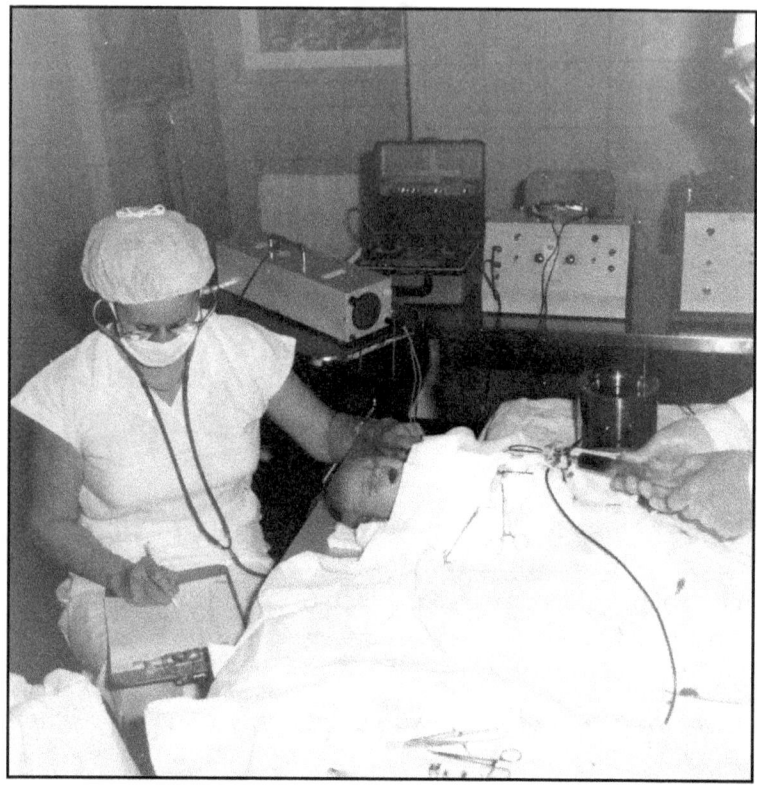

Checking the vitals on a newborn.

In 1961, to celebrate the 30th anniversary of the founding of the hospital an Italian marble fountain at the building's entrance was erected to commemorate. Included was a sculpture of a small joyful child inscribed with the hospital founder's name, M. Grace Nordlund Jorgensen, the dates of her life, 1904-1959 and the inscription: *"Humility, Courage, Strength: Love, Her Greatest Gift."* This became the official symbol of the hospital.

Delivery With Grace

In 1962, Albert Dettbarn, a building and grounds employee, was approached by Aram Atashian and was asked if he had an interest in learning about the operation of the pathology laboratory that Atashian directed. Mr. Dettbarn saw this as an opportunity to advance himself and enrolled in online training

Portrait of founder Mary Grace Jorgensen painted by Rachel MacDonald of Galway in 1966 and hung in the mansion.

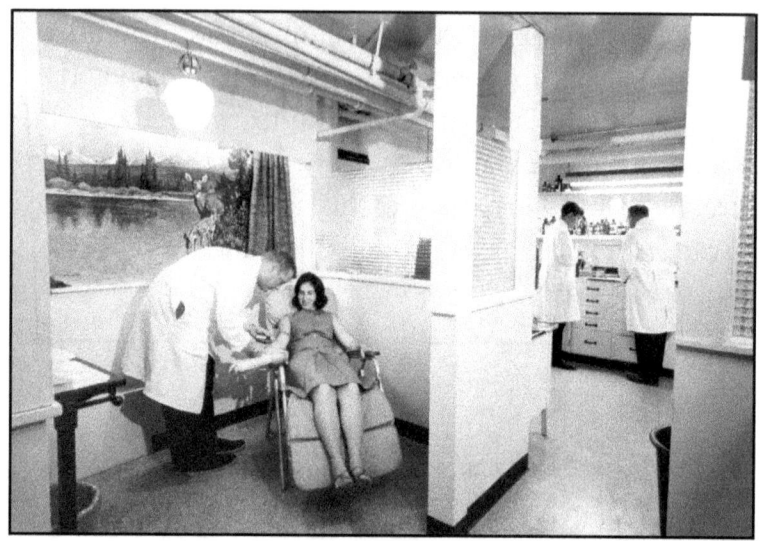

Aram Atashian prenatal testing a patient. It was one of many services offered at Bellevue.

courses from Centers for Disease Control and Prevention (CDC) and also pursued classes at Russell Sage College and Hudson Valley Community College, both in Troy, New York, to learn the fundamentals of working in a hospital pathology laboratory. In 1965, Mr. Dettbarn became licensed by the State of New York as a Medical Laboratory Technician. In 1971, based on his performance and acquired knowledge in the hospital's lab, he was appointed as Lab Supervisor and in 1982 he was promoted as the Administrative Manager of Bellevue Pathology Laboratory under director Aram Atashian, his mentor. Mr. Dettbarn left Bellevue in 2003. This was a prime example of what Bellevue Hospital stood for: training, educating, and

Delivery With Grace

Dr. Grace G. Jorgensen, seen here around 1930, would follow her mother in directing Bellevue. Her grandmother belonged to a quilting club in Galway and they always were talking about women's suffragette issues, instilling a sense of strong female roles into Grace's consciousness which prepared her for taking over Bellevue when her mother passed.

promoting good and loyal employees from within the hospital.

Beginning on October 27, 1966, Bellevue conducted a weeklong celebration of its 35th anniversary by presenting a $50 US savings bond to the first

"Goldie." Katherine (Katie) Gold.

Delivery With Grace

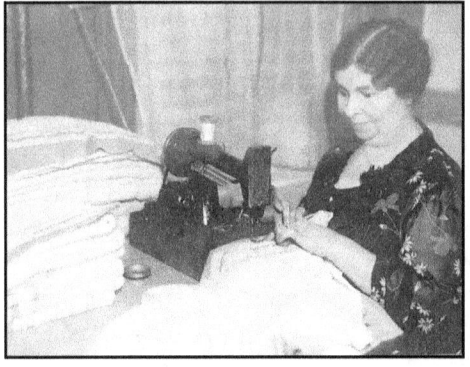 

Dr. Grace G. Jorgensen's grandmother, seen here sewing, belonged to a quilting club in Galway where discussions about women's suffragette issues was a common event, instilling a sense of strong female roles into Grace's consciousness.

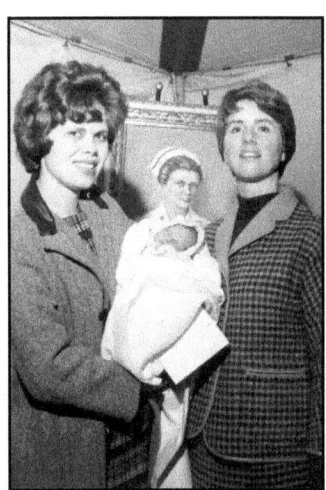

A proud mother and her new infant with Dr. J. on the right with the portrait of her mother in the background.

baby born at Bellevue after noon time on Monday (Oct 31). Having first babies on New Year's Day was common at Bellevue. First arrival contests began in area hospitals beginning in 1936 and from 1949 to 1966. During the 31 years since 1936 a mother at Bellevue was the winner except for four years. There was a celebration of the first baby born to Mrs. Stephen Urban, and a portrait of the founder painted by Rachel MacDonald of Galway was

Delivery With Grace

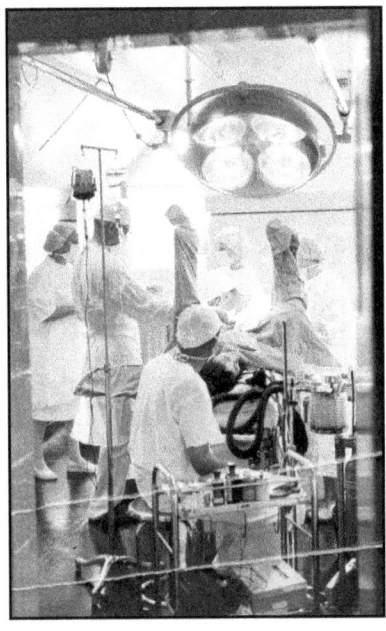

A delivery scene at Bellevue.

hung at the mansion. Ten years later, a memorial service was held in the founder's name and to honor the hospital that she, at only 26 years old, and her husband Elmer founded as the only one of its kind in 13 counties in New York State.

That same year, 1966, Bellevue opened a sterility-fertility division. The division was created to do basic research on the causes of sterility and fertility and the implications on the woman who has had difficulties in conceiving and maintaining pregnancy. At the same time Bellevue became one of the first institutions to use the gas chromatographs for routine clinical studies on pregnancy in the Northeastern United States. It made it possible to identify minute substances by physical methods, providing the ability to measure parts per billion in substance measurements, something not possible before.

Costs continued to rise for hospitals throughout the area. Hospital rates for Medicaid in New York in

Delivery With Grace

1967 increased significantly. Bellevue's rate with 37 beds was $36.85, a 25.7% increase.

On June 22, 1968, long time employee Katherine (Katie) Gold retired. She was the delivery room supervisor for Bellevue who directed, or participated in delivery of an estimated 24,000 babies. A nurse since 1942, "Goldie" was honored by the staff at a reception in her honor. Dr. J presented her with a certificate and employees gave her a gift. Some 200 guests attended including Dr. C.F. Ackerknecht, who was Miss Gold's employer over 35 years ago, and her mentor for a nursing career. Katie was appointed delivery room supervisor in May 1947 by the late Mrs. Mary Grace Jorgensen, then head of Bellevue. Since 1943 she was a resident nurse living on the hospital grounds in order to be available in all

Priority one was taking care of the newborns and mothers at Bellevue.

emergency situations. She was a native of Nurnberg, Germany, and came to the United States in 1931 and lived with the Ackerknecht family for five years. She went to the former Nott Terrace High school and took classes in English and became a naturalized citizen.

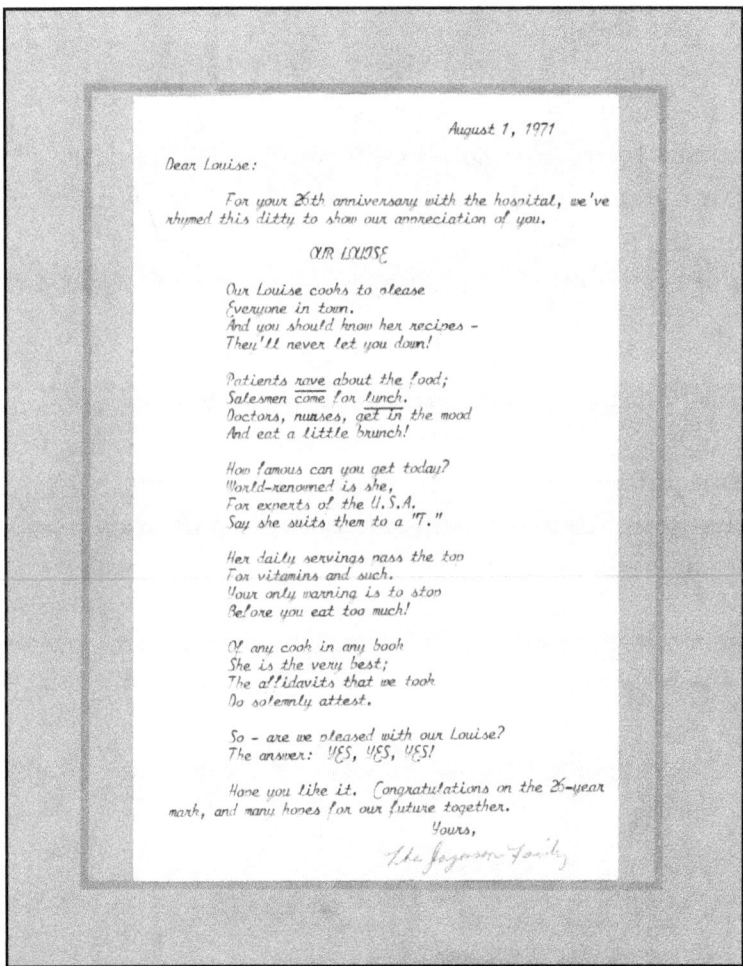

Bellevue often recognized its long-term employees. Shown here a poem written by the Jorgensens for one of their cooks who was celebrating 26 years with the hospital.

Delivery With Grace

The Ackerknechts encouraged her to become a nurse with their financial help. She became a special nurse going home with mothers who had new babies to care for them. When Bellevue expanded for the third time, Ackerknecht suggested she work there. When the hospital moved in April 1942 to Niskayuna she accepted a two month job as a nurse. She said, *"The job became my life."* The late Mrs. Jorgensen assigned her duties leading to the supervisor role of from 7 to 10 persons from 1947 on. She moved back to Germany upon retirement. During this year, 1968, 1418 babies were born at Bellevue with an estimated total 45,000 babies born up to that date.

On November 4, 1968, Dr. Ira S. Fink was appointed chief anesthesiologist at Bellevue. A native of New York City he had held staff appointments in anesthesia in Virginia and in Memphis, Louisville and St. Petersburg, Florida, and St Clare's in Schenectady.

Albany Memorial Hospital in the 1950s.

Delivery With Grace

In 1969, Memorial Hospital in Albany closed its maternity services and Bellevue allowed the student nurses from Memorial to train in obstetrics for two months. An 8-week maternity nursing class program in maternal and newborn nursing for second year students of Memorial Hospital was conducted as a joint endeavor between the nursing school and Bellevue. At this time over 1400 babies were born annually at Bellevue. Students assisted the Bellevue staff with care of mothers during their labors, observed deliveries, and assisted with care of mothers and newborn infants. They were also encouraged to assist with bedside teaching of mothers on the care of newborns.

Also in May 1969 a major policy shift occurred. Bellevue announced its new policies on natural childbirth procedures and admittance of fathers to labor delivery units. Fathers were allowed to enter if permission was signed by the mother and doctor beforehand but the fathers had to be educationally prepared. The new policy providing admittance to closed units was permissible if witnessed signatures, particularly of the mother and her doctor, were filed with the hospital beforehand. And if both parents had been educationally prepared and provided that no extenuating circumstances such as a medical emergency would entail protest should the husband be asked to leave the delivery area. *"In other words, the vast majority of patients at Bellevue will be able to deliver as they wish,"* Stated Dr. Harry T. Wood, medical chief of staff at the time.

Intermittent visits by her husband to the patient in labor have always been encouraged he noted as well as the custom of allowing the husband to visit his wife and newborn baby immediately after birth. Small children were also allowed to visit the new mother.

Two popular concepts of natural childbirth were the Reade Method of English derivation and the Lamaze method of prepared children, first popularized in France. Birth involved education of the prospective parents, control of emotional reactions by breathing and relaxation techniques, and positive rather than negative mental attitudes for emotional support of the mother during her labor. Participation of the husband, especially in the delivery room was a peculiarly American development and was not a part of natural childbirth elsewhere in the world.

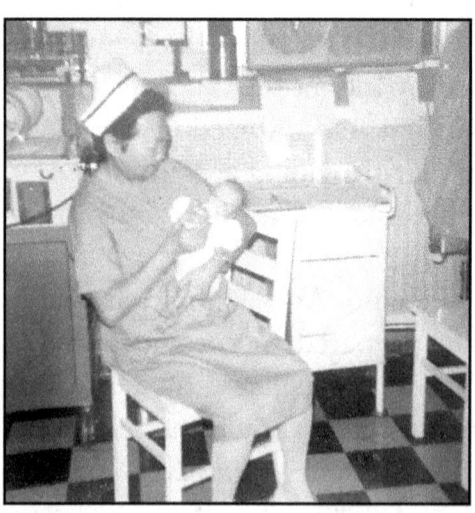

Mabel Fan attending a newbie.

Delivery With Grace

In 1970 some 51,115 diagnostic procedures were handled by Bellevue staff. Bellevue added an X-ray and radiology department and all of this was approved and accredited by the Joint Commission on Accreditation of Hospitals. Now simply called the Joint Commission it is a nonprofit tax-exempt 501(c)3 organization that accredits more than 21,000 American health care organizations and programs.

Bellevue's Christmas party in 1968. L to R: Mrs. Harry T. Wood, Mrs. Robert B. Hamilton, Jr., Mrs. William B. Jameson, Jr. (The dinner chairperson), Mrs. Ira S. Fink, and Dr. Jameson, Jr.

Today a majority of state governments recognize Joint Commission accreditation as a condition of licensure for the receipt of Medicaid and Medicare reimbursements.

In 1970 there were 143 doctors on the medical staff at Bellevue. Continuing to add staff to the

Delivery With Grace

expanding hospital in September 1970, Dr. Virgil J. Sager was named resident and consulting physician at Bellevue. He had a private practice in medicine and surgery from 1944 to 1951 and then confined his practice to general surgery, as assistant attending in surgery at Ellis and St. Clare's hospital. He later became medical consultant for Knolls Atomic Power Labs in 1964-65 and then from 1966 to 1970 was a member of the five-person group Schenectady Emergency Room Associates covering the emergency room at Ellis Hospital.

Births at the hospital were up 18 percent from the previous year (1969) as it increased its gynecological services. Bellevue had three fully staffed operating rooms fully capable of elective major or minor surgery, radiological and laboratory services which encompassed hematology, clinical chemistry and

New York State license to operate at Bellevue.

Delivery With Grace

hormonal studies, and created a department for rubella testing in connection with New York State's drive to eradicate German measles, a dangerous disease to pregnant women and their unborn. Bellevue, through its non-profit Research

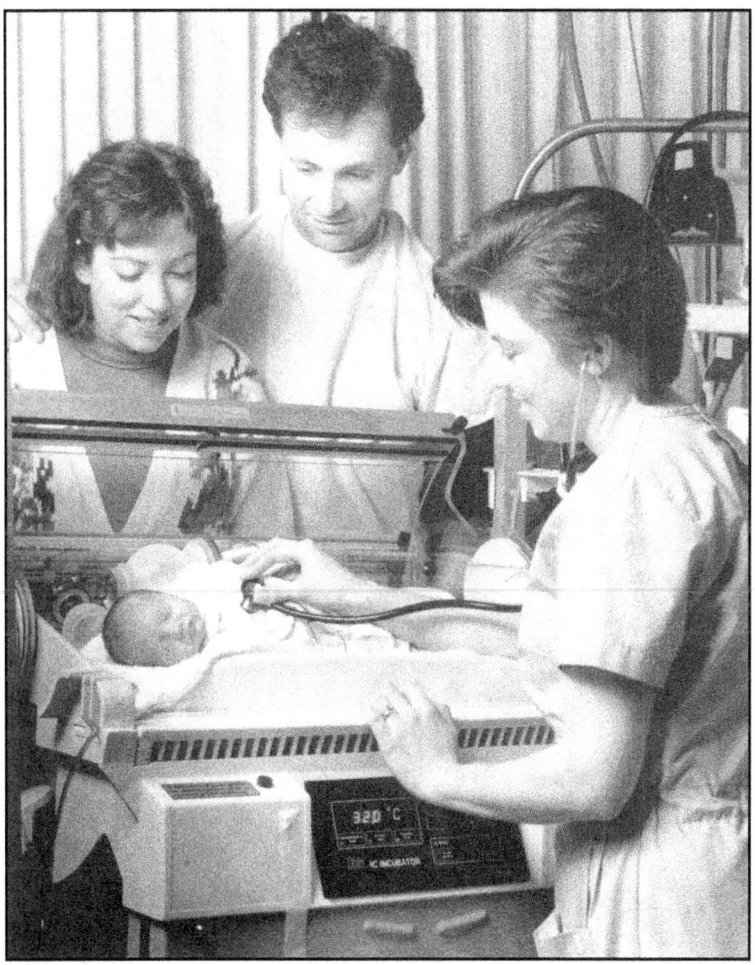

"By blending the advantages of today's most advanced equipment with a personal, caring approach. Bellevue assures that every patient receives optimum care." From a Bellevue brochure, 1991.

Foundation, founded on July 16, 1962, was devoted to basic research of anomalies in newborns and increased its research with results in hematology (RH-factor), premature births and genetic studies. Chauncey A. Welch of Elnora was hired as assistant administrator of Bellevue. Chauncey was formerly an administrative assistant at Child's Hospital in Albany, N.Y. Welch was formerly an anesthesiologist at Albany Medical Center.

"Responding to a woman's needs before, during and after her stay, our Perioperative Nursing Care Program keeps patients informed during all phases of the surgical experience." From a Bellevue brochure, 1991. Karen Lawson, left, attending a patient.

Delivery With Grace

Bellevue's laboratory expanded its research into the retardation field. Aram A. Atashian, director of Bellevue's clinical lab cited breakthroughs in RH and ABO incompatibilities, and rubella. All three causes were now preventable.

Bellevue recognized its long-term employees in 1970 with a special observance. Those recognized were Mrs. Louise Borghardt, 25 years; Mrs. Lina Ott, 26 years; Miss Dora Wiltse, 27 years; Mrs. Marie Boule, 28 years; Mrs. Sophia Weber, 24 years; Mrs. Theresa Logios, 24 years; and Miss Katherine Gold, 28 years. Thirty-five employees with more than 5 years service

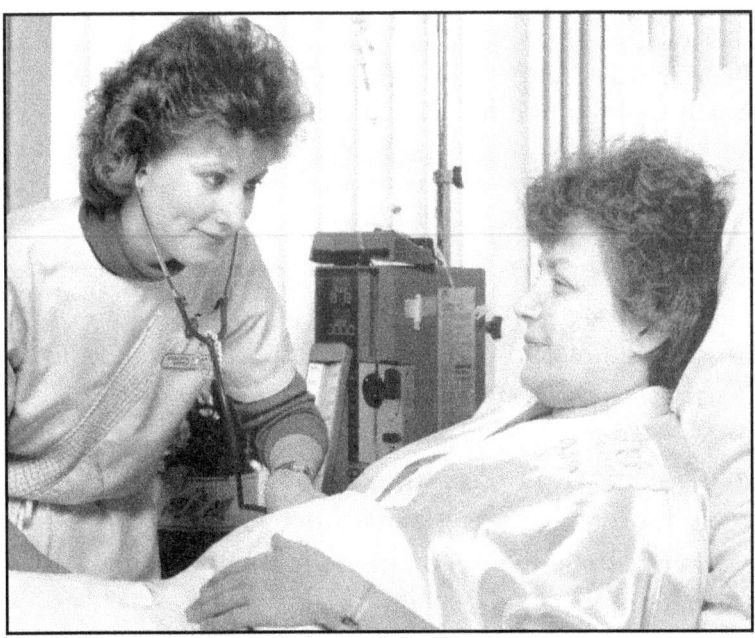

"A total commitment to our patients' well-being and personal comfort is one of Bellevue's hallmarks." Patient being cared for by Roberta Nolan. From a Bellevue brochure, 1991.

Delivery With Grace

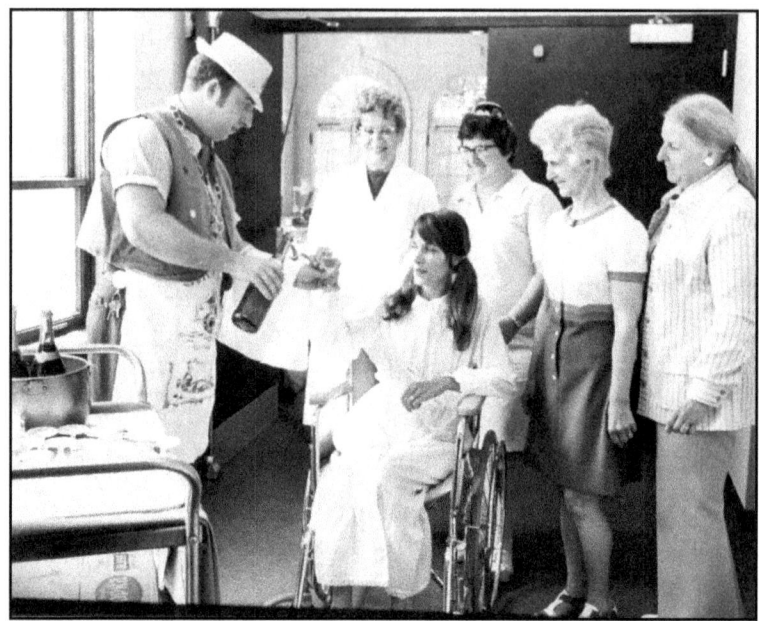

On August 1, 1973, Bellevue's hospital steward pours glass of champaign for the first patient in the new wing. Elnora Smith from Rotterdam had the honors. From left to right, Bellevue staff, Wayne Mabee (cook), Katie Gold, Connie Geganbagh, Sophie Weber and Rita Curran.

were also honored. Ten were on active duty after more than 20 years. The five with more than 25 were presented jeweled pins by Paul Jorgensen, Bellevue Business Administrator.

In 1970 abortion reform went into effect in New York State which was a controversial subject for many. Bellevue performed 70 abortions in 1970 within the law but the hospital declared *"implementation of abortion procedures beyond a 20 week pregnancy entails certain medical dangers and that Bellevue*

Delivery With Grace

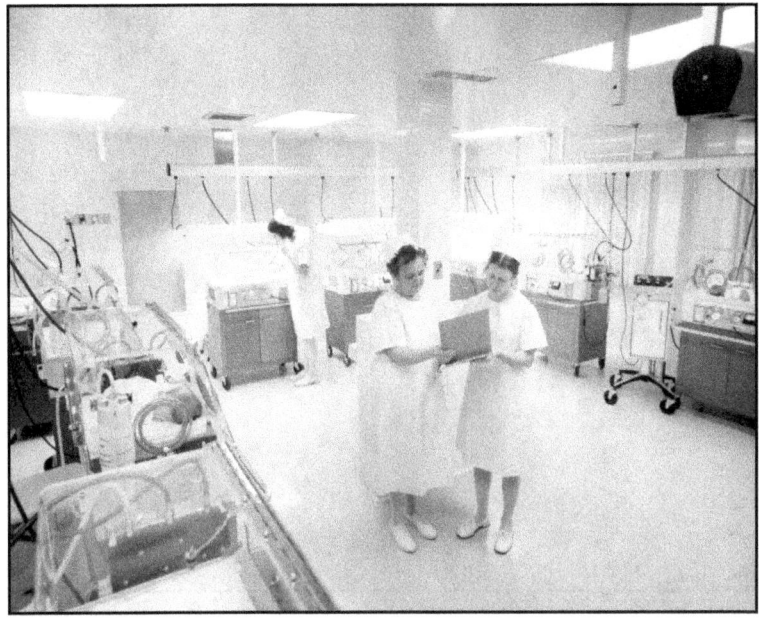

Bellevue had a Level III Nursery. The nursery had personnel and equipment to provide continuous life support and comprehensive care for extremely high-risk newborn infants and those with complex and critical illness. Dora Wiltse (middle).

physicians would prefer not to stretch the deadline to 24 weeks." A spokesman said the reform measure caused *"no surprises"* or problems at his hospital and that, *"everything was preceding smoothly."* Bellevue was averaging about two abortions a day, he said. Abortion was being viewed, "conservatively" with outside consultation required on abortions proposed after the 18th to 20th week. However Albany Medical Center was handling the most abortions in the Capital area.

Delivery With Grace

"One form of care that every Bellevue patient receives is love." From a Bellevue brochure, 1991. Veda Strader holding baby.

Marking its 40th year of operation in 1971, Bellevue, then the only investor-owned hospital in Northeastern New York, announced plans to construct a three story, $4 million addition to the right side of the mansion building. This was the fourth expansion project from its humble beginnings. The plan was to expand the 37 bed hospital to 40 beds, add patients services, operating and delivery rooms, and the laboratory moved to the new addition making it the new hospital with the present mansion used only for offices. This was announced as other hospitals such as Ellis reduced their cases by 50 percent while maternity facilities in Albany and Cohoes eliminated them altogether.

Delivery With Grace

When the hospital first opened in 1931 it delivered 94 babies that year. In 1970 there were 1,759 deliveries made (bringing the total to over 45,000 since it opened in 1931). However a price freeze for health care services was applied at a national level during the first phase of the Nixon Administration's Economic Stabilization Program (ESP) from August-November 1971. ESP began as a result of Congressional and other pressures to control costs. Before ESP, President Nixon steadfastly refused to consider wage and price controls as inflation control policy. Fortunately, Bellevue personnel had discussions with the head of this agency and permission was granted to go ahead with the Bellevue expansion. The ESP operated nationwide from August 1971 to April 1974. It was a four-phase wage and price control program intended to reduce U.S. wage and price inflation by one-half. At five percent annually in the first quarter of 1971, inflationary pressures were perceived as high and there was strong political pressure on the administration to take action.

In 1972, Mrs. Sandra Nava was appointed assistant director of nursing for in-service education to aid Mrs. Josephine A. Nealon, nursing director in all phases of in-service education. Sandra was a five year employee of the hospital nursing staff, and was former head nurse of a surgical unit at Albany Med where she obtained her RN in 1960. Sandra came to Bellevue in May 1967. In addition, Dr. Krikor W.

James Glavin

Rita Glavin

Boyagian was appointed head anesthesiologist for the specialized entity of maternity and gynecological care at Bellevue. He had been a staff member at St. Josephs hospital in Baltimore, MD. Boyagian directed all anesthesiology procedures at Bellevue. He was assisted by Dr. Ira S. Fink, the former anesthesiologist in semi retirement with 12 years of service.

When the new wing opened in 1973 it was said to be *"like a hotel."* What the public did not know is that Dr. Grace G. Jorgensen had to personally guarantee the loan of millions of dollars. On August 2, 1973, 17 gynecology patients were moved into the third floor of the new building. While the patients' floor was the third floor of the new building it was the same level as the lowest floor of the old building built into ancient sand dunes. The addition of four bedrooms in addition to private and semi private and the homey atmosphere was a hit with the public.

The year 1974 also was the year that Bellevue could legally incorporate as a business with approval from the State Hospital Review and Planning Council although the law was approved in 1971. Hospitals such as Bellevue could not incorporate in New York previously. As a private institution all liability rested on the owners of the hospital, and in this case Grace G. Jorgensen. Bellevue became Bellevue Maternity Hospital, Inc., on October 11, 1974, with John Westney as the CEO, (Bellevue also created DBA's [Doing Business As]) later in 1986 as Bellevue Hospital, and just Bellevue. In essence Bellevue was now run by the Jorgensen family: Grace G, daughter Clarissa, and son John.

While it seemed that incorporating Bellevue would be an easy task - thousands of companies are incorporated each year in New York - no lawyer in the Capital District wanted the task in 1971. Grace Jorgensen approached every legal body in the area but none would take the case. Since Bellevue would have been the first to incorporate as such, local law firms felt it would be too much of a struggle. And it was. It took two years to incorporate Bellevue. In 1971 Public Health Law 2801 established that private hospitals could be incorporated under certain conditions and with approval of the Public Health Council. Bellevue applied for approval on October 7, 1974, and received permission from the Council four days later. Fortunately Dr. Jorgensen found the legal team of Glavin and Glavin. Rita Glavin and her husband James were from nearby Waterford, New York. Rita was the first female judge in Saratoga County and former president of the Saratoga Bar Association. They filed the necessary papers and Bellevue was officially incorporated on November 19, 1974.

Bellevue became the first independent hospital to be incorporated in New York. Later in 1996 Bellevue created a DBA (Doing Business As) Bellevue Woman's Hospital.

In 1974, Frances E. Vosburgh, MD, became Woman of the Year by Branch 18 of NYS American Women's Medical Association. She practiced obstetrics, gynecology and pediatrics at Bellevue for more than 25 years and was president of the medical staff from 1971-73. Vosburgh marched in the 1914 Suffragette rally in Albany as a teen and later in the 1930s opened the first birth control clinic in Albany.

The growth of Bellevue in the 1970s had a financial impact on the hospital. In 1973, the tax assessment increased more than ten fold since the previous year reflecting the $1.5 million dollar addition that was

Delivery With Grace

underway. Town Assessor Richard Strong had put an assessment of $693,000 on the property and grounds but an appeal brought it down to $337,000. The previous year it was $31,250.

Bellevue began providing childbirth education classes in 1979. The 8-week program focused on women who were in their third month of pregnancy and taught about their psychological and emotional needs through each phase of childbearing. It also

In 1890, this house was located in what became the garden fountain in front of Bellevue Hospital. This was the home of George Westinghouse Jones when he first moved out of Schenectady in 1900. Jones sold it to Harriet Westinghouse Stone, his cousin in 1911 and both she and her husband lived here until 1920 when it was picked up and moved to 901 Morgan Avenue at the corner of St. David's Lane where it still sits today. Stone then built the mansion.

diversified its volunteer program with flexible hours. Volunteers were a much needed workforce.

Volunteers focused on staffing a mobile gift cart, clerical jobs such as scheduling, mail distribution, filling and typing, patient education programs and staffing the medical library. Hostesses supervised gift cart sales on weekdays and weekends during visitation hours. The hospital also supported an ongoing education fund which provided loans or grants to hospital employees who wished to obtain continuing education credits or update their training. Mrs. Mims Bendall was the volunteer coordinator.

Aerial photo of the Stone Mansion/Bellevue. It was torn down by Ellis Hospital in January 2012 after the merger.

Delivery With Grace

The 1980s and 1990s saw an increase in specialized care and services. Bellevue went from simply a birthing center to offer comprehensive breast care, women's surgical services, ten private labor delivery recovery suits, midwife care, a Level III High Risk Neonatal Unit, Comprehensive Women's Center (Woman's Healthcare Plus), In vitro fertilization (IVF) including Intracytoplasmic Sperm Injection (ICSI) for male infertility, plastic & reconstructive surgery, podiatry, women's urology & continence center, osteoporosis screening and prevention center, nutrition counseling, physical referral, education, exercise programs and support groups, dermatology, oncology services, complete medical imaging services including Level III Ultrasound and community conferences and seminars and a women's health resource phone line. All of this started

Winter view of the Stone Mansion/Bellevue.

from a small former church parsonage in 1931 with six beds.

In 1981, Doctor Thomas Frede was hired by Bellevue and became the head of the Radiology Department. His previous experience was in the Radiology Department at the Veterans Hospital in Albany, Albany Medical Center, and St. Peters Hospital. When he arrived at Bellevue they were using a French mammography instrument that used water-cooling and a B-scanner ultra sound equipment. The mammography unit was the first instrument of its kind in the Capital District and had been imported from Europe. Shortly after Dr. Frede's arrival Bellevue purchased a GE RT 3000 ultrasound instrument with crystal detectors and a 5 megahertz transmitter. The ultrasound widely used at the time in the United States was a SAVOX, a Xerox product with poor resolution.

The hospital also purchased a new mammography machine at the same time. While ultrasound was invented back in the 18th century the use of high frequency sound waves for detecting pregnancy is given credit to England's Dr. Ian Donald. In 1942 an Austrian neurologist/psychiatrist used ultrasonic beams to diagnose brain tumors. A decade later, in 1952, the American Institute of Ultrasound in Medicine (AIUM) was founded and ultrasound began to be used to view pregnancies. And yet Bellevue was ahead of the curve in the United States

Delivery With Grace

Dr. Dominick Mele, here at age 104, Dr. Maria Fort, Dr. Grace G. Jorgensen, and Sanford (Sandy) Roth discuss the history of Bellevue with the author in November 2018. Dr. Mele was still on the staff at Bellevue in 2019. Both Mele and Roth died in 2020.

in its use. Bellevue used free ultrasound in conjunction with mammography. Bellevue's reputation grew for having the best equipment and knowledgeable staff so that many local obstetricians who earlier did not send their patients to Bellevue began sending them, prenatal at about 18 weeks, for thorough combined examinations and review by Bellevue staff. One example notable for its success was a local doctor sending his patient for an examination. However she had extremely large breasts and the mammography machine could not penetrate the full depth of the breast. After a combined examination, Dr. Frede was about to announce that he had located a tumor deep in the breast. Her doctor's surgeon was initially reluctant to go ahead but was persuaded and they removed a malignant tumor. This incident bolstered the reputation of Bellevue staff locally to detect and remedy severe medical problems, for example preventing cancer.

Bellevue continued to be creative and progressive when it was the first to report radiological results to the patient. Following the examinations and their interpretation by the radiological staff and technicians, the attending physician would meet with the patient and explain the results. Dr. Frede's reputation grew as well. He constantly stayed on top of breaking research in his field and encouraged his staff and younger radiologists to do the same. Having a patient ask for him by name was not a rare event. Another innovation was the short time between radiology and pathology procedures. This resulted in shorter times between the radiological produced, a biopsy taken, and a result for the patients and appropriate physicians and surgeons to agree and proceed with further tests or surgery.

Ten years after Dr. Frede came to Bellevue he moved to the University Hospital in Innsbruck, Austria, and continued his work in radiology and pathology. His procedure was following a core biopsy, pathology, then prepared frozen sections and was able to return results within 15 minutes. When this procedure was reported on at a physicians meeting in Switzerland, they found the procedure was quite unique and other physicians quickly followed. At Innsbruck, Dr. Frede and his colleagues had such a high rate of success in analyzing and curing mammary growths that their reputation was world wide and they were curing 300 or more breast cancers per year.

In 1988 Dr. Herbert F. Gretz was appointed Chief of Staff after Dr. Harry T. Wood assumed the title of Chief of Staff Emeritus after 22 years of service. Gretz joined Bellevue in 1970 and was president of the medical staff. He took over duties which included being responsible for all medical activities within the hospital,

Helen Urban photographed on January 26, 1987, holding Marcel Lauren Moll, the 70,000 baby born at Bellevue Hospital. Helen was the first baby born at Bellevue on July 8, 1931, six days after Bellevue opened. Baby Marcel received a $700 US Savings Bond.

the quality of patient care and for implementing changes in medical polices. He was a board certified physician who graduated from Lehigh University, the University of Pennsylvania School of Medicine and Albany Law School. He served his internship at St Luke's Hospital, Bethlehem Pennsylvania and residences there and at the University of California at San Francisco.

In 1991 Bellevue continued to grow now adding an eight-room ambulatory suite, a breast care center and 10 private suites allowing each mother to labor and give birth in a single room. An addition to the staff was Dr. Clarrisa Westney, daughter of Dr. Grace G. Jorgensen, now the third generation in her family to work at Bellevue. Bellevue became the only women's health center in Northeastern New York specializing in obstetrics, gynecology, infertility, neonatology and urology. Many friendships were developed by those who worked at Bellevue over the years. In September, 1991 five Bellevue employees and one retired employee formed a group who liked to play bocce, shoot the game of darts, and primarily enhance the very popular game of poker. Sanford Roth, Carl Pucci, Walt Chambers, Al Dettbarn, Steve Knapp and retiree Joe Ross rented a cabin for a weekend on Indian Lake, N.Y. Based on a meeting of the six people, a decision was made to have the group meet for a weekend every September and by a unanimous vote the name Indian Lake Group, usually going by the acronym "ILG" was socially incorporated. The group celebrated its 29th weekend in September 2019. Roth died shortly after.

Bellevue's reputation was also getting recognition in many areas. It was listed as "One of the 10 Best Hospitals for Woman's Health Care" by *Self Magazine*. A Gallup patient satisfaction poll gave the hospital 99 percent ratings of "excellent" and "very good" for its quality of service as rated by its patients. It was also rated among the top ten employers in the Capital Region for five years.

In 1995 Mohawk Anesthesia Associates (formerly George A. Albright, MD, P.C) became Director of Anesthesia and assumed responsibility for those services at Bellevue. At this time there were six anesthesiologists (four Board Certified and two Board Eligible) and one Certified Nurse Anesthetist. Robert A. Chuda, D.O was Chief, Gynecological Anesthesia and Richard M. Forster, MD, appointed Chief, Obstetrical Anesthesia. Doctors Paik, Rosenberg and Tang were staff anesthesiologists. Important milestones during those first two years at Bellevue is it had continuous 24 hour day in-house call starting in July 1, 1994, and there was a complete repayment of a hospital loan to the Anesthesia Department on October 15, 1995. This new department modified a number of former Bellevue anesthesia procedures and forms. There was a major effort to improve "Post Operative Pain Relief" and there was the modernization of anesthesia equipment and supplies.

The 1990s provided financial struggles for many private hospitals throughout New York. In 1996, at least a dozen private New York City hospitals were laying off staff, or were late paying bills as a result of sharp Medicaid cuts and the rise of Health Maintenance Organizations (HMOs). Bellevue had to continue to fight for women's health care as a right. HMO's such as CDHPC allowed two primary care doctors, one of which could be obstetrics. MVP did not allow an obstetrician to be a primary care doctor.

In 2001 due to rising local taxes, the sheer number of mandated programs from more than 130 government agencies and having to deal with hundreds of different insurance providers, Bellevue switched from an investor owned hospital and became a non-profit organization in 2001. The town of Niskayuna was not happy to lose the tax base considering that Bellevue's budget was around $20 million.

The Berger Commission

In 2005, George Pataki, Governor of New York, proposed the most comprehensive
attempt to restructure the state's system of acute- and long-term care. The New York State Legislature

approved a budget that gave the Commission on Health Care Facilities in the 21st century a year or more to *"examine the needs and capacities of the health care system and make recommendations to right-size hospitals and nursing homes."* With a December 2006 report pending, some hospital executives were opposed to the changes arguing that reducing hospital capacity would harm New York's health care. The commission, chaired by former state official Stephen Berger, was to recommend major changes such as closing of some institutions, expansion or redevelopment of others in each region of the state.

Their conclusions followed:

"Per its statutory obligation, the Commission makes the following recommendations to rightsize and reconfigure health care facilities in each region of the state. The recommendations apply equitably across all regions. The acute care recommendations address 57 hospitals, or one-quarter of all hospitals in the state. The acute care recommendations include 48 reconfiguration, affiliation, and conversion schemes, and 9 facility closures. Collectively, the recommendations will reduce inpatient capacity by approximately 4,200 beds, or 7 percent of the states' supply. The long-term recommendations for downsizing or closing nursing homes will make highly targeted nursing bed reductions of approximately 3,000, or 2.6 percent of the state's supply. Twice as many nursing homes will be downsized as closed. In addition, the long-term care

recommendations will create more than 1,000 new non-institutional slots."

Six sections of the state were affected. The Northern Section conclusions, which included Bellevue, were:

Northern:

• *Bellevue Woman's Hospital should close in an orderly fashion and its maternity, neonatal, eating disorders, and mobile outpatient services should be added to another hospital in Schenectady County.*

• *St. Clare's Hospital and Ellis Hospital should be joined under a single unified governance structure and the resulting entity should be licensed for 300 to 400 beds.*

• *Ann Lee Infirmary and Albany County Home should merge, downsize by at least 345 nursing home beds, rebuild a unified facility, and simultaneously add or provide financial support for non-institutional services.*

• *The Avenue and Dutch Manor should merge and downsize by approximately 200 nursing home beds in a rebuilt Avenue facility and should add assisted living, adult day care and possibly other non-institutional services.*
  • *The Glendale Home should downsize by approximately 192 beds.*

The report goes on to say:

Delivery With Grace

Bellevue Woman's Hospital is one of two remaining not-for-profit women's specialty hospitals in the nation, and the only one in the State. It has 55 certified beds, 40 of which were staffed in 2004. Its average daily census was 22 patients in 2004. Its chief service line is low-risk obstetrics. It had approximately 2,200 deliveries in 2004. It also had approximately 2,000 ambulatory surgeries in 2004, and houses breast and pelvic care health centers. Bellevue has partnered with a local mental health provider and the local medical college to train specialists in eating disorder treatment. It does not offer high-risk maternity care, medical surgical care, or emergency services. Eighteen percent of Bellevue's patients in 2004 were Medicaid-covered.

The hospital's financial situation is dire and its future viability is in serious jeopardy. It has a substantial debt load and its business model is dependent on the provision of poorly reimbursed obstetrical services. As of 2004, the hospital's (non-DASNY) long-term debt was approximately $15.5 million. Bellevue has tried to address its financial problems by diversifying the hospital's service base and securing philanthropic support. These measures, however, have proven to be insufficient. Financial statements for 2004 and 2005 indicate a negative net worth, significant debt, and losses from operations. The hospital's net deficits at the end of 2004 and 2005 were respectively $1.192 million and $1.320 million, and its total deficit as of the end of 2005 was $17.690 million. Additionally, Bellevue is unaffiliated with any other hospitals or systems that could provide substantial financial or management assistance to improve the current financial situation.

Delivery With Grace

A capacity to close analysis confirms that Bellevue's patients readily could be absorbed by its coverage partners, including St. Clare's, St. Peter's in Albany and Albany Medical Center hospitals. Provided that its distinctive level II neonatal intensive care and an eating disorder program services are transferred to one of the other area hospitals, Bellevue's closure will not affect availability of care. Furthermore, most complicated obstetric and neonatal cases are already diverted to the larger area hospitals, so closing Bellevue will not affect provision of these more high-tech services.

Consolidation of services offered by Bellevue with another area hospital will have quality of care and financial benefits. Consolidating all of Schenectady institutions' deliveries (approximately 3,000 annual births in 2004) into a single area hospital would allow investment in a more comprehensive neonatal intensive care unit than is currently offered by Bellevue. Its closure will also improve the viability of the remaining hospitals in Schenectady by allowing them to capture

Bellevue's patient base, a high percentage of which is privately insured. Bellevue employed approximately 275 FTEs in 2003, which was less than 0.5% of the workforce in Schenectady County. If Bellevue closes, its employees will be easily employed by other institutions because the elimination of services at Bellevue will be accompanied by a transfer of its services elsewhere in the area.

Delivery With Grace

A decision to close the only women centered hospital in over a dozen counties based on bureaucratic meetings and by people who never administered medical care forced the dissolution of Bellevue as it was incorporated. No one from the Berger Commission ever visited Bellevue nor did they even know that Bellevue was not just a maternity hospital but had a full function laboratory and offered other services.

Ironically, a report written in May 2018, a decade later, by Bill Hammond of the Empire Center for Public Policy, titled "Profit Potential: Revisiting New York's Restrictive Hospital Ownership Laws" deals with revisiting New York's restrictive hospital ownership laws. Its executive summary states these key findings:

- *"Despite a concentration of world-famous institutions in Manhattan, New York's hospitals collectively rank at the bottom of the federal government's quality ratings and score substantially lower than the national average on other major report cards"*

- *The amount of free care provided by New York's not-for-profits in 2015—1.9 percent of operating revenues—was a third lower than the national averages for both not-for-profits and for-profits.*

- *As of 2014, New York's per capita spending on hospital care was 19 percent higher than the US average.*

- *Tax exemptions for New York's not-for-profit hospitals likely cost federal, state and local governments about $2 billion a year.*

- *In spite of high spending on hospital care and their tax-exempt status, New York's hospitals collectively had the sixth-lowest profit margins, and the highest ratio of liabilities to assets, among the 50 states as of 2015. These factors compromise the hospitals' ability to raise capital.*

- *Hospitals are increasingly relying on government funds to finance capital projects. In just the past five years, the state has allocated $3.8 billion in capital grants to hospitals and other health care providers.*

- *While for-profit hospitals score lower, on average, than not-for-profit hospitals nationwide, they score higher, on average, than New York hospitals of all types.*

The final chapter titled Discussion makes the case for allowing for-profit hospitals, which Bellevue was before it was forced to go non profit.

DISCUSSION

New York's longstanding restrictions on for-profit hospital ownership are an unusual and consequential intervention in the state's health care industry.

Delivery With Grace

These laws have not merely limited the presence of for-profit general hospitals in the state but eliminated them completely.

Based on the evidence presented in this report, there is little indication that excluding for-profit hospitals has resulted in a public health advantage for New York. As discussed previously, the average quality ratings of the state's hospitals rank at or near the bottom of national report cards; the state's per capita spending on hospital care is higher than the norm, and its not-for-profit institutions provide lower-than-average levels of uncompensated care to the indigent, among other negative indicators.
Longstanding ownership restrictions did not necessarily cause these shortcomings, but the restrictions do not appear to have ameliorated them, either.

Also weighing against the status quo are financial factors, such as the loss of tax revenue that for-profit hospitals would otherwise pay and the loss of capital investment that for-profit hospital companies might otherwise make in New York's health care system.

It could be argued that lack of effectiveness alone is reason enough to reverse a restrictive policy that applies to no other major sector of New York's economy.

As a practical matter, however, any proposal to change the policy must address concerns that introducing for-profit hospitals into New York would have a further negative effect on quality, cost and access.

Evidence presented in this paper indicates that some of these concerns are exaggerated or misplaced. Financial data, for example, show that for-profit hospitals, in the aggregate, provide roughly the same levels of Medicaid care and uncompensated care as not-for-profit hospitals.

Meanwhile, data show that for-profit hospitals maintain larger profit margins, more cash reserves and lower debt levels than not-for-profit hospitals, meaning they are less dependent on government for subsidies, loans and capital infusions.

On quality, the evidence is harder to parse.
On one hand, the comparative research summarized above, coupled with scores for Hospital Compare and other report cards, indicate that for-profit hospitals tend to be of lower quality, on average, than not-for-profit and government-owned hospitals at the national level. That gap appears to be narrowing with the advent of improved quality measurement and value-based financial incentives, but has not disappeared.

On the other hand, New York—where for-profit hospitals are effectively banned— has some of the lowest quality scores of any state.

A possible explanation for New York's quality gap is that hospital performance is being dragged down by underlying features of the state's operating environment—such as demographics, economics or regulatory structure. Those features would presumably diminish the quality of for-profit hospitals as well. If so, a change in ownership laws by itself would have little impact.

Delivery With Grace

Another possible explanation is that the absence of for-profit owners has contributed to the performance gap by insulating the state's hospital industry from competition and limiting its access to innovative managers and their successful practices. If so, the state would stand to gain from a change in ownership policy.

In weighing this mix of evidence, it's important to remember that a change in ownership laws would not authorize any particular for-profit company to operate in New York. Rather, it would give such a company the right to apply for an ownership license, in some cases in competition with other bidders.

For-profit bidders would be subject to the multiple layers of review that any change in hospital ownership would necessarily undergo. This process could be used to screen out lower-quality options.

The most likely avenue for a for-profit company to enter New York is not opening a new facility in a crowded market, but converting one that already exists. To start, such a conversion would need support from the institution's board of directors. As volunteers with a demonstrated concern for both the hospital in question and its community, and with no prospect of financial gain, hospital directors could be expected to vet would-be buyers and reject those with poor track records.

The next layer would be the state Health Department and its Public Health and Health Planning Council. Even if the restrictions on for-profit ownership were loosened, these regulators would retain authority to review the history of the acquiring company and its management—and check the background of major owners involved in operations. They could be specifically empowered to reject would-be buyers who have operated low-rated hospitals in other states.

The reorganized company would also have a legal obligation to compensate the public for the loss of a charitable asset, which often means endowing a health oriented foundation or simply making payments to the state. That process would need approval from both New York's attorney general and a court, both of which would be duty-bound to reject deals that work to the disadvantage of the public.

How much interest for-profit hospital companies and other investors would have in acquiring New York facilities is difficult to gauge. There was little public campaigning in favor of the reform proposals floated over the past several years, possibly because the state's hospitals have been effectively closed to private investment for so long.

Some industry officials anticipate that the big chains would be discouraged by New York's environment of relatively tight regulations and slim financial margins. Others see the state's market as too big and lucrative to go untapped forever.

One prominent hospital system CEO, Michael Dowling of Long Island's Northwell Health, has said the entry of for-profit operators into New York's market is "inevitable."

Delivery With Grace

A change in New York's hospital ownership laws would not mandate the conversion of any hospital to for-profit status. Rather, it would provide hospital managers with an additional option for managing the financial futures of their institutions.

For-profit conversions would be voluntary, require both a willing seller and a willing buyer, and be subject to multiple layers of regulation. Current laws effectively veto all such deals in advance. A changed policy would allow each to be weighed on the merits.

Conversion would hold relatively less appeal for big-name academic medical centers and other high-quality, financially strong institutions that have thrived as not-for-profits. The more likely candidates would be lower-quality, financially weaker institutions—of which there are many scattered across the state. For them, buy-outs might represent a lifeline, the chance for increased stability rather than continuing decline and bankruptcy.

Small shareholders with no role in running a hospital, and their routine sales of stock, would no longer be subject to background checks—a procedure that is, at best, an indirect form of oversight. The Health Department would still have full licensing authority over the company and its management, as well as all of the doctors, nurses and other medical professionals on its staff.

Through its "certificate of need" law, the state would continue to control which types of care—such as delivering babies or performing heart surgery—hospitals can add or subtract from *their menu of services. This would limit the risk that a for-profit company would aggressively "poach" lucrative patients from not-for-profit rivals.*

Not-for-profit hospitals would also continue to enjoy the significant competitive advantage of exemption from taxes and access to government-backed low-interest bonds. For-profits, meanwhile, would pay full corporate income, sales and property taxes, becoming a potentially significant source of revenue, especially for local government.

A 2014 study in the Journal of the American Medical Association, referenced earlier, offers perhaps the most pertinent lessons for New York's situation.

The study analyzed the outcome of 237 for-profit hospital conversions, comparing their financial status, quality performance and patient mix to a control group of 631 hospitals that remained not-for-profit or government-owned. The analysis used Medicare data from 1.8 million patients from 2002 to 2010—a more recent period than most other studies.

The authors found that converting hospitals improved their operating margins by an average of 2.2 percentage points—shifting from modest losses to modest gains—compared to 0.4 points for non-converting hospitals.

At the same time, they found that mortality rates and other quality metrics generally improved at all hospitals, with no statistically significant difference between those that converted to for-profit and those that retained their former status.

The authors further found that converting hospitals as a group treated more patients who were African-American, Hispanic and recipients of Medicaid than the control group—and that there was no significant change in their collective patient mix after conversion.

Ownership reform that produced similar results for New York —an improvement in the financial status of converting hospitals without any harm to quality or access—would be a positive for the state.

In other words, the report suggests "For-Profit" hospitals are a benefit to patients.

The author's personal communication with author Bill Hammond further supported this:

My report argued that the laws restricting hospital ownership — which effectively bar corporate chains and make it difficult to operate as a for-profit — aren't doing any good and should be dropped.

The laws are not improving quality — according to most report cards, NY's hospitals are collectively among the worst in the country — but they are shutting out potential investors and denying local governments a lot of tax revenue.

From what I can tell Bellevue was one of the last two or three for-profit general hospitals in the state.

Delivery With Grace

Obviously, most hospitals would prefer to avoid that cost if they can. But if a hospital's management wants to go for-profit — even if it means paying more in taxes — I don't see why the state should stand in the way.

The End of an Era

As a direct result of the Berger Commission Report in 2007 Bellevue Hospital's control was transferred to Ellis Hospital in Schenectady ending an era for the Jorgensen family. During all the years that Bellevue was a private hospital it received no government loans, grants, charity or handouts. The majority of the profits went back into the hospital.

To survive the increasing burden of regulations — reimbursement rate formulas were deregulated and budget funds had to go toward staff, equipment and mandatory inspections required by state and national rules and regulation — and dealing with 135 different agencies, Bellevue was forced to go non- profit in 2001 due to these "managed care" regulations. The new non-profit was named Bellevue Women's Medical Center, Inc. A non-profit team moved in and replaced the Jorgensen family, in effect, ending the family-owned hospital. The new board consisted of Anne Saile as CEO, Neil Golub, president of Golub Corp (Price Chopper, Market 32) brand, Jeanne Neff, president of Sage Colleges became Vice President, and the only medical doctor on the new board Dr. Fe Mondragon became secretary. She was the former president of the Bellevue medical staff. In the year 2000 when the Jorgensens operated the facility there were fifteen medical doctors on the advisory board and the board was ethnically diverse.

The feeling of family, the clambakes and picnics, and the sense of camaraderie among the staff all came to an end.

Ironically, while the hospital was free from paying taxes to the Town of Niskayuna, saving money, the cost of doing business at the hospital under new leadership rose considerably and in one example the cost of doing an official audit more than doubled according to Sanforth Roth, former CFO of Bellevue.

In 2007, Ellis Medicine assumed responsibility for Bellevue services as a direct result of the Berger Commission report. While Bellevue continues under the aegis of Ellis Hospital, the latter made it clear of the responsibility they took on:

"Bellevue has long been a trusted name in women's health care and remains the region's premier facility dedicated to the care of women and infants. Bellevue Woman's center proves quality health care for women of all ages, with services ranging from maternity and breast care, to survey and pelvic health. At Bellevue, women benefit from the expertise of our medical and nursing staff, state of the art technology, as well as the

compassionate care and comfortable settings that have helped drive Bellevue's deputation for over three-three-quarter of a century. When it comes to welcoming babies to the world,

The Jorgensen family, founders and leaders of Bellevue. Left to right, bottom. Mary Grace Jorgensen, little Pamela, Elmer Jorgensen. Top row: Paul Jorgensen, Grace G. Jorgensen.

Delivery With Grace

there's no place in the region that's more trusted and renowned than Bellevue Woman's Center."

Ellis continued under the legal entity Bellevue Woman's Medical Center, Inc. until February 1, 2011, when it dissolved the corporation and absorbed it into the Ellis umbrella, officially ending the hospital that Mary Grace Jorgensen had created in 1931, exactly 80 years previous. In recent years, other institutions have added services that Bellevue pioneered such as University of Chicago Medicine.

When Dr. Grace G. Jorgensen turned over the reigns of Bellevue to the non-profit version in 2001-2002, she personally had by then delivered 8,000 babies, (including the author's three sons). While under the Jorgensen's family tenure, 120,000 babies were born at Bellevue. That is more than the entire current population of the nearby city of Albany (98,251), New York State's Capital.

In 2008, the town of Charlton, N.Y. dedicated its annual Founder's Day Parade on June 1 to the nurses of Charlton and in particular Mary Grace Jorgensen, founder of Bellevue. Her daughter, Dr. Grace Jorgensen, who lived for a time in Charlton, was Grand Marshall of the parade. Mary Grace graduated Galway High School in 1922 and went to nursing school in Amsterdam after graduation.

Delivery With Grace

For several months following the issue of the Commission's Report, the continued existence of Bellevue Hospital was in doubt. Finally, a solution was reached wherein Bellevue and St. Clares Hospital were merged with Ellis to form Ellis Medicine and Bellevue became the Women's Healthcare Campus for Ellis Medicine.

Fast forward to the present (Year 2021) and Ellis Medicine is in merger talks with St. Peters Hospital Partners which in turn is part of Trinity Health, a Catholic controlled organization. Because of the known restrictive medical procedures for Women heath treatments, which Trinity requires, this proposed merger by Ellis is raising many challenges to Bellevue' traditional practices. A solution still awaits.

It is certainly true that *Delivery with Grace*, both Grace Jorgensens, had an impact on thousands of lives throughout the Capital District. The family's remarkable ability to hire the best and brightest staff and administrators is a testimony to their commitment to providing the best care for expectant mothers and their babies.

Their legacy will live on.

"Do the Right Thing and Do It Right."
—Mary Grace Jorgensen

Bellevue's Legal Historic Time Line
by Rita Glavin

Two attorneys, James and Rita Glavin were a major help to Dr. J. in helping formulate the legal and business needs of Bellevue over the years. This timeline by Rita Glavin highlights many of Bellevue's accomplishments.

BELLEVUE MATERNITY HOSPITAL
1931-1975 and beyond

1931-1964   *Early Establishment Years*

July 1, 1931- Bellevue Maternity Home under direction of M. Grace Norlund Jorgensen, R.N. and Elmer Jorgensen opened in the Bellevue section of Schenectady.
1930's-1942-
Growing and requiring more room, Bellevue located to Union Street in Schenectady.
1942- Relocated to Troy Road in Niskayuna, Bellevue had space to expand and evolve.
1957-Bellevue passed its first inspection by the Joint Commission on Accreditation of Hospitals. (JCOAH)
May 1959- Founder M. Grace Norlund Jorgensen passed away.
October 20, 1959-Grace G. Jorgensen Westney filed her Certificate of doing business under the Assumed name of BELLEVUE MATERNITY HOSPITAL. The founder's daughter, Grace, a medical doctor, took over the hospital business, her son, Paul, took over the real property, which was later transferred to The Brookbridge Estate.
Bellevue (Dr. J.) joined various hospital associations.

1964-1975   *Transition and Expansion years*

1964-
J.A. Reitfort P.E. was engaged to develop plans for additional hospital facilities. Bellevue was encouraged and under some pressure from NYSDOH and JCOAH to plan a new hospital conforming to DOH building codes and health regulations.

1966-

Spring and Fall 1966-
Contacts made with the FAH (Federation of American Hospitals), Sen. Robert Kennedy's office, SBA (Small Business Administration) concerning construction loans and reimbursement issues; NYSDOH, NYS Assembly, regarding public and private financing for hospitals. Actively involved were: Dr. Grace Jorgensen (Dr. J.), Dr. Howard Westney, accountants, Paul Jorgensen, and attorneys A. Rita Chandellier Glavin (ARCG) and James H. Glavin III (JHGIII).

May 26, 1966- Attended first (FAH) meeting in NYC (Paul Jorgensen with ARCG), topics: Medicare and Medicaid issues, financing small business construction.

June 3, 1966- Conference with NYS Regional Health Director Dr. Daniel McMahon.

July, 1966- Communication with NYSDOH and with IRS (Internal Revenue Service)- loan application process. Reimbursement formulas for private hospitals, garnering letters of support. Communications with various architects; Re: construction.

1967-

January 31, 1967- Attended FAH convention in NYC (Dr. J. and ARCG).
Held lengthy communications, meetings, etc. with FAH regarding reimbursement issues for proprietary hospital. Lux and Quakenbush architects (August Lux) chosen. Contract with architects negotiated.

Communications made with various banks and lenders including Key Bank.

Relationship with The Brookbridge Estate and Niskayuna Realty regarding the real property. Issues re: Deed restriction, Town zoning and neighbors.

Surveyor retained (C. Hartnett) to survey the real property.
Communication with IRS and tax exempt status applied for and obtained for Bellevue Research Foundation.
Zoning issues discussed and resolved with Town of Niskayuna.
Numerous meetings regarding construction plans, ownership of the hospital, financing, zoning and government loan. (Mr. Lux, accountant, Dr. J., Dr. H. Westney, Paul Jorgensen.)
Continuing communications with federal and state politicians exploring construction financing and reimbursement of hospital charges under Medicare and Medicaid.
Meetings with the hospital Medical Board to inform the medical staff, doctors and nurses of the plans for construction.
Selection of and engaged appraiser for the appraisal of the real property.

June, 1967- LETTER OF INTENT by Dr. J. with plot plans and architect drawings was prepared and delivered to Dr. Daniel McMahon, NYS Regional Health Director.

November 1, 1967-Meeting took place with the Regional Planning
Council in Albany to review the construction plans.
(Dr. J., Paul Jorgensen, James Nelson and ARCG)

Incorporation of Niskayuna Realty Ltd. to acquire
the land from The Brookbridge Estate, construct the
new building, and lease the land and buildings to
Bellevue Maternity Hospital (BMH).

November 8, 1967-
Approval of the LETTER OF INTENT was
recommended by John H. Servis, Executive Director of
the Regional Hospital Review and Planning Council of
NENY.

1968/1969-

March, 1968-
BMH was advised by the office of the Commissioner of
Health that the NYSDOH approved the "architectural
planning" of the project.

Working with the FAH, it was learned bill introduced to
NYS legislature to allow incorporation of a private
proprietary hospital under certain defined conditions.

Letter and communications to and with area, state and
federal elected representatives to support incorporation.

In depth discussion had with banks for financing. Continued dealings with neighbors and Mr. Ernest Fullam, spokesperson.

1970-

September, 1970-
Numerous meetings with counsel led to success in obtaining Waiver of the deed restriction from 38 neighbors in neighboring properties. (ARCG)

December 1, 1970-
Letter received from William Leavy, Director, NYS Bureau of Facility Planning, approving the functional program.
Bellevue was now in a position to apply for construction of the new hospital.

1971-

June, 1971-
Bellevue administration with counsel, accountant, and investment banker, Gordon Berg & Co, for the presentation, obtained approval of financing for the construction from Marine Midland Bank of Northeastern Eastern N.Y. N.A. (William Kelly, V.P.).

July, 1971-
NYSDOH per Deputy Commissioner approved the application for construction with recommendations for approval from Regional Hospital Review and Planning Council of NENY and the State Hospital Review and Planning Council.

July, 1971-
Sweet Associates, Inc., the construction contractor, was engaged for construction and moved heavy construction equipment to the BMH building site.

BMH celebrated its fortieth anniversary and ground was broken for construction of the new hospital.

August, 1971-
Anthony J.J. Rourke, hospital consultant, prepared an extensive favorable report concerning the future continued growth and success of the hospital and community support.

1972-1973-
Construction of the new hospital continued.

Price Controls under the Federal Economic Stabilization Act presented a new challenge. It was a financial imperative that the services provided in the new BMH qualified as " new services" for purposes of financial reimbursement.

Meetings with FAH, Peat Marwick C.P.A.s, hospital counsel and State health officials took place.

Incorporation of BMH as a business corporation under the new Public Health Law section was explored.

Area hospitals were closing the obstetrical services; BMH is the #1 in births.

State pressures were felt for general hospitals to consolidate obstetric departments as a cost saving measure.

<u>May-October, 1973-</u>
With extensive documentation gathered and support obtained from state officials (Hollis Ingraham, M.D., Commissioner of Health, and Daniel McMahon, M.D., Regional Health Director, and Mary Jane Stern M.D., (acting Regional Health Director), Dr. J., JHGIII, Kenneth Parker, CPA, presented a Request for a Ruling from the District Director of Internal Revenue (U.S, Department of the Treasury) that the new hospital being constructed qualified as a new hospital service. This meant that Bellevue would qualify for the reimbursement rates at normal operating profit markup or rates comparable to those in the hospital's marketing area. The in-person presentation was in Washington D.C. and was facilitated in no small way by contacts made by counsel JHGIII through FAH. (Greg Moses*)

*Gregory H. Moses, Jr., Director, Health and Exceptions Division, Office of Price Monitoring, Cost of Living Council, Washington, D.C.

By letter from the Economic Stabilization Program Cost of Living Council, general Counsel, in Washington D.C., BMH was notified "...the services offered by Bellevue Maternity Hospital are to be considered new services and the base price for each service determined in accordance with 6 CFR 300.409 (b)".... **Attachment A**

Bellevue Maternity Hospital, Inc.-

Incorporation was on the agenda but had not been possible under existing law. This was especially important with Bellevue capturing increasing share of the births in the service area, construction plans and necessary financing.

1971-1973-

Public Health Law (PHL) Section 2801-a "Establishment or Incorporation of hospitals". Through FAH contacts it was learned that the Public Health Council (PHC) was on board for incorporation of proprietary hospitals. It was anticipated that the NYS Health Department would sponsor the legislation. New Section 2810-a Public Health Law became law. It provided that a business corporation, with approval of the Public Health Council and according to Sec 2801-a subsections 2, 3 and 9 could own and operate a hospital for profit provided it did not discriminate based on race, color, creed or national origin or sponsor in admission or retention of patients.

Once the new PHL section 2801-a 9 became law, Dr. J., as sole proprietor doing business as BMH, could begin the process of applying for state approval of operating the hospital as a business corporation.

Reorganization of the BMH board had taken place. There were five board members: Dr. J., Paul Jorgensen, JHGIII, ARCG and Edward Curren.

Tax issues were handled by accountants Peat Marwick, hospital counsel, and Welch England and Joseph Donawick in the Bellevue administration. In 1973 with financing in place, among issues to be worked out were: The name of the new corporation, filing for approval of incorporation with the NYSDOH, filing the Certificate of Incorporation with the State Department of State, financial and tax advice to determine best time to accomplish the transfer to the new corporation, after permanent financing, merger of the building construction corporation (Niskayuna Realty) into the new Bellevue corporation.

Reservation of the name Bellevue Maternity Hospital, Inc. was made by counsel on July 10, 1973 and again on November 20, 1973 with the NYS Department of State.

November, 1973-
: Dr. J. signed "Application for Approval of Incorporation of Bellevue Maternity Hospital, Inc." for filing with the Department of Health. The Application included a pro forma balance sheet and information on each member of the Board. By her affidavit, Dr. J. agreed to be the sole shareholder.

December 5, 1973 –
: Staff report from the NYSDOH to the Public Health Council acknowledged actual filing of the Application for Establishment designated No. ALB-38 i.e. of a business corporation to operate the existing 40 bed maternity hospital.

<u>1974-</u>

January 2-
: Regional Hospital Review and Planning Council of NENY recommended Approval of the application for BMH, Inc., *subject to compliance with all requirements as determined by the NYSDOH.*

April 4-
: Maternity and nursing services survey was conducted by three NYSDOH nurses.

April 25-
: State Hospital Review and Planning Council recommended approval of the application for incorporation, *contingent upon determination that the "proposal is financially feasible".*

April 26-
: Additional information requested by NYSDOH.

May 1-
: NYSDOH recommended approval to Public Health Council for establishment of BMH, Inc. contingent upon compliance with certain items identified in a recent Article 28 survey.

May 9 and May 10-
: Management Assessment survey was conducted by Edwin Augustin of NYSDOH.

May 15-
: Maternity and nursing survey was conducted.

May 23-
: Materials requested by NYSDOH were prepared and filed.

May 24-
: PHC referred Application to the Establishment Committee.

June 25-
: Received first recommendations of NYSDOH nursing services.

June 28-
: Dr. J. was notified that the Public Health Council (PHC) having considered the advice of the Regional Councils, the State Hospital Review and Planning Council, the Staff of the NYSDOH and the Establishment Committee of the PHC, approved the application for establishment of BMH, Inc. at the location and number of beds *with the contingencies fulfilled.*

July 9-
: Management assessment recommendations sent to BMH by Edwin Augustin.

July 16-
: Bellevue responded to management assessment review.

August 14-
: Communication made to Bellevue from deputy NYSDOH Commissioner Dr. Dickson concerning Bellevue's July 16 response.

August 20-
: Received copy of Maternity and Nursing Services Survey from Mary Jane Stern, M.D., NYSDOH Commissioner's office. (Survey made April 4, with follow-up in May).

September 17-
: Bellevue responded at length by letter to the "suggested studies" and "administrative actions for consideration" received from NYSDOH Deputy Commissioner Dickson (Preventive Services and Medical Care). Copy was sent to Dr. Hollis Ingraham, Commissioner NYSDOH.

September 18-
: Dr. J. and ARCG requested and attended in person meeting at the office of the NYSDOH Commissioner Dr. Hollis Ingraham in Albany. Also in attendance were Assistant Commissioner Dr. Frank Cicero (Hospital Affairs and Health Facilities, Financing and Development) and George Meitch (NYSDOH Health Economics in charge of Bureau of Health Care Reimbursement). George Meitch had discussed the cost of living matter with JHGIII.

October 7-
: Public Health Council notification was sent to attorneys Glavin and Glavin and Dr. J.: KNOW ALL MEN BY THESE PRESENTS: ...Certificate of Incorporation of Bellevue Maternity Hospital, Inc is APPROVED....
Attachment B

October 11-
: Certificate of Incorporation of BELLEVUE MATERNITY HOSPITAL, INC. under Section 402 of the Business Corporation Law was filed with the New York State Secretary of State.

October-December-
: Multiple meetings and discussions took place with counsel, accountants and administration with Dr. J. relative to ceasing the hospital business under the name of BMH and beginning January 1, 1975 and thereafter conducting business as a business corporation, i.e. Bellevue Maternity Hospital, Inc.

Dr. J. was issued all the shares (200) of BMH, Inc. in accordance with requirements of NYSDOH.
Dr. J. was replaced as guarantor of the financing by the Bellevue corporation.
Dr. J. established the board of directors to include:
Dr. Jorgensen, Paul Jorgensen,
A. Rita Chandellier Glavin, Edward Curren and James H. Glavin III. Administration appointed were: Welch England, administrator, Joseph Donawick, comptroller, Dr. J., Medical Director.

December 31-
Effective date of Certificate of Discontinuance of sole proprietorship (Bellevue Maternity Hospital) filed with the Schenectady County Clerk i.e. December 31, 1974.

1975-

January 1-
Official start of business of Bellevue Maternity Hospital, Inc., i.e. January 1, 1975.

Mid 1970's-During this period of cost containment and changing demographics, obstetrical and newborn services were under study in the seventeen counties of northeastern NY and its 24 hospitals. A plan for regionalization of those services and levels of care was finalized by the Health Systems Agency of NENY for implementation by the NYS Commissioner of Health.

The Regional Hospital Review and Planning Council of NENY developed a plan for Maternity and Pediatric Care in the seventeen counties, divided into 10 subareas.

Bellevue was an important component of and participant in those plans. (ARCG, Paul Jorgensen)

Other dates of note:

October 23, 1979-
Bellevue Maternity Hospital Inc. filed with the New York State Department of State: Certificate of Assumed name: BELLEVUE MATERNITY HOSPITAL.

January 13, 1986-
Bellevue Maternity Hospital Inc. filed with the New York State Department of State: Certificate of Assumed name: BELLEVUE HOSPITAL.

January 13, 1986-
Bellevue Maternity Hospital Inc. filed with the New York State Department of State: Certificate of Assumed name: BELLEVUE.

December 18, 1996-
Bellevue Maternity Hospital Inc. filed with the New York State Department of State: Certificate of Assumed name: BELLEVUE WOMAN'S HOSPITAL.

ECONOMIC STABILIZATION PROGRAM
COST OF LIVING COUNCIL
WASHINGTON, D.C. 20508

Office of
The General Counsel

OCT 1 8 1973

Mr. Kenneth R. Parker
Peat, Marwick, Mitchell & Co.
50 Wolf Road
Albany, New York 12205

Dear Mr. Parker:

This is in response to your request for a ruling as to whether "new services" are being provided by Bellevue Maternity Hospital within the meaning of Section 300.409 of the Economic Stabilization Regulations (6 Code of Federal Regulations). Ordinarily, the establishment of a new facility in and of itself is not sufficient to qualify the services offered as "new services." See Price Commission Ruling 1972-270, 37 F.R. 23321 (November 2, 1972). However, the improvements in services being offered at the new Bellevue facility, when looked at in totality, are of such a nature that the quality of all services is substantially different from those previously offered. Therefore, the services offered by Bellevue Maternity Hospital are to be considered new services and the base price for each service determined in accordance with 6 CFR 300.409(b).

Thank you for your interest in the Economic Stabilization Program.

Sincerely,

William N. Walker
General Counsel

ATTACHMENT A

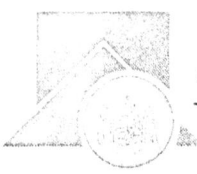

STATE OF NEW YORK
DEPARTMENT OF HEALTH
ALBANY

PUBLIC HEALTH COUNCIL

October 7, 1974

KNOW ALL MEN BY THESE PRESENTS:

                         In accordance with action taken after inquiry and investigation at a meeting of the Public Health Council held on the 28th day of June, 1974, I hereby certify that the Certificate of Incorporation of Bellevue Maternity Hospital, Inc. is APPROVED. Of the 200 authorized shares of no par common stock, Grace G. Jorgensen, M.D. will hold 200 shares and no shares will be retained by the corporation.

                     Public Health Council approval is not to be construed as approval of property costs or the lease submitted in support of the application. Such approval is not to be construed as an assurance or recommendation that property costs or lease amounts as specified in the application will be reimbursable under third party payor reimbursement guidelines.

                                                  MARIANNE K. ADAMS
                                                       Secretary

Sent to: James H. Glavin, III, Esq.
              Glavin and Glavin
              P.O. Box 40
              69 Second Street
              Waterford, New York 12188

              Dr. Grace G. Jorgensen
              P.O. Box 1030
              Schenectady, New York 12301

ATTACHMENT B

COUNCIL

NORMAN S. MOORE, M.D.
    CHAIRMAN
GEORGE BAEHR, M.D.
ALONEVA P. BOND
DETLEV BRONK, Ph.D.
GORDON C. BROWN

MORTON P. HYMAN
CHARLES T. LANIGAN
GERALD B. MENSKY, M.D.
GEORGE R. METCALF
W. KENNETH RILAND, D.O.
JOHN F. ROACH, M.D.

HOWARD A. RUSK, M.D.
JOHN M. AARON

HOLLIS S. INGRAHAM, M.D.

124

Biographies of Bellevue Maternity Hospital Personnel: The People that made Bellevue a Success

Clarence F. Ackerknecht, M.D.
1895-1987

Specializing in obstetrical practice, Dr. Clarence F. Ackerknecht was one of Schenectady's leading physicians and hospital workers of his day.

Dr. Ackerknecht was born September 15, 1895, in Johnstown, N. Y., son of Ernest and Martha I. (Klaus) Ackerknecht. His paternal grandfather, Ferdinand Ackerknecht, became the founder of a leather business in Johnstown in 1859, and was active in it for the rest of his life, also serving in the Civil War as a member of the 10th New York Infantry Regiment. Ernest Ackerknecht, who was born in 1858 in New York City and died May 26, 1915, carried on the leather manufacturing business in Johnstown until his death. His wife, Dr. Clarence Ackerknecht's mother, Mrs. Martha I (Klaus) Ackerknecht was born in 1870 near Leipzig, Germany.

Public schools in Johnstown, his New York birthplace, provided Clarence F. Ackerknecht's early formal education, and he graduated from high school there in 1913. He then became a student at

Cornell University in Ithaca, where he received a degree of Bachelor of Arts in 1918. In 1923 he was made a Doctor of Medicine by Albany Medical

College, after which he served a year internship at Ellis Hospital in Schenectady then began his general practice of medicine in Schenectady. In 1934 he limited his practice to obstetrics.

He was assistant attending obstetrician at Ellis Hospital and held membership in the Schenectady County Medical Society, the New York State Medical Society and the American Medical Association. He served his country in a professional capacity during World War I, being stationed for six months with Mobile H, No. 100, overseas, in the American Expeditionary forces. Honors to Dr Ackerknecht came in the course of his medical work, among them his election as president of the County Medical Society for the year 1937-38 and his appointment to the board of Glen Ridge Sanitarium on which he serviced for six years. Politically Dr. Ackerknecht was a Republican. He belonged to the Mohawk Golf Club and St. Patrick's Lodge, No. 4 Free and Accepted Masons (in Johnstown). He attended St. George's Protestant Episcopal Church. His fraternal membership was with Sigma Pi at Cornell University and Nu Sigma Nu medical fraternity.

Dr. Charles F. Ackerknecht married September 17, 1923, to May Elizabeth L. Kleitz, of Albany N. Y., daughter of William Kleitz. They became the parents of three children: William Charles Ackerknecht, born in 1923; Carol Ackerknecht, born in 1927; and Grace Elizabeth Ackerknecht, born in 1932.

His son William was killed in action in Luxembourg, Germany, in December 1944. Nurses at Bellevue held a blood drive in his honor. The drive was created by fellow employees of the GE publicity Division (where Kurt Vonnegut worked). William was the first member of the group to give his life in the war. He was overseas only two months before he was killed.

Dr. Ackerknecht was the chief of obstetrics at Bellevue and was active since its founding in 1931.

On August 17, 2017, the statue dedicated to Dr. Ackerknecht was given to his family in a ceremony.

On November 9, 1974, Dr. Ackerknecht was honored at Bellevue. A portrait done by his daughter and an Alfo Faggi bronze statue of mother and child purchased in 1946 by former patients as a memorial to his son lost in World War II was presented to the hospital. That statue was recently removed from Bellevue and given to the family at a ceremony in 2017.

Dr. William J. Jameson (1896-1970)

In December 29, 1922, the local paper reported that Dr. William Jameson, for several years the physician at Camp Dudley, the Y. M. C. A. summer camp at Westport, had given up a large practice in Schenectady to take up a seven-years course in tropical diseases in order to become a medical missionary in the Orient.

On Feb 19, 1929 a group of his friends sent an annual purse together with a large amount of linen to Dr. Jameson for his hospital work at Manepay, Ceylon, now called Sri Lanka. It was Dr. Jameson's seventh year in the field. He wrote enthusiastically of his work, that included building and equipping a new hospital, the first in that

country, and was recognized by premier civil rights leader, Mahatma Gandhi for his efforts. In a letter, Dr. Jameson wrote of the difficulty in suppressing a serious epidemic. Dr. Jameson was formerly an Intern at the Ellis Hospital, while Mrs. Jameson was dietitian there. They were married before their departure for Ceylon. Dr. Jameson was the son of Mr. and Mrs. William Jameson of 227 Utterly St. and was born here. When he returned after seven years in the field both he and his wife gave many talks on their missionary work in Ceylon in the 1920s and earlier to many church and local groups. The Jamesons also lived at 1574 Union St. (1944)

In 1966, Dr. William J. Jameson Sr. and his son William J. Jameson, Jr. announced an association with Dr. August C. Schwenk, Jr., a practice of obstetrics and gynecology with offices and home at 1574 Union St.

and 130 Old Niskayuna Rd., Loudonville (1971) where an old fashioned picnic was given to the public at their home named "Taprobane."

He was a graduate of Union College and Albany Medical College in 1921. He served an internship at Ellis Hospital in Schenectady and in 1923 did graduate work in London, receiving a diploma in tropical medicine while there. He went to Ceylon as a medical missionary from 1923 to 1938 and helped establish and run a hospital in Manipay and an auxiliary one in Kodalkanal. When he returned to America he worked doing post-graduate work at the Women's Hospital in New York City and Harvard Medical School. He opened a private practice in Schenectady in 1939.

William John Jameson, Jr. (1924-2017)

Dr. William John Jameson, Jr., of Loudonville and Beaufort, S.C., died on April 5, 2017. He was born in Ceylon (Sri Lanka) on July 30, 1924, to Dr. William John Jameson, Sr., an esteemed medical missionary, and Gladys Thompson Jameson. Dr. Jameson, Jr., had the opportunity during his visit to meet Mr. Gandhi in recognition of his father's efforts. He was married to his wife, Judith Latch Jameson, for nearly 50 years. His son was William John Jameson III. In 1942, he was inducted into the US Navy and served in the Asiatic/Pacific Theater, including the Battle of

Guadalcanal, where he was a corpsman. He went on to become a Scout and Raider (Navy Seal).

He graduated from Union College and New York Medical College. Dr. Jameson, an obstetrician and

Dr. William Jameson, Jr..

gynecological surgeon for over 50 years, served as chief of staff at Bellevue Hospital for Women.

Though widely recognized for his many achievements, Dr. Jameson was a private and unassuming man. His compassionate care and love of his patients were the guiding principles of his practice. His funeral was held in Beaufort with Graveside services on April 29, 2017, in Memory Gardens, Colonie.

Grace Gertrude Jorgensen, M.D.

"Dr. J." as she is known, is the daughter of the founder of Bellevue, M. Grace Jorgensen and was delivered on the kitchen table at her mother's home. Her birth in 1928 was the impetus for the founding of Bellevue. As she puts it, *"Only 40 percent of the women in Schenectady birthed at hospitals in those years. There were social pressures, economic pressures, and you didn't go to a*

hospital unless you were sick. But I guess it wasn't the best experience for her. My mother felt there had to be a better way."

Dr. J. grew up in Schenectady living on the first floor of the new Bellevue Maternity Hospital on Bradt St. along with her brother Paul. Patients were situated on the second floor.

She attended Union College in Schenectady and received a BA at Russell Sage College in Troy. After completing her medical training at New York Medical College in 1954, she interned at Ellis Hospital in Schenectady. Her postgrad experience was at Presbyterian Hospital in New York City as an obstetric aesthetician. After her mother passed in 1959, she became the medical director at Bellevue and dedicated her life's work at Bellevue until she retired in 2001 when the hospital was changd to a

Grace Van Der Voort who taught Grace chemistry at Russell Sage.

non-profit organiztion. Dr. J served on a number of boards and had her own private practice. She has won numerous awards and recognition for her work such as the Science Award, Russell Sage College (1950) and Doris L. Crockett Award, Russell Sage College; Leadership Award YWCA (2001), Leadership Award, Girl Scouts (2001); Woman of Excellence - Life Achievement, Albany - Colonie Regional Chamber of Commerce (2001); Aiden March Award, Albany Medical (2003); Certificate of Appreciation, Niskayuna Foundation (2005); Doctor of Excellence Leaders in Healthcare(2014); Flah's Tribute to Women; Golden Leadership Award International Award for Kay, Sons & Daughters, LTD, England; National Hospital Association National Award for Patient Education; and Phi Kappa Phi Honorary Society, to name a few.

She was the first women to be elected a board member to the Marine Midland Bank Eastern NA in 1973. The success of Bellevue in becoming the leading women's hospital in upstate New York is due to her untiring devotion to her work.

Dr. Thomas G. Adinolfi.

Grace was fortunate to meet Pope Pius XII in 1946 at the Vatican for her 18th birthday. She was taken to Italy by Dr. Thomas G. Adinolfi, Schenectady's coroner physician and was accompanied by her friend Katie Gold. Grace spent more than 30 minutes with the Pope alone discussing her interest in the medical field and about her family and Bellevue Medical Hospital. While in Italy she was able to see their underground hospital built during WW II. Another one of Grace's memorable moments was dancing with President Ronald Reagan at the Inaugural Ball.

Her experiences in visiting Europe after the war were useful in her later work. She saw first hand the ruins of war in Germany. She visited underground hospitals, went to Switzerland and studied with a professor who was a leader in translation of herbal medicines from Asia to western medicine. The doctor became a role model for Grace and how to treat people who were sick. She visited Danish hospitals which were government controlled and impressed her on how not to run a hospital. Her visit to Iceland exposed her to genetic research, and later as a board member of HSBC Bank she travelled to England to learn the English ways of delivery management, and visited many banks. The Soviet-American Citizens Summit II: Restoring the Global Environment, held in Moscow from January 21-26th, 1990 was an eye opener about Soviet medicine. Her visit to Russia allowed her to see how Soviet medicine was applied and learned that

Grace and Howard on their wedding day in May 1954.

men and women were treated differently and that most of the people involved in medical care were women.

**"Union Days"
By Grace G. Jorgensen
English 101B,
September 30, 1947**

Due to the crowded colleges, I had just resigned myself to the thought of working home for a year before entering college. To my rescue came an announcement from Union College that they were going to take coeds. At first I was dubious but when I saw all of the feminine faces taking the entrance examinations, I was relieved. I took my examinations and was duly accepted as a full-fledged freshman at Union College.

The first day was a day I will not soon forget. I knew no more about the college than I would have had it been in Asia. My first shock came when I went into the class meeting and found that all of the inquisitive eyes that I looked into were of the opposite sex. That is, with the exception of one Pair. We two were the first two girls to attend Union College, and right from there we had to play the part together.

Fellows were human too I discovered, and felt just as peculiar about having us around as I felt about being there. Not only did we disturb them, but also put a cramp in the style of teaching of many of the professors. The lectures all had to be cut down to the bear facts, this left the lectures very uninteresting compared to those enjoyed by the fellows without "women" in their classes. The boys were good, however, about taking us in their stride. The first class was a Chemistry laboratory and the work was given to us by the pound. I was at first just a little overwhelmed, but with the helping hands and patient answers of my fellow classmates the Chemistry laboratory was conquered.

History was another subject that took a lot of patience on both the part of the professor and the poor fellows who had the hard luck of being in my class. The teacher lectured many times about the women at Union having to become use to the men and not worry about them looking, talking or whistling when it might injure their work. No matter how many times he lectured, and no matter how many library assignments had to be failed, that library still looked unbearable. All the men seemed to be

Dr. J's school days.

just sitting in there waiting a chance to watch you fumble your book or trip over the last step. Just the thought of it made me feel like curling up and dying in some inconspicuous spot. Although it did take time, I finally did accustom myself to this new life. I had to be a lady and I knew it. It was hard sometimes to put my hair up when homework had kept me up very late, but all I had to do was think of what the boys would say and think of my hair. I never went a night uncurled.

Dinner was also a big problem for me because the dining hall was all filled with fellows and my only coed companion went home regularly for her evening meal. This left me alone. So I spent my dinner in the sandwich bar. It was from here that I met all the people who were later to be such good friends and influences. While I was eating my sandwich one evening, a fellow sat watching me until he made every piece of sandwich stick in my throat. I was sure I had forgotten to wear my shoes.

When finally I could take it no longer and was preparing to leave, he very meekly requested me to sit down a moment and talk with him. I found out he wanted to ask me to write on the college paper. I was to write on what I thought of Union. When I arrived at the paper office, I was slowly but surely talked into

Dr. J. made sure there were parties during the year for her staff and family.

Clarissa, John and Diana (John's graduation from Dartmouth). Dr. J.'s children.

starting a campaign to make Union coed. After an exasperating evening I delivered my masterpiece. I later discovered that only I thought it was to be a masterpiece. The day following its publication was completely ruined by the peculiar stares and remarks such as "I read your article" with that terrible long pause following. At least these were the reactions of the faculty. Among the students I made many friends. As anyone might guess, Union is still a college for men only. (Union became Co-Ed in 1970- DR).

As the school year wore on, transportation grew to become more and more a problem. The roads were slippery and the busses always failed to meet with the Union schedules. After due consideration and much strong opposition, I was allowed to drive our one ton, orange truck to college. All the way from the constant bumps to the smiles and frowns of the many pedestrians who barely escaped with their lives, the truck was one thing that will never let me forget Union College. No matter how much criticism it received, those who could squeeze on always did, for a nightly trip down to the local meeting place.

Two years ago, Union College was the last place I ever considered going to.

Never once did I think that the most outstanding year of my life would be lived at Union.

"The Way it Was"
by Grace Jorgensen

Mona Lisa Smile, *the name of a movie, was on the money for women's colleges of the 50's. Manners and "Marriage training," were part of an eduction.*

One of the deans taught us how to eat ice cream "never take a bite from the spoon, the bowl is cleared and no ice cream should remain on the spoon."

One needed permission from the college before marrying. It didn't matter if your parents said it was fine, if the dean didn't say OK, (and neither of them were married) you would have been in big trouble.

Tea parties were held several time a year in each dorm and these were social events.

A movie was to be held on campus, shooting the birth of a baby. In order to see the movie, a student had to take a particular class in home economics or as it would be called today, Family and Consumer Sciences an hour for one semester period. This turned out to be a course not in caring for a child after the birth, but rather a course about establishing a home and buying groceries. This was taught by one of the same unmarried deans. The movie was indeed about the birth of a baby, but as today would evaluate, a third grade edition as regards to the thoroughness of the education.

In our class, there are two women that held MD degrees and a few who received PhD's. To my knowledge, we had no JDs (Juris Doctor, Lawyer), CPA's (Certified Public Accountant), but quite a few happy MRS.

Paul Jorgensen (1930-2016)

Brother of Dr. Grace Jorgensen. Paul was in charge of Wage & Price Control (he kept the data from the Government 1099 forms). See p. 229.

William F. Nealon, M.D. (1888-1958)

Engaged in the general practice of medicine in Schenectady, Dr. William F. Nealon was one his city's beloved citizens and the principal supporter of Grace Jorgensen in the establishment of the Bellevue Maternity Home.

Paul Jorgensen.

Dr. Nealon was born December 7, 1888, in Hoosick Falls, N.Y., son of Lawrence and Catherine (Byrnes) Nealon. His father was born in Stephentown, N.Y.

Public Schools in Hoosick Falls provided Dr. William F. Nealon's early formal education. After graduating from high school in 1907, he became a student at Albany Medical College, where he took the degree of Doctor of Medicine in 1915. He served an internship at Gouverneur Hospital and at Bellevue and Allied Hospitals, in New York City, for two years. Then came the entry of the United States into the World War, during which conflict Dr. Nealon served with the 27th Division, 106th Field Hospital, and was overseas for a year, with the commission of captain. He was honorably discharged from the service April 4, 1919.

Coming to Schenectady at the time, he engaged in general practice, covering all the varying phases of his profession, and was widely known and respected in medical circles. He was on the staff of Ellis and St. Clare's Hospitals. He was a member of the Schenectady County Medical Society where he served as president, the New York State Medical Society and the American Medical Association. Politically Republican, Dr. Nealon was deeply interested in the affairs of his adopted city. He was official surgeon of the police department, and was affiliated with many organizations. He was a member of the Lodge No. 480, Benevolent and Protective Order of Elks, and Post No. 1002 of the American Legion, and also belonged to the Phi Sigma Kappa Fraternity in which he joined Beta Chapter in his undergraduate days. He was a member of the Church of St. John the Baptist.

On January 29, 1918, Dr. Nealon married Anna M. Gregg, of Brockwayville, Pa. They became the parents of three sons: William F. Nealon, Jr., Joseph B. Nealon, and James H. Nealon.[1] Joseph, who was a sergeant in the air force, served 12 months in the European Theater of operations during World War II. James was seriously injured but survived when he was struck by a car on November 29, 1937. The Nealons resided at 2126 Broadway in 1937. He was the official Schenectady Police Department surgeon

---

[1] Kimball, Francis P. The Capital Region of New York State: Crossroads of Empire. 1942. Vol. III, pgs. 181-82.

for 33 years. He died at his son Joseph's home after a long illness and was buried in St. John's Cemetery.

Dr. Harry T. Wood Jr. (1927-1995)

Dr. Wood served as Chief of Staff at Bellevue from 1965-1988, and Chief of Staff Emeritus from 1988 until his passing in 1995. He was also Chief of OB-GYN. He helped raise and maintain high standards throughout the range of Bellevue medical services. He was the founder of the Harry T. Wood Memorial Library at Bellevue.

Born in Westport, Conn., Wood also lived in West Hartford. He earned his Bachelor's at Dartmouth, his Master's in Psychology at Yale and his medical degree at the New York Medical College in 1954. He was in the same class as Grace Jorgensen and Howard Westney. Dr. Wood did his residence in OB-GYN at the New York Medical College Metropolitan Medical Center. He moved to Schenectady and to Bellevue in 1961, with a private practice and was board-certified for

Dr. Harry T. Wood Jr.

OB-GYN since 1962, practicing at Bellevue, St. Clare's and Women's HealthCarePlus.

Harry and Doris Wood.

When not studying and practicing medicine, Dr. Wood was a commodore of the Dartmouth Yacht Club and a member of the Mohawk Golf Club. He served in WW II with the US Navy. For eight years Dr. Wood did medical commentary for radio station WGY, one of the first doctors to discuss women's health.

Wood was a Fellow of the American College of OB-GYN, a diplomat of the American Board of Medical Examiners, a Fellow of the OB-GYN Society of New York Medical College, a member of the Northeastern OB-GYNN Society, a member of the Board of Planned Parenthood in Schenectady and the Schenectady County Medical Society and the New York Medical Society. In a tribute for Dr. Wood, Dr. Navin Pardanani wrote that he lived like Sinatra's song, *"I did it my way."* *"He lived his life authentically as he perceived life. He did not live life according to other*

In 1969 Dr. Wood moved to 1370 Union St. to practice.

people's reactions or opinion. He lived his life totally."

He was well known as an intelligent conversationist and avid reader and was always current on the latest developments in obstetrics and gynecology and could *"always comment on any topic with great authority and wisdom."*

He was married to Doris Lane, a popular model and actress during the 1940s and 50s and she was an important volunteer with the interior decoration of the 1971 expansion at Bellevue.

In 1969 Wood moved his offices to 1370 Union for the practice of obstetric, gynecology and infertility. The announcement stated that he was:

"Chief of the medical staff at Bellevue Maternity-HospitaL Dr. Wood is an attending physician at Ellis and St. Clare's Hospital. Certified by the American Board of Obstetrics and Gynecology, he is a fellow of the American College of Obstetricians and Gynecologists, a diplomate of the American Board of Medical Examiners, and a fellow of the Obstetrical and Gynecological Society of New York , a diplomat of the American Board of Medical Examiners, and a fellow of the Obstetrical and gynecological Society of New York Medical College."

"The author of a number of scientific articles, he practiced in Hartford, Conn, where he was on the staffs of Hartford, St. Francis, Mt. Sinai and McCook Memorial hospitals from

1958 to 1961. Since coming to Schenectady, he practiced in association with the two Doctors William Jameson at 1574 Union St."

"A native of Westport, Conn., he is a graduate of Dartmouth College and did post-graduate work at Yale University School of Physiology. He graduated from New York Medical College in 1954, interned at Jefferson Memorial College Hospital in Philadelphia; and was chief resident in obstetrics-gynecology at New York Medical College, Metropolitan Medical Center in 1957-58."

He lived with his wife, the former Doris Lane of Brunswick, Ga. and their son, Wesley, at 3186 Rosendale Rd., Niskayuna. Doris died during the Spring of 2021.

Selected Personnel Affiliated With Bellevue Hospital

ABBE, ROBERT T.

Mr. Abbe was a consultant with expertise in material management and purchasing. He was invited to act as a consultant for Bellevue personnel regarding purchasing practices in 1984.

Mr. Abbe, from Massachusetts, attended high school in Winchester (1942), Union College with a BA in Economics (1949), and in between spent three years serving with the U.S. Navy Submarine Service (1943-1946).

He worked for General Electric from 1949-1983 in various management positions relating to all aspects of material control. He worked at five locations, spending the last ten years in Division and Corporate positions focusing on the purchase of steel for GE as a whole.

Having interviewed several Bellevue staff members at the director level, Mr. Abbe recommended for Bellevue Hospital that the position of Purchasing Agent he established as the recognized person in control of all purchases, reporting to the Finance Manager. He also recommended that the National

Association of Purchasing Managers be a source for learning about purchasing practices and procedures, and a that proper clerical support staff be put into place.

Mr. Abbe was also on the Advisory Board of Directors for Bellevue.

ALBRIGHT, GEORGE, DR.

Dr. Albright came to Bellevue Maternity Hospital in 1992 and served as Chief of Anesthesia Services for seven years, assembling an excellent team and leading the area in research and education. In 2000, he moved to the Department of Anesthesia at the Stanford School of Medicine, California.

Dr. George Albright.

Albright attended Franklin & Marshall College in Lancaster, Pa. (1951), and graduated from Temple University School of Medicine in 1956. He did postgraduate work in the U.S., Canada, and as far afield as Finland and Australia, including flight surgery training at the US Navy School of

Aviation Medicine. Albright was board-certified by the American Board of Anesthesiology and Basic Cardiac Life Support. He held positions in Anesthesiology across the US, and was a member of various related institutes and societies in the US and Europe.

He published two books (1978, 1986), and many articles in several professional journals in the fields of Anesthesiology and Obstetrics/Gynecology. George wrote numerous articles, one of which is in the top 10 cited articles in obstetrical anesthesia. His presence at Bellevue raised the level of respect for delivery of babies since it was not considered important at the time.

After three years in the Navy, George began a residency in internal medicine at the Mayo Clinic in Rochester, MN. Following the birth of their fourth child Greg, the family moved to Long Island, New York where George worked in aerospace medicine with Republic Aviation. This eventually led him to relocate to California to work at Lockheed Missiles and Space Company and settle down in Los Altos Hills. While at Lockheed, George participated in the space program helping to design the space suits worn by the Apollo astronauts.

Recollections of Dr. George Albright at Bellevue Hospital

Grace Jorgensen MD

As Medical Director of Bellevue, one of my principal responsibilities was to make sure that the hospital had the best available equipment, was using the most up-to-date protocols and was staffed by the best physicians, technicians and other personnel as it was possible to draw to Bellevue. You may recall that Bellevue as a privately owned solely Female Healthcare facility was certainly unique in New York State and perhaps in the whole of the US. I therefore made an effort to aLend national and international scientific meetings, covering all the medical specialities involved in the hospital, both for the content but also to meet and aLempt to recruit top-notch physicians to our staff.

Dr. Albright and I met for the first time at an OBGYN meeting in Chicago sometime in 1991, at which he may have been one of the invited speakers. I was aware of him through his reputation, since he was the author of a book on OBGYN Anesthesia which had become a standard in the field. During our conversation I must have men&oned that one of my grandsons was attending Franklin & Marshall and he said that that was his Alma Mater and that the college had been good for him. He spoke of his interest in his field of OBGYN anesthesia because he felt that women should have a good experience during childbirth. He was interested in Bellevue's plan to increase its Anesthesia Department and he agreed to come to Bellevue to be in charge of that development. Luckily, his wife was also interested and they arrived in Schenectady in early 1992.

Together they developed a lovely home and his wife Dolly became a close friend of several Niskayuna women. Dr. Albright completely overhauled the department, upgrading the equipment, creating new office space, including an anesthesia call-room, as well as building a strong staff. By 1996, the Department was fully staffed with six board qualified anesthesia physicians and operated 24/7, offering a wide range of protocols and drugs. An important contribution at that time was the development of two patient pamphlets, "Pain Relief for Labor & Delivery" and "Surgical Anesthesia". In addition the group insisted on a protocol requiring a meeting with every patient for a pre-anesthesia evaluation. Meetings of this nature greatly reduced anxiety especially in complicated cases. Standardized anesthesia records were developed, as were standing orders for epidural procedure (more commonly known as 'paradise') during Labor and Delivery. These were warmly appreciated by the patients. Also a major effort was made to reduce post-op pain using spinal narcotics in addition to epidural. These methods for reducing post-op pain resulted in an 80 percent increase in patient satisfaction with post-op comfort.

Looking back, I must say that Dr. Albright and his colleagues had a great and lasting impact on the anesthesia procedures at Bellevue. Whereas the national average for the surgical failure rate for regional anesthesia (conversion to general anesthesia) was 5-10%, Bellevue's rate over the period 1993 to 1995 decreased from 2.4% to 1.8% and the national spinal "wet tap" was 0.5 to 2.0%, whereas the Bellevue rate decreased from 0.5% to 0.1%. In fact, our procedures in this area earned national renown and I was chosen to be a faculty member at one of the scientific meetings at the Snowmass Conference Center located in Aspen, Co., at which Bellevue was honored with an award for being a unique private hospital solely for women's healthcare and emphasizing its high quality of patient care.

I deeply respected Dr. Albright because he was his own man. He was a kind, considerate, caring gentleman. As a professional, he was a giant in his field. His commitment to provide pain relief under the patient's full control in a sure and dependable manner fitted-in admirably with the hospital's complete emphasis on providing the patient with a wonderful experience whilst undergoing childbirth.

Grace Jorgensen MD, April 3, 2020

APPERSON, JOY, RN

Joy Apperson began in 1973 working nights with Mabel Fan. After her two daughters were born at Bellevue, Joy worked the evening shift. She later transferred to days as the Nursery Manager. She was always interested in expanding her clinical knowledge and experience, so she moved to Labor and Delivery and then to AM Surge, retiring in 2014 after 41 years of service. Joy had a great sense of fun and every unit she worked was always decorated appropriately for every single holiday.

She recently recalled one memorable Bellevue incident, *"One time I travelled in the parent's truck to Hartford Connecticut in order to transport a preemie baby back to our nursery. Such personalized service to the patient would be unheard of today."*

Her final comment was, *"The thing that made Bellevue so safe for parents was the nursing chain of command had strong clinically skilled nurses which made for effective and efficient management. As a result we were alway able to do our best for the patients because every boss had worked as staff on the unit they managed."*

APPLE, DOROTHY, RN

Dorothy Apple was a nurse at Bellevue Hospital.

ATASHIAN, ARAM, DIRECTOR OF CLINICAL LABORATORY

In 1953, Atashian's laboratory at Bellevue was hardly more than a microscope, a Bunsen burner, and four walls. His work, his professional ambition, and his dedication to his work and to Bellevue turned that start-up laboratory into one of the pre-eminent laboratories in the Capital District, with Atashian as director. He was also the Executive Director of the Bellevue Research Foundation. Atashian retired after 35 years of service in 1989. He passed away in 1991.

Aram Atashian.

Roasted and toasted after his three-decades-plus service to Bellevue, Atashian is remembered by his successor, Dr. John M. Donhowe, as the epitome of a laboratory scientist: professional, quality-conscious, full of initiative, always on top of developments and activities in his field. He was also practical, direct with his patients, and not shy about telling patient's doctors how things could be, or should be changed for the better. Nurse Printsky, who came to Bellevue as a teenager to earn money for a class trip and stayed to become one of Bellevue's longest and most loyal staff members, recalls Atashian as always being willing to help her and others with their studies. He was also a cigar and rummy partner with Sanford Roth, Bellevue's Chief Financial Officer from 1985-1994 , and chief operational officer from 1994-1998. Some of those employed in the Laboratory remember him not only as "boss," but also as a friend, a man conscious of his position, his responsibilities, with drive and determination to live up to the high standards he stood for and inspired in those around him.

BAUM, JANE, RN

Jane Bailey Baum grew up in Syracuse, N.Y. She graduated in 1945 from Johns Hopkins Hospital School of Nursing, and earned her BSN/ RN, working at Johns Hopkins and other hospitals before joining the staff at Bellevue in 1971 as Director of Nursing Services. She served at Bellevue

Jane Baum, Head Nurse.

for fifteen years. Nurse Mary Printsky remembers her as being very active in recruiting an absolutely first-rate nursing staff for Bellevue.

Working through some years of great changes at Bellevue as the hospital expanded both in physical and staff size, Baum is remembered by those who know her well and worked with her, especially members of the Jorgensen-Westney family and Nurse Printsky, as being extremely good at her job, professional, organized, and committed to recruiting an absolutely first-rate nursing staff for Bellevue. Jane Bailey married Parker Baum. They had three children. Baum passed away in 2015.

BELLOWS, FRANCES, RN

Frances Bellows was a nurse at Bellevue Hospital.

BEST, MARTHA, RN

Martha Best was a nurse at Bellevue Hospital, earning her twenty-year award in 1964.

BORGHARDT, LOUISE

Louise Borghardt was a nurse at Bellevue Hospital, earning a twenty-five year award.

BORICHEVSKY, JOAN F. (BOARD, PROFESSIONAL)

Appointed Director of Human Resources at Bellevue Hospital, Joan Borichevsky attended Fischer Junior College in Boston, and received her BS in Business Administration from the Vermont State College at Castleton State College. She spent two years as an adjunct teacher at Ethan Allen Community College.

Before coming to Bellevue, Borichevsky worked at Whitney Blake of Vermont as a private consultant in personnel services. She established and developed the Personnel Department for the National Sales Force, field official, and administrative offices of the Norton Company of Granville, Vt. She also worked for nine years at Emma Laing Stevens Hospital of Granville, Vt.

BOULE, MARIE MOREAU, RN

Marie Moreau Boule was a nurse at Bellevue Hospital, and earned her twenty-year award.

BOWDEN, JUDY, RN, MED FACCE

Nurse Judy Bowden was also a health educator, a manager, and a community volunteer. She graduated from the nursing school of Russell Sage College, then took her masters in education at Columbia University.

She was an assistant professor in the Department of Nursing at Russell Sage, and Director of education for the OB/GYN Birthing Center Association. Bowden was the Manager of Women's Health Care Plus in Guilderland and Colonie, and of the Women's Health Center of Bellevue Hospital since 1998.

Bowden was a member of Sigma Theta Tau, the National Honors Society for Nursing. She was a fellow of the American College of Childbirth Educators, and was a certified childbirth educator with Lamaze International.

BUTLER, ELIZABETH A., RN

Nurse Practitioner Butler worked with the Women's Health Care Group. As witnessed by Dr. Clarissa Westney, collaborating physician, Sept. 27, 1999.

CASEY, MARGUERITE, Professional

Marguerite Casey was Manager of Employee Relations at Bellevue Hospital.

Casey earned her BA from Heights College in Michigan, and her MA from Mundelein College in Chicago. Casey taught school for ten years, then became Director of Religious Education from 1971-1978 at St. Ambrose Parish. She was an adjunct faculty member at the State University of New York School of Business, and served on the Board of the New York State Public Health Association and of the American Red Cross Albany Chapter.

Before coming to Bellevue, Casey worked for ten years at Empire Blue Cross & Blue Shield of Albany, formlery Director of Health Promotion and Education, Director of Community Affairs, and Personnel Manager and Staff Trainer.

CHAUDHRY, MUSSARAT, MD

Dr. Chaudhry is a diplomate of the American Board of Radiology. She was appointed to the staff of

Bellevue Maternity Hospital in 1980. Dr. Chaudhry had worked previously for St. Clare's Hospital from 1976-1978.

She was an instructor in the Dept. of Radiology and assistant attending in Radiology at Albany Medical. A Pakistani-born American citizen, she and her husband Dr. Muhammad Ashaff Chaudhry, a cardiologist, took up residence in the Albany area.

CHEON, DR. HONG KYU

Dr. Cheon served as vice president of the Bellevue Medical Staff under President Fred Pulver in 1979.

Dr. Cheon was a diplomate of the American Board of Obstetrics & Gynecology. He trained at Roswell Park Memorial Institute in gynecologic cancer, and as an MD at Anderson Hospital & Tumor Institute in Houston.

Dr. Cheon was the author of "Prognosis of Endometrial Carcinoma," *Obstetrics-Gynecology* (1969), and he was a speaker at the Meeting of the Association of O-R Nurses, Nov. 9, 1979, his topic "CA Insitu."

CHESKY, DEBBIE, PROFESSIONAL

Debbie Chesky was Head of Marketing and Public Relations at Bellevue Hospital.

COSICO, DANILO, MD

In an agreement dated September 6, 1995, and notarized July 11, 1996, Dr. Cosico, with a specialty in surgery, became Director of the Scrub Assist Service at Bellevue and part of the multi-disciplinary operating room team along with the Surgical Services Manager.

The agreement also allowed for Dr. Cosico's private practice.

Dr. Cosico became ACLS certified and thus qualified for in-house coverage for emergencies and to evaluate patients for surgical complications at the request of the attending physician. Dr. Lugaya Cosico, his wife, partnered in pediatric practice.

CURREN, EDWARD, BOARD, PROFESSIONAL

As Chairman of the Advisory Board of Bellevue Hospital, it was Edward Curren's duty and honor to present Bellevue Hospital Service Awards to the staff for their years of loyalty and skilled and faithful discharge of their duties. His wife Rita was an interior designer who helped in the design of Bellevue's building additions.

DAVIS, DELPHINE, BOARD

Delphine Davis was considered for and joined the Board for Bellevue ca. 2000.

DeROCHER, EDMOND

Edmond DeRocher, professional interior decorator and designer, served Bellevue Hospital in both capacities. Based in Glens Falls and N.Y., Mr. DeRocher chose furniture and fabrics and colors for the various areas of the hospital. He also did space planning for the commons and staff areas.

DONHOWE, DR. JOHN M.

Dr. John M. Donhowe was appointed Director of Laboratory Services at Bellevue Hospital in 1987. He was responsible for all clinical and pathological lab services. Before coming to Bellevue, Dr. Donhowe was Director of Clinical Chemistry and the Neural Tube Defect Laboratories at SUNY-Stony-Brook with the rank of Assistant Professor.

Donhowe graduated from Oberlin College and the University of Wisconsin Medical School. He was certified by the American Board of Pathology in clinical and chemical pathology.

Donhowe has co-authored several papers for various medical journals.

He and his family (in 1987) settled in Niskayuna, N.Y.

Donhowe was instrumental in bringing in-vitro fertilization procedures to Bellevue and the program was considered a great success at the hospital.

DOUCET, ROLAND E., MD

Canton-born Dr. Roland Doucet was elected President of the Bellevue Hospital Medical Staff in 1988. Active on the Bellevue staff since 1966, he was a graduate of St. Lawrence University of New York with a BA in chemistry. He worked for Krafts Foods for five years as a biochemist before graduating from Queens University of Kingston, Ontario. Dr. Doucet did his internship at Ellis Hospital and his residency at Maryland General Hospital in Baltimore specializing in OB-GYN. He was board certified in OB-GYN by the American Board of Obstetrics and Gynecology.

DUPREE MARSA, MD

Joined the Bellevue staff in 1999 as part of the Department of Anatomic Pathology. Dr. DuPree was a board certified Dermatopathologist with a focus on vulvar lesions. She worked with Dr. Marin Mihm at Massachusetts General Hospital, a world authority on melanomas.

DYKEMAN, MAE, RN

Mae Dykeman was the Head Nurse in charge of the night shift in the Maternity Ward of Bellevue Hospital.

ELSON, CLIFFORD, MD

Dr. Elson, OB/GYN, worked for Women's health Care Plus, affiliated with Bellevue Hospital, through the Extension Clinics in Colonie and Guilderland which opened in 1995. The Colonie Clinic was made full-time in 2000.

ENGLAND, WELCH, PROFESSIONAL

Born in 1926, Mr. England earned his BS in 1948 with a major in psychology and a minor in chemistry and zoology. In 1950, he served a one-year administrative residency at Harrisburg Polyclinic Hospital at Purdue and earned an MA with a major in clinical psychology and a minor in speech therapy. He served in the U.S. Army as a clinical psychologist for two years, and as a clinical psychologist at the West Virginia Penitentiary in Morgantown. England graduated from Northwestern University Graduate School with an MS in Hospital Administration in 1955. From 1954-56, he served as Administrative Assistant at Harrisburg, overseeing the renovation and updating of the building.

From 1956-1970, England was Head Administrator at Hershey Hospital in Hershey, Pa., working to get the hospital accredited by the JCAH. Under his administration, the hospital was enlarged, reorganized, and put on sound fiscal standing. From 1968-1970, England also served as Assistant Administrator at the Milton S. Hershey Medical Center. His position before coming to Bellevue was as Associate Hospital Administrator for the Milton S. Hershey Medical Center, Penn. State University. Directly under his administration at Bellevue were the anesthesiology department, inhalation & physical & occupational therapy, housekeeping and laundry, all food services, medical records, patient nutrition, pharmacy central, and services for supplies, stores, linens, material handling, as well as the accreditation program, and he acted as liaison with government agencies relating to inspection, certification, and licensing.

England joined the staff at Bellevue as Administrator in 1974. He resigned as Administrator and Chief Executive Officer for Bellevue in 1982.

ENOS, JENNIFER, NURSE

Jennifer Enos was hired as a Staff Nurse for the Upper Level Night shift right after her graduation from Maria College in 1982, working mainly in PCC (Patient Care Coordinator) and Labor & Delivery. By 1984, she was transferred to the evening shift in

Labor & Delivery, adding relief PCC duties in 1985. In 1986, Enos was promoted to Clinical PCC, responsible for Labor & Delivery, Surgical Services and Central Supply.

Enos achieved NAACOG certification in June 1989. She was nominated to represent the American Nurses Association "Search for Excellence Contest" in April in 1989. She was also nominated for the Capital District Nurses Association, District Nine award for excellence in leadership and management in 1990. Enos was also a nominee for the Ackerknecht Award.

FAN, MABEL, RN

Mabel Fan was a British-trained nurse from China. She never felt that her English was fluent enough for dealing with the patients and the public in general, and also suffered from facial scarring, which made her prefer to work the night shift in the Bellevue Maternity nursery.

FINK, IRA S., MD

Dr. Fink was Chief of Anesthesiology at Bellevue Hospital.

Before becoming Chief of Anesthesiology at Bellevue in 1968, Fink graduated from the University of Louisville, Kentucky School of Medicine. He served his residency in anesthesiology at John Gaston Hospital of the University of Tennessee, Memphis. He held staff appointments in anesthesiology in VA hospitals in Memphis, Louisville, St. Petersburg, Fl., and St. Clare's in Schenectady. He also worked in the emergency wards in St. Clare's Hospital and Ellis Hospital, and since 1960, part time at Bellevue Hospital.

Dr. Fink was a member of the AMA, the Schenectady County Medical Society, the American Society of Anesthesiologists, and the New York State Society of Anesthesiologists.

FORT, MARIA D., MD

Dr. Fort was born and raised in Valencia, Spain. She attended Our Lady of Loreto High School, Our Lady of Pilar University Orientation Course, and graduated from the University of Valencia Medical School in 1978. She came to Bellevue in 1986. She was the only neonatologist in Schenectady at that time. She brought to Bellevue CPAP (continuous positive airway pressure) used to keep the lungs of newborns open. She also brought to Bellevue parental nutrition in the form of intravenous.

Her post-graduate medical training from 1979-1985 was at the University of Medicine and Dentistry of New Jersey (UMDNJ)-Rutgers Medical School in New Brunswick, New Jersey as a pediatric resident, as Chief Pediatric Resident, and as a Fellow in Neonatology, completed as a Fellow in Pediatric Pulmonology at the Children's Hospital of Pittsburgh.

From 1983-1984, Dr. Fort was a Clinical Instructor in the Department of Pediatrics at UMDNJ, then an instructor in the Dept. of Pediatrics at the University of Cincinnati Medical Center from 1985 until her appointment at Bellevue Hospital in 1986.

Dr. Fort was licensed by the Educational Commission for Foreign Medical Graduates, took the (US) Federal Licensing Examination in 1981, and obtained a New Jersey Medical License, a Pennsylvania Medical License, was licensed by the American Board of Pediatrics, and obtained an Ohio Medical License (1970-1985). Dr. Fort became a junior member of the American Academy of Pediatrics in 1983, and has published in her fields from the 1980s.

Dr. Fort is currently taking care of babies of mothers who themselves were born at Bellevue.

FRALEY, SUSAN, RN

Susan Fraley was director of nurses at Bellevue Hospital.

FREDE, THOMAS E., MD

Dr. Thomas Edmund Frede joined the staff at Bellevue in 1981. He brought the technique of ultrasound to Bellevue Hospital. He was Chief Operating Officer of the Thomas E. Frede Corporation of New York as a 50 percent shareholder. He became, with the Jan. 1, 1992 agreement, Director of the Bellevue Hospital Medical Imaging Service.

Dr. Frede retired from full-time medical practice in 1994.

GAFFIGAN, MARY, RN

Mary Gaffigan was a nurse at Bellevue Hospital.

GALLO, SALLY, RN

Sally Gallo was a nurse at Bellevue Hospital.

GLASGOW, CONNIE, MD

Dr. Glasgow was the wife of Mr. Twitty Styles, a member of the Advisory Board at Bellevue, pediatrician. Still practicing in 2018 part time at Capital Care Pediatrics in Clifton Park. She was chief of Newborn Services at Bellevue from 1986-2003.

GLENN, BETTY, RN

Betty Glenn was a nurse at Bellevue Hospital.

GOLD, KATHERINE A., RN

Katherine Gold was a licensed practical nurse at Bellevue Hospital in charge of the evening nursing staff.

GRETZ, HERBERT F., MD

Appointed Chief of Staff at Bellevue Hospital in 1988, Dr. Gretz succeeded Dr. Harry T. Wood, who served for 22 years. Dr. William Jameson, Jr., was the Associate Chief.

Gretz graduated from Lehigh University, the University of Pennsylvania School of Medicine, and Albany Law School. He interned at St. Luke's Hospital in Bethlehem, Pa., and did his residency at St. Luke's and at the University of California-San Francisco. Dr. Gretz joined the Bellevue staff in 1970, was active on many committees, and served as president of the medical staff. As Chief of Staff he was responsible for all medical activities at Bellevue and was accountable to the Board of Directors for the quality of patient care and the implementation of any changes in medical practices.

GROVER, JOHN, MD

Dr. John Grover, former Chairman of the OB/GYN Department of the Lutheran General Medical Group, SC. of Park Ridge, Illinois, was not only a patient at Bellevue's Medical Imaging Department, but he became a valued consultant to Bellevue. He was especially interested in the development and expansion of healthcare for professional women. As a consultant, he was able to provide significant knowledge and experience for assisting in unusual and difficult diagnoses. He was always ready to visit when called upon, and he often participated in the Hospital's Lecture Series.

He contended that as more and more women entered the business world in many fields, including medicine, that access to healthcare choices for diagnosis, treatments, and therapies would require constant updating and upgrading by Women's Healthcare institutions. Dr. Grover was born and raised in Moorefield, W.V. and after service in the U.S. Navy, he graduated summa cum laude from Harvard College and then from Harvard Medical School. In his professional career he delivered over 5,000 babies. He authored "No More Babies: a Novel," penned while he was recuperating from surgery in early 1986 and distributed copies to his friends in 1988. Died in 2021

GUTSCHE, B. B., MD

Dr. Gutsche was an anesthesiologist from the University of Pennsylvania.

HAMILTON, CYNTHIA

Cynthia Hamilton was Director of Medical Records at Bellevue from 1968-1999. She was often the person who represented Bellevue in court, saw to it that Bellevue was always up to code and accredited, and kept records for all the committee meetings at which all manner of cases were discussed. She also dealt with the Joint Committee on Accreditation. She was also head of the medical library.

In 2006, NYS Senator Hugh T. Farley announced she was awarded the Breast Cancer Research and Education Award. She was coordinator of the Bellevue Woman's Hospital's Mobile Mammography program, and received the Health Professional Award, one of the 2005 Innovation in Breast Cancer Research and Education Awards.

HENNESSEY, WILLIAM 2ND, MD

Dr. Hennessey served as a pediatric and adolescent gynecology doctor at Bellevue, focusing on gynecological surgery, laser surgery, and infertility. His surgery for Bellevue often focused on pelvic relaxation.

HIATELLA, GERRY, RN

Nurse Gerry Hiatella was personal nurse to Dr. Grace Jorgensen.

KEOUGH-AMYOT, KRISTINA, MD

Dr. Keough was Medical Director of Bellevue Woman's Hospital from 1988 until she resigned her position on January 24, 2001.

Dr. Keough graduated from the University of New York at Buffalo, summa cum laude, with a BS in Nursing in 1970. She attended Russell Sage College for her MS in Maternal and Child Health Nursing, graduating in 1974. From 1976-1978, she was a non-matriculated student at SUNY Albany, then graduated from Albany Medical College in 1982. She did her internship in OB/GYN at Albany Medical Center Hospital 1982-83, and her residency in Anatomic Pathology 1983-1985.

Dr. Keough worked in Clinical Pathology at the Albany Veterans Administration Medical Center 1985-1987, had a fellowship in OB/GYN and Perinatal Pathology at Brigham and Women's Hospital, Boston, 1987-1988, as well as a fellowship in Clinical Pathology at Harvard Medical School. She received her permanent license from the State of New York, and became Board-certified in Anatomic & Clinical Pathology by the American Board of Pathology in 1988.

Dr. Keough belonged to several professional organizations: International Academy of Pathology, the Society for Pediatric Pathology, the American

College of OB/GYN, the American Medical Association, the American Medical Women's Association, the Association of Professors of Ob/GYN, the New York State Perinatal Association, the New York State Health Labs Association, and the Albany Medical College Alumni Association.

From 1970 through 1994, Dr. Keough earned many awards, worked on many professionally related projects, acted as a consultant and was an Associate Professor of Pathology, worked as a nurse instructor, and kept up her professional skills with continuing education in her fields.

She instituted the practice of meeting the parents of dead babies personally, explaining the autopsy results with great empathy, and answering their questions.

KULBIDA, DR. NICOLAS S.

Bronx-born Nicholas Kulbida graduated from New York University and worked as a research assistant in the Department of Chronobiology at the Cornell Medical Center. He earned his MD at the Universidad Del Noreste School of Medicine in Tampico, Mexico. Back home in New York, he did his residency in internal medicine at Mt. Sinai School of Medicine and Beth Israel Medical Center, then completed his OB-GYN residency at Children's Hospital in Buffalo, N. Y., and was board- certified by the American Board of OB-GYN and the Society of Laparoendoscopic Surgery. He served as Chair of the Department of OB-GYN at Johnson Memorial Hospital in Stafford, Ct. before coming to the Capital Region where his wife, Lydia, was recruited for the anchor position for BT News for Albany.

Dr. Kulbida was a clinical instructor at SUNY Buffalo Medical/Dental Consortium, clinical associate professor of medicine at Springfield College, clinical instructor and full- time faculty in the Department of OB-GYN at St. Francis Hospital in Hartford, Conn.

In January of 2000, Dr. Kulbida attended a group exploration of eating disorders at Bellevue. His wife is Lydia Kulbida, a well known local newscaster. He is currently Chief Medical Officer of the current Bellvue Hospital.

LATIMER, SUZANNE, RN

Suzanne Latimer was appointed Assistant to the Administrator of Bellevue Maternity Hospital in 1980, her overseeing duties including: infection control, risk management and safety, the physicians' assistant program, social services, patient representative activities, community education for patients and staff, and the development of policies and procedures required by law.

Latimer was from Watervliet, N.Y. She graduated from Guilderland Central High School, then attended the

Albany Medical Center Hospital School of Nursing and the Albany/Hudson Valley Physician's Assistant Program. At the time of her appointment, Latimer was enrolled at Russell Sage College.

Latimer became part of the Bellevue Staff as Interim Nursing Director only the year before her appointment, and had received a post-graduate position as physician's assistant for training at Montefiore Hospital and Medical Center in the surgical residency program.

Latimer is a member of the New York State Society of Physician's Assistants and the American Society of Physician's Assistants. She worked for the American Red Cross as a CPR instructor, was a volunteer for the American Cancer Society, and a speaker for the Girl Scouts and other youth groups.

LIM, DR. DAI M.

Dr. Lim attended Kyunggi High School in Seoul, Korea, finished a course in Biology at the College of Sciences & Engineering at Yonset University, a course in Biology at the College of Liberal Arts & Sciences at Seoul University, did his pre-med at Seoul National University, and earned his MD at Seoul National University College of Medicine in 1964.

Dr. Lima completed his Surgical Rotating II internship at Buffalo General Hospital in Buffalo,

New York, Pediatric Residency at Vincent's Hospital & Medical Center of New York, and his second year of pediatric residency then as Chief Resident at City Hospital Center at Elmshurst, N.Y. He was a Pediatric Fellow at Mount Sinai Hospital in Hartford, Conn. In April Of 1972, he presented a case of Galactosemia at the New York Academy of Medicine: "Inadvertent Temporary Treatment by Exchange Transfusion."

De Lim was the first neonatologist in the Pediatrics Department, coming to Bellevue in 1975 (leaving 1985). Dr. Lim helped set up and expand the neonatology department, obtained the newest equipment, such as a respirator, and made testing protocols such as that for sepsis (blood, spinal, urine workups).

He died in 2019.

LOGIOS, THERESA, RN

Theresa Logios worked as a nurse at Bellevue Hospital. She was given an award for 24 years of service.

MACPHERSON, TREVOR A., MD

Born in 1946 in Port Elizabeth, South Africa, Dr. MacPherson graduated from the University of Cape

Town with an MB and ChB in 1970. He interned with the Cape Provincial Administration, Groote Schuur Hospital in 1971-72. He was Medical Officer OB-GYN/Senior Medical Officer-Surgery at McCord Hospital in Durban in 1972-73, Registrar-Resident OB-GYN at the University of Zimbabwe in 1973-74, Registrar-Resident in Pathology at the University of Zimbabwe in 1975, Registrar-Resident in OB-GYN at the University of Natal in Durban in 1975-76, Resident in Pathology at the Hospital of the University Health Center of Pittsburgh in 1977-1979.

From 1976 through 1998, Dr. MacPherson split his time and medical skills between the University of Natal, earning his MS in Administrative Medicine at the University of Wisconsin, and being a consultant and resident in administrative positions such as Chief of Pathology at Magee Women's Hospital in Pittsburgh, and CMO of Quest Diagnostics Venture at the University of Pittsburgh.

Dr. Macpherson was a member of various professional societies in South Africa, London, and Pennsylvania. He was certified on all three continents since the 1990s. He published in medical journals, contributed chapters to several books, spoke at lectures and symposia and chaired panels internationally, and did research in OB-GYN-related fields.

Dr. MacPherson joined the staff at Bellevue in 2001 for a five-year term as Senior Vice President and Medical Director reporting directly to the CEO.

McGRINDER, GERARD J., MD

Named Chief Medical Officer at Bellevue Woman's Hospital in 2002 directing all aspects of medical care, staff functions in the hospital, and acting as liaison between the medical staff and the Board of Directors.

Dr. McGrinder earned his New York State license in 1991, completed his residency at the Brooklyn Hospital Center, and joined the staff at Bellevue in 1992. He was board-certified by the American College of OB-GYN and named a Fellow of the American College of OB-GYN in 1995. He served as Bellevue's Chief of Medical Staff from 1997-2002 when he was named Chief Medical Officer.

Dr. McGrinder, a first-generation American, was the ninth of twelve children of immigrant Irish parents. He showed an in-depth interest, if also somewhat unsafe now and then, in the context of a large family household, in science, manifested at the time through home-devised chemical experiments.

He was very good in school and was allowed to skip the 8th grade, heading to senior high school a year early and getting a year's head start toward medical school. He knew he wanted to be a physician. In fact, with two brothers who became pharmacists and five sisters who became nurses, the medical professional seemed to be the focus of almost his entire family.

McGrinder got into an early intern program the last year of high school through which he worked five days a week at Manhattan Hospital instead of attending regular classes. On the side, he studied to pass the Physics Regents Examination. He worked as an orderly every school vacation until he earned his MD. He was the resident advisor throughout his college years and prone to trying to persuade his friends to go to medical school. "All work and no play," was, however, not entirely his lot as he was known for giving great parties.

Medical school proved no different as McGrinder passed all his exams and thrived in all his rotations, narrowing his choices to OB/GYN or Pediatric Oncology, OB/GYN finally winning out. During his residency, McGrinder also worked as an inner-city physician in New York City. The fact that he could speak Spanish was a great asset to such work. The need to live in a safer neighborhood had him moving to the Capital District though without giving up contacts in the city.

Dr. McGrinder was known to be a very kind, very caring doctor, loving his work and always keeping his cool in emergencies. He seemed able to get along with all manner of people in all manner of situations, self-confident in his work and his abilities, yet never above trying to learn anything worthwhile from others and always open to new experiences.

When not deeply involved in his chosen profession, Dr. McGrinder enjoyed a good meal, the spicier the better, and a variety of sports such as bicycling, hiking, skating, and scuba-diving.

MALLOY, JOAN, LPN

Nurse Malloy was an LPN at Bellevue from 1972-2002, for many years working the third shift in the nursery and was in charge of the other LPNs until the State of New York decided LPN's should not be in charge.

The quality of the staff as well as quality assurance through evaluations, the management, the opportunities for professional development, the outreach through community involvement and education, and the "fun times" such as the staff Christmas parties and pool-side clam-bakes, all aided in attracting the best staff, keeping the best staff, and keeping that best staff at the highest levels of professional and personal satisfaction with work and workplace.

Nurse Malloy went to Draper for three years, switching to Linton as a senior, though she did not finish her nursing degree immediately, her marriage and the birth of her children interrupting. Once she finished her nursing degree, she began working at St. Mary's, then at Leonard, both of which eventually closed their maternity wards; she then came to Bellevue; Mr. Welch was administrator at the time, and Nurse Baum her supervisor. Like many of Bellevue's staff, Nurse Malloy was pleased and felt supported by the family atmosphere surrounding the staff as well as the mothers and babies being cared for. She has fond memories of her colleagues each as Nurse Willsie's uncanny ability to know exactly what each individual baby and mother needed, and Nurse Mabel Fan's desire to popularize acupuncture and to have all the nurses taste her cooking. She well remembers the overall spirit of the nursing staff, always willing to learn on the job to make Bellevue's nursery the best, and the doctors such as Dr. Lim and Dr. Mele who were willing to teach.

MANGINI, MICHAEL, CEO

Michael Mangini was the CEO of Bellevue Hospital and a member of the Board from 1984-2001.

MARTING, FRANK, MD

Dr. Marting was the first Chief of Pediatrics at Bellevue, 1971, bringing with him new concepts in the field, especially the monitoring of high-risk pregnancies. He performed the first exchange due to rh+ and rh- blood differences between mother and baby.

Dr. Marting was born in Columbus, Ohio. He graduated from the Exeter Academy, Yale, and from the Yale Medical School. There, he was a member of Phi Gamma and the Aurelian Honor Society. Marting served in World War II in the US Navy, retiring with the rank of Lt. Commander.

A pediatric doctor in Schenectady for over forty years, Marting was affiliated with the Pediatrics Association and served as Chief of Staff at Ellis Hospital from 1958-1972, doing double-duty as part of Bellevue's staff from 1956 till his retirement in 1974. He was a consultant at St. Clare's and at Sunnyview Hospital, and an honorary member of staff at St. Clare's and Ellis Hospitals.

Dr. Marting was a member of the Schenectady County Medical Society, the American Academy of Pediatrics, the New York Central Pediatrics Society, Sigma Xi, the AOA honor Society, and also the Rotary Club, the Mohawk Golf Club, and the Schenectady Curling Club.

Dr. Marting passed away in 1980.

MAURO, JACQUELINE, MD

Dr. Mauro served as a pathologist at Bellevue for nine years, becoming Head of the Testing Laboratory at Bellevue for nine years. He passed away in 1976. The Bellevue Board composed a resolution for inclusion in the 1976 official records, copy of which was given to her husband and children. It was a tribute to her professionalism and dedication during her tenure at Bellevue.

McCARTHY, FE TERESA, MD

Dr. McCarthy worked with Dr. Grace Jorgensen in partnership and was still practicing in 2020.

McGINNIS, MARY JOYCE, MD

Dr. Mary Joyce McGinnis worked at Bellevue Hospital.

MELE, DOMINICK, MD

Dr. Mele was born December 3, 1914, in Schenectady, N.Y., but his family moved back to their country of origin, Italy, returning to U.S. at different times as economic conditions and job opportunities varied in both countries.

Dr. Mele attended Union College, finishing in three years, 1937, instead of four because he took pre-college classes in Albany. He lived at the time in the Woodlawn area, the family moving to the Bellevue area when his father opened a restaurant and eventually bought two homes. In 1941, he graduated from the Albany Medical School, and then found himself working as a military doctor with the rank of 1st Lt. in California when he was drafted in 1942. Though it took a few years to reconnect and marry, Dr. Mele and his future wife, Elma, met while he was in the military (1942-1940).

Unable to obtain a residency in Albany at first, Mele, coming back to the Capital District from working in Chicago, was aided in setting up is own practice in pediatrics with the help of Dr. Ackerknecht, and worked with Welfare part time for little or no money with Dr. D'Orio. It was twenty years before he got a partner of his own. Dr. Mele was known for his kind and gentle ways and his common sense when it came to health care; however, he was also known for pushing an annual check-up for everyone rather than the prevailing attitude of seeing a doctor only when a problem had already manifested itself. He also worked to make medical check-ups and vaccinations for school children a regular event, earning him the nickname "feely Mele" because he checked the whole body, not just a quick look at ear-nose-and throat.

Dr. Mele took over as Chief Pediatrician at Bellevue Hospital from Dr. Marting, again stressing the need for thorough check-ups and preventative care for mothers, babies, and older children. He was known to let those doctors working under him make their rounds without micro-managing their work, but regular staff meetings made sure that everyone knew what needed to be done and who was going to do it. Dr. Mele retired from Bellevue in the 1990. He died in 2019.

MISTHAL, HOWARD, PROFESSIONAL

Mr. Howard Misthal of David Berdon & Company, worked for Bellevue Hospital as an accountant.

MONDRAGON-TIU, FE, MD

Dr. Mondragon was elected Vice President of the Bellevue Hospital Medical Staff under Dr. Roland E. Doucet, in 1988.

NAMKOONG, WON, MD

Dr. Namkoong was appointed Director of Anesthesia at Bellevue Maternity Hospital responsible for all anesthesia services round the clock.

Dr. Namkoong was a native of Seoul, Korea. He graduated from Kyngpook University College of Liberal Arts and School of Medicine. Before his internship at the Capital Hospital in Seoul, Dr. Namkoong served in the Medical Corps of the Military Academy for Basic Military Training. He held a residency in anesthesia at Capital Hospital from 1961-1963, after which he came to the U.S. for postgraduate training in Military Medicine at Walter Reed Army Medical Center in Washington, DC

Dr. Namkoone served in Vietnam at more than one U.S. Army Hospital from 1964-1971, finally returning to the U.S. to serve nine years as a rotating intern at Mercy Hospital in Rockville Center, New York, then on to anesthesiology training internship at Nassau Medical Center Hospital in East Meadow, N.Y. His training in epidural anesthesia qualified him for an Assistant Professorship in Anesthesiology at Albany Medical College in 1974, becoming the clinical attending anesthesiologist till taking up the position at Bellevue.

Namkoone was a member of the American College of Anesthesiology and a diplomate of the American Board of Anesthesiology.

NADHERNY, CHRISTOPHER C., PROFESSIONAL

Christopher C. Nadherny worked for Bellevue in the professional capacity of public relations and accounting. He earned his BS from Union College in 1975, and graduated from Wharton Business School in 1979.

From 1979 to the present, he has worked in the field of marketing and spending plans for such diverse companies as Funyuns Onions, Tostitos Tortilla Chips, Frito-Lay, Johnson & Johnson, and Burke Communications Industries. Before being employed by Bellevue, Nadherny worked as a consultant for international Spencer Stuart in/out of Chicago, an executive search firm. He was made a senior director/partner but left forming his own firm, The Proactive Executive.

NEALON, JOSEPHINE, R. N.

Director of Nursing; her father-in-law helped M. Grace start Bellevue on Bradt St.

NELSON, JAMES W., PROFESSIONAL

Mr. Nelson was Administrator for Personnel and Administrative Serves. He earned his AB from the University of Denver and worked ten years in advertising and insurance. In 1962, he became Senior Manager for Veterans of Foreign Wars, the National Home in Eaton MI. He is also a former Kiwanis Club Officer, PTA President, Boy Scout Chair, and MI Radiological Monitor for the Local Defense Unit.

NIAZ, ASMA, MD

Dr. Asma MD, was an obstetrics & gynecology specialist in Schenectady, N.Y. She graduated from Fatima Jinnah Med College For Women University of Punjab Lahore Pakistan and specializes in obstetrics and gynecology. Practiced at Bellevue while she had her own private practice. Has been practicing for over 20 years. She now is one of 32 doctors at Ellis Hospital who specialize in Obstetrics & Gynecology.

OSTRANDER, HENRIETTA, "HANK," RN

Ostrander was on staff at Bellevue as an obstetrics nurse for forty years before retiring in 1987. Before coming to Bellevue in 1947, she worked at Leonard Hospital in Troy, N.Y. during a time when, she recalled, the "old fashioned" rules kept women in hospital for up to ten-twelve days after giving birth even if no emergency or irregularities occurred and the nurses worked up to twelve-hour shifts tending them.

PATTISON, THETA. S., M.D.

New York City-born Theta S. Pattison is a doctor of dermatology and dermatological surgery with offices in Niskayuna at Bellevue Hospital and Guilderland, N.Y. since 1995. Dr. Pattison entered into an agreement to work with and take patients referred from Bellevue and the Woman's Health Care Group.

Dr. Pattison earned her BA in biochemistry from SUNY Geneseo in 1985, and her MD from Albert Einstein College of Medicine in 1989. She did her internship at Rhode Island Hospital, 1989-1998, and her residency at New York University in the Dept. of Dermatology, 1990-1993. She was board certified in Dermatology in 1993, was a clinical instructor at New York University and an assistant clinical professor at Columbia's Mary Imogene Bassett Hospital 1990-1994. Dr. Pattison opened her private practice in Niskayuna in 1995.

Dr. Pattison has received several awards and honors in her field, belongs to national and regional medical/dermatological associations and societies, and has given professional presentations on several occasions.

PRINTSKY, MARY, O-R, LABOR & DELIVERY NURSE

Mary Printsky went to work at Bellevue when it was in the Stone Mansion and when she was in high school. She wanted to go on a class trip to Spain and needed to earn the money to do so. A friend already working at Bellevue helped get her a job in the Housekeeping/Kitchen division. She worked the 6:00 a.m.- 2:30 p.m. shift. She remembers feeling a little scared at the tight-ship professional atmosphere under the direction of then CEO Paul Jorgensen, but she also remembered how quickly she came to feel the tight-knit family ambience that offered its staff rides to and from work in bad weather or other transportation difficulties, set out one or two hot meals a day for all levels of staff from the same kitchen which served the patients (full capacity 40 beds + ca. 20 staff), the quality of the food, and the fact that absolutely nothing was wasted as unused food stuffs were handed over to the "pig man" farmer to feed his pigs.

Mary washed dishes, peeled potatoes, cleaned around the patients (new mothers stayed in hospital longer than is usual today), sanitized the one shower on the second floor after each use, and, one task in particular which sticks in her mind to this day, washed the black and white staircase twice a day, which had to be kept clean and above all dry to prevent slipping, for all hospital foot traffic. The staff was not supposed to use the elevator unless transporting something for the hospital and/or patients, bringing food carts, or, for the nurses, carrying babies to their mothers. Sturdy, laced shoes were the rule. The extension built in 1972 added much needed space and better elevator service, but it also added distance to many of the housekeeping and kitchen tasks. Fire drills were a constant occurrence people, including patients, could smoke in the hospital in those days.

When Mary decided to go to nursing school at the Junior College of Albany, Paul Jorgensen helped with scheduling her work hours to allow her to go to school and keep her job. Printsky recalls that the doctors and nurses, especially Aram Atashian and Dr. Wood, always found time to help her with her studies. And she remembers that Bellevue, looked down upon as a "maternity home" rather than a "real hospital," took extra pains to attract and keep experts in the various medical fields, keeping to national standards striving to add services, and open to bringing in new techniques and equipment as they became available. Printsky was officially hired as a nurse at Bellevue in 1977. Bellevue by then, had brought in the newest techniques in ultra-sound, a true "Bellevue first."

While Printsky had thought to find a position in a hospital venue larger than Bellevue, there was, at the time, more nurses than nursing positions in the region, So she remained at Bellevue; saying that they remained strict and professional but fair, and it never lost that tight-knit family feeling. The head nurse at the time, Jane Baum, was attracting a first-rate nursing staff and Bellevue offered not only the basics for healthy birthing, but also surgery related to childbirth with its own anesthesiologist on staff, laperscopics ultra-sound, and a range of outreach as blood work for reasons other than just maternity matters, done by staff sent out to those who could not, for a variety of reasons, get themselves to

Bellevue. Also remembered was Mabel Fan, a British-trained nurse from China who, due to her broken English and facial scars, preferred to work the night-shift in the nursery, and Sophie Weber, mother of "Miss Diane" who hosted Romper Room, an early children's television show. The nursing staff rotated through the various activities, except for surgery, learning what needed to be learned on the job, coached and mentored by the staff: labor, birth, recovery, and nursery which was never left unattended.

Along with the professional yet tight-knit atmosphere at Bellevue and roster of perks such as meals, transport, and the occasional staff parties, Printsky remembered when the birthing suite was added in 1991, when a rose brought all the way from Germany was planted by the fountain which was, in itself, a memorial to M. Grace Jorgensen, founder of Bellevue: staff like Joe Ross who made sure that no matter the weather, the drives in and around Bellevue were always cleared and passable. Even when Bellevue was brought under new management, many of the staff stayed on to continue the "patient-first" professionalism demanded and freely given from its founding. From high-school-hired kitchen staff through junior then senior nursing staff, Printsky never regretted her choice to stay on at Bellevue. Indeed, she retired in 2018.

PUCCI, CARL, PROFESSIONAL

He was the Professional Chief Operating Officer.

PULVER, FRED, MD

Dr. Pulver, a obstetrician was a pioneer in the use of epidurals. Active on the staff at Bellevue for 38 years, he was elected President of the Medical Staff of Bellevue Maternity Hospital in 1979 with Dr. Cheon as Vice President, both of whom were re-elected in 1980. He retired in 1988.

Active in the Pacific arena during World War II, Dr. Pulver was a graduate of Syracuse University and the Syracuse University School of Medicine He did his internship at Ellis Hospital, and his residency at Ellis Memorial Hospital and Glen Cove Community Hospital on Long Island. He was an attending physician at Ellis Hospital from 1947 on.

From 1954-1974, Dr. Pulver served as Medical Director of Planned Parenthood in Schenectady. He was the first physician to use caudal anesthesia in obstetrics in the Schenectady region. He was a member of the American Medical Association, the American Academy of Family Practice, and the NE New York OB-GYN Society.

Pulver was the first to initiate epidurals in Bellevue with Grace G. Jorgensen following.

When not practicing medicine, this family man played the violin with the Schenectady Doctors' Quartet and the Schenectady Symphony. He is also a master bridge player.

RENZI, MAE ELLEN, RN

Mae Ellen had worked nine years at St Clare's Hospital before she started at Bellevue, working nights with Mei Fan. She then moved to evenings, working with Mary Guarneri. During her time at Bellevue, Mary was a nursery nurse, but during the day worked in Dr. Parillo's proctologist office. She also did all of Bellevue's x-rays, since she was a certified Radiology tech. She ended her time at Bellevue working days with Sophie Weber and Dora Wiltse.

Known by everyone as "Renzi" she is remembered by her co-workers as funny and outspoken. Like all bellevue employees she was also known for her hard work ethic. One co-worker laughed and recalled *"Renzi ran her nursery with a tight fist. Her babies did not disturb her swaddling."*

Renzi was quick and unafraid to confront the hierarchy whenever an issue or problem occurred. Even the most obstreperous doctors respectfully backed off when Renzi spoke. She recently was quoted as saying, *"We did not know how good we had it working for the old Bellevue until the new management took over."*

REUSS, MART LYNN, MD

Dr. Reuss was Senior Research Scientist for the Bellevue Research Foundation, Inc. Dr. Reuss was also a member of the Woman's Health Care Group, for which she specialized in ultra-sonography, all the while running her own private practice.

Dr. Reuss graduated from Penn State (1968-1971) and Thomas Jefferson University (1969-1973) for her BS and MD, followed by a four year-residency in OB/GYN at the Hospital of the Albert Einstein College of Medicine (1973-1977) in the Bronx, and a two-year fellowship in maternal fetal medicine at the University of California in San Francisco (1977-1979). For eleven years, she worked as a specialist in obstetric gynecologic Ultrasonography. She was an attending physician in the OB/GYN Division at Columbia Presbyterian Hospital. In 2001, she applied for the fall-term faculty position at the Center for Research in Women's Health & Reproductive Science at Stanford University.

From 1980 through 1996, Dr. Reuss held several positions in California and in New York in OB/GYN in private practice and as a member of a faculty at university. Before joining the Woman's Health Care Group, Dr. Reuss was an Assistant

Professor in the Dept. of OB/GYN at Columbia. She was certified by the American Board of OB/GYN in 1981, in Maternal Fetal Medicine in 1982, the American Registry of Diagnostic Medical Sonography in 1996. Her research experience runs from 1977 to the present, and her published materials, solo and with co-authors, from 1979 to the present.

ROSS, JOE, PROFESSIONAL

Joe was the head of the maintenance department.

ROTH, SANFORD, PROFESSIONAL

Mr. Roth, an accountant, was hired as Vice President Financial Officer for all services at Bellevue. He came from St. Peters where he had been Vice President of Finance. Mr. Roth earned his MA at Russell Sage College in Albany while working at Bellevue. He was a great friend and rummy partner of Aram Atashian.

Roth became CFO during the time of changes being made in the way of insurance in the 1990s with PPO's and HMO's. He recommended changes be made at Bellevue, such as going from a for-profit family-run hospital to a not-for-profit, with Dr. Grace Jorgensen and others from the Bellevue Board remaining on the new Board with new management. At Bellevue from 1985-98, Roth became Chief

Operations Officer in 1994. On his retirement John Westney stepped into his position; Roth worked part-time a few months later and remained for three more years in the finance department. Sanford continued to have a long friendship with the Jorgensen family. He died in 2020.

SACKETT, LINANNE, PROFESSIONAL CONSULTANT

Dr. Linanne Sackett, PhD, first earned her MA at Syracuse University; then her doctorate at the University of Albany. Now President of the Brunswick Institute, Dr. Sackett founded four organizations for establishing work strategies for building effective, properly managed, financially successful businesses.

Dr. Sackett worked in management positions involving computer fiber-optic technology, technology development, economic growth, and web-based approaches to business. Academic-related activities include a year as an adjunct professor in the doctoral program at the University Center at Albany, eleven years as Vice President for Academic Affairs at Hudson Valley Community College, seven years an program evaluator, a Verizon Next-Step Project Consultant responsible for evaluating the progress of twenty-six colleges in the establishment of cultural exchanges of student employees, and two years as principal investigator for the Next Step

Program NYNEX University regarding the coalition of the fifteen SUNY and CUNY colleges.

One of her main goals is to enable her constituencies to develop and build consensus while clarifying roles and formulating a vision.

SCHWAB, CONSTANCE, RN

Started the first volunteer program at Bellevue (candy stripers), teaching basic functions, how to answer the phone professionally and other basics.

SONI, SUSAN, MD

May 1, 1988, Dr. Susan Sony became Associate Chief of Staff at Bellevue, a board appointed position, to assist Dr. McGrinder.

SPINK, BONNIE JO, BSN

Bonnie began her career at Bellevue working the night shift. She was one of the more formally educated nurses, with a BSN. After some time she moved to day-shift working the RR. She took annual medical trips to third world countries, monitoring post-op patients, after the surgeons, who had also volunteered their services, had done their work. Bonnie also took one medical trip to China and she returned to report on the operation she saw done with acupuncture.

Bonnie was our quiet example of Christian Faith. Working with her as a co-worker was to experience a serene and peaceful room for both patients and fellow nurses. She was universally liked by all. Her one single transgression in all the years occurred one quiet low census night when Dr. Jorgensen came along and caught Bonnie with her feet upon on a desk, knitting. Bonnie later reported, *"She didn't say anything, she just gave me a look."*

STORY, DAVID S., MD

With temporary privileges to practice granted in 1987 until officially joining the Bellevue Staff and being licensed to practice in the State of New York, Dr. David Story had completed his residency at the University of Texas at San Antonio with specialties in obstetrics, gynecology, infertility and women's health.

Dr. Story earned his BA at Notre Dame in 1974 and his MD at the Medical College of Virginia OB- GYN residency at the Medical College of Virginia Hospital. Story served in the ER in Richmond Memorial Hospital in Virginia before his medical practice took an international turn. He volunteered as a staff physician at the Evangelical Hospital Khanar in Orissa, India, the Raleigh Fitkin Memorial Hospital in Manzini, Swaziland, and St. Jude Hospital in Vieux Fort, St. Lucia.

Dr. Skory took his licensing exam in 1980 and was board certified in internal medicine in 1982. In 1985, he was board eligible in OB-GYN by the American OB-GYN Board.

STRACHER, BARBARA, RN

In 1979, Nurse Stracher, operating room nurse at Bellevue, received certification in maternal gynecological-neonatal nursing by the American Nurses' Association, Division on Maternal & Childbirth Health Nursing Practice and NAACOG Certification Corporation.

STYLES, TWITTY, BOARD

Professor Styles, professor at Union College, was on the Bellevue Business Board of Trustees. His wife, Dr. Constance Glasgow served as Chief of Newborn Services at Bellevue from 1986-2003. He talks about his experience at Bellevue in his book, *Son of Prince Edward County* (Dorance Publishing, 2019). The story of Twitty J. Styles is his firsthand experience with the strike that took place in Prince Edward County and Farmville, Va. He shares the hardships that he experienced in grade school, the military, and college. Although this book is a collection of Styles's struggles, it also shows the glory of the people and students that he has affected over the years.

SWIATEK, BOBBI

Bobbi was one of the nursery nurses who was instrumental in initiating and setting up a formal lactation program at Bellevue. She authored a published article in Neonatal Network, a peer reviewed professional journal assisting neonatal nurses to remain current in their field. One co-worker recalled, *"Bobbi's calm, quiet demeanor was especially helpful to those frantic new moms attempting to navigate the art of successful breast feeding."*

TOMS, MARY ELEANOR, MD

Mary Elenanor Toms was born in Beaumont, Texas and went to the College of St. Elizabeth, Convent Station, N.J., John Hopkins School of Public Health: MS in Genetics, Temple University School of Medicine: MD, and did her Residency: Boston Children's Hospital. Boards: AAPM&R — Physical Medicine & Rehabilitation. AAHPM — Hospice & Palliative Medicine

Mary Toms

My Memories of Bellevue by Mary Elenanor Toms

It has been my pleasure to be both a patient (3 times) as well as a Consulting Physician over some 15 years at Bellevue, so I have experienced both sides of the service protocols of the hospital. In 1973, I arrived in Albany from my training in Boston and knew no one. I was dreadfully unhappy with the difference in the caliber of medical practice that I witnessed, and then I met Dr. G. Jorgensen and Dr. Howard Westney. The happiest journey of my life had begun.

As Dr. J and I began to form a professional relationship, she asked if I would consider a staff position at Bellevue. My specialty was medical genetics and counseling. I accepted, and this has resulted in a lasting relationship with Dr. J, with Bellevue, and to this day, with some of the families with whom I had the blessing of working with, both parents and children.

Dr. J was very strong in her advocacy for all her patients: that was, for all the patients in the Hospital. Knowing that a pregnancy or delivery of a compromised baby brought much tension and questioning, having a medical geneticist at Bellevue was unique for the Capital of the State of New York! My service continued until I left Albany 15 years later.

Much ensued at Bellevue during those years, involving my family and my memories of the incredible care, love and laughter which were always present. The year my husband was the Bellevue Santa Claus, the outfit was so good that even my children didn't know who it was. The Christmas party was a yearly event, anticipated eagerly by the staff and some very surprised patients in the hospital for the holidays.

Personally, Dr. J. helped and saved me from infertility. It wasn't easy, and her compassion and utmost caring made possible the birth of my three precious children. It didn't end there either, because my oldest daughter chose to imitate Grace in many ways, including becoming an Obstetrician Gynecologist herself. Now with four children of her own, she is a full-time practitioner and they named their last angel "Lily Grace."

One of the many highlights of Bellevue was the newest in a diagnostic tool of the day — i.e. ultrasound. I was the "test" subject for the "new" machine. For the expectant mother it gave great joy to realize the "miracle" she was carrying.

In my view, the ethics and professionalism at Bellevue exceeded the standard in all areas. One example of Dr. J's awareness, sensitivity and tenacity, occurred when I was hospitalized after a C-section delivery for my son. Grace had a patient who came into the hospital with major genetic issues. Dr. J. asked me if I could please see her ASAP. Well, sure, but I only had my hospital garb with me, and the only shoes that fit me were green satin and gold — not what I would usually wear to conduct a consultation. The father who was sitting in the room was a very high ranking military officer who couldn't have been more gracious then I should be up in my "fatigue" attire. In cases such as this, early consultation and education are important steps to make the patient and other members of the family capable of accommodating what might be an unanticipated situation.

This same time that my son was born was the coldest winter I believe in over 75 years in the Capital District. The snow was three quarters way up the flagpole. On December 24, at 4 o'clock in the morning, the fire alarm sounded throughout the hospital. Without any regard for my recent C-section, I flew out of my room to join the wonderfully efficient nurses who were carrying the noisy infants in their cradles out into the lobby, preparing for possible evacuation. The Niskayuna firemen were already in the lobby, with icicles hanging from their beards, glasses and hats. I shall never forget the joy we all shared when it turned out that a pipe in the basement had something wrong and that had triggered the alarm. We were all well! Just another Bellevue experience.

Another wonderful memory was the painting of Grace Jorgensen, the Founder of the Bellevue Hospital. I watched it being done by "Pat," who herself was a marvelous example of tenacity. She was quite immobilized by severe rheumatoid arthritis, but with her fingers manipulated small pastel chalks. She achieved a very remarkable portrait of Grace Jorgensen, RN.

Breakfast in the Bellevue Cafeteria for staff and attending physicians, was almost always gifted by Elmer's presence! Most often as chef! He was a strong deeply caring Scandinavian man who handcrafted many items in the new extension, and who had been indispensable in handling the business side of the hospital in the early decades of its existence.

Bellevue Hospital operated like a family. Families, including mine and all my children for multiple pregnancies and deliveries, and some of us felt so strongly about Bellevue and Dr. J. that we even named a daughter GRACE! The tradition lives on in even a great way — some of us who became mothers because of Dr. J have a daughter who became an OBSTETRICIAN, all because the person saw how she had brought life and joy to so many — All through the spirit of excellence at Bellevue.

At the side of Dr. J. was Dr. Howard. He was her husband and a man among men. You never knew exactly when he would show up at Bellevue as he had his own large family medical practice in Latham and he had established many new programs including developing a medical training program for New York State Emergency Medical Services (EMS). Whenever he spoke you wanted to listen! He was not loquacious, but had great content in everything he said.

It was the morning of my C-section at 6 a.m. on December 23, 1980. I was very peaceful and dozing on the stretcher outside of the Operating Room. Suddenly I felt a pair of very cold hands on my face and I looked up and he simply, so thoughtfully said, "You did a good job kid." It was a few short years later that he threw the same baby (now 2 ½ years old) into the swimming pool. I screamed "Howard, he doesn't know how to swim!" He smiled and reached out his arm to Sean and said: "Mama-watch!" Sure enough that little guy intently looked and listened to Howard and started and bobbed and started again and kicked his way over to Howard. He's been swimming ever since.

Spring-time was always beautiful at Bellevue. The entrance to the new extension had hanging flower baskets and the grounds were always well groomed. Every year, I can remember the birds made a nest in the eaves for at least one or two years. What a spectacular way to welcome life!

VAUGHN, JUDY, RN

Nurse-epidemiologist Vaughn worked as a consultant for the ASSIST Program developed by Bellevue Hospital to help individuals and couples deal with sexually transmitted diseases, supplying information, and support for those afflicted with STD's (Sexually Transmitted Disease).

Nurse Vaughn is the consultant for the service, which is designed to provide information and support to those diagnosed as having herpes or other STD's. Confidential phone inquiries are accepted, and private office consultations can be arranged for a small fee.

"Affected couples have feelings of shame, anger, fear and embarrassment. They feel alone, but in reality are among 10 million Americans affected by STD's." These conditions include *chlamydia, herpes, gonorrhea, venereal warts, vaginitis, syphilis, cytomegalovirus and more,"* says Vaughn.

VIETZ, PAUL, MD

Obstetrician/gynecologist Dr. Paul Vietz was born in Berlin in 1931, and attended school there from 1938-1951, then travelled to the U.S. and graduated from Bard College, Annandale-on-Hudson (1951-1952) as an exchange student. He graduated from the Medical School of the Frele Universitaet in (West) Berlin (1952-1958) with a license to practice in Germany and all countries of the Common Market, and in 1959 received his *"Approbation als Arzt,"* his medical license.

From 1958-1959, Dr. Vietz did a rotating internship at the Glens Falls Hospital in New York. From 1959-1963, he did his OB/GYN residency at the Union Memorial Hospital in Baltimore, the Hospital for the Women of Maryland, and his chief residency rotation at the Johns Hopkins Hospital.

In 1963, Dr. Vietz was licensed to work in Maryland and began his private practice in Baltimore and Westminster. He was affiliated with three hospitals in and around Baltimore, was Board certified in OB/GYN in 1972 and recertified in 1979.

At Bellevue Hospital, Dr. Vietz studied, demonstrated, and taught laparoscopic techniques for hysterectomy surgery. Dr. Gerard McGrinder,

Bellevue's Chief of Staff at the time, studied the technique with Dr. Vietz.

Developed in the 1990s, Dr. Vietz supported the use of and taught techniques for pelviscopic/ laparoscopic intrafacial hysterectomy surgery done using a laparoscope and thus able to omit the need for incisions and causing only minor pain during recovery.

Dr. Vietz held memberships in several medical societies and associations relating to OB/GYN, cervical pathology, and laparoscopy. He has published many papers, and has been engaged as a speaker and a tutor in pelviscopy since 1986 in the U.S. and abroad. In 1992, Dr. Vietz was awarded the Piannenstiel Medal from the Christian-Albrechts-Universitaet in Kiel for his contributions in the field of pelviscopic surgery.

VIGLIOTTI, GEMMA A., PROFESSIONAL

Gemma Vigliotti was appointed Personnel Director of Bellevue Hospital in 1979. Medical-related work ran in the family as her husband, John Vigliotti, was Laboratory Manager at Amsterdam Memorial Hospital where their daughter was a coronary care nurse at St. Mary's Hospital and where Mrs. Vigliotti served as assistant to the comptroller for five years.

Vigliotti graduated from Nott Terrace High School and the Mildred Secretarial School in Albany. She attended Fulton-Montgomery Community, the Wharton School of Finance, and New York University through the American Management Association, making her more than qualified to work at the Schenectady Operations Office of the Atomic Energy commission, as an assistant to the St. Mary's Comptroller, President of St. Mary's Hospital Auxiliary, and as Administrative Assistant to the Vice President of Corporate Planning at MOHASCO Headquarters before coming to Bellevue.

VOSBURGH, FRANCES E., MD (1897-1989)

This pioneer in women's health care and women in a male-dominated profession, was born in Voorheesville, New York. She was a doctor and a force to be reckoned within the Capital Region all her ninety-two years.

Vosburgh graduated from Vassar College in 1918, majoring in chemistry and biology, subjects not usually studied by young women. The post Workd War I flu epidemic saw her caring for victims of the disease as a civilian employee of the Army. The Army, a most-male dominated company, actually recommended to her the possibility of a career in medicine. For three years she worked for the Health Department Laboratory in Bridgeport, Conn., but in 1921, she enrolled in the Cornell Medical School, graduating with honors in 1925.

Vosburgh home-delivered her first baby while still in medical school, and went on to intern at Albany Hospital (now Albany Medical School), qualifying for special training in OB-GYN. Right after graduation, Vosburgh joined the practice of an Albany physician. The next great milestone in her professional career was the establishment of her own practice in 1948.

For thirty-two years, Vosburgh maintained her practice, provided services to the New York Telephone Company, mentored students at Albany School of Practical Nursing, joined the Ames Women's Medical Association (establishing a local group in 1972), kept up her membership in several professional organizations including the Albany County Medical Society, and held various honorary staff positions at other hospitals.

Vosburgh served as President of the Bellevue Medical Staff from 1971-1973, and was affiliated with Bellevue Hospital for thirty years plus. Her professionalism, always tempered by her genuine love of her work and for her patients, is remembered by the Bellevue staff and all who knew her during her sixty-four years of practice. Birth control was still an explosive and controversial subject when Vosburgh took up the cause, opening her own home to single pregnant women. In 1935, due to the efforts of Frances Vosburgh, the Mother's Health Center was opened on State St. in Schenectady. She was still actively speaking on the subject forty- four years later, supporting family planning choices publicly and in the face of editorial opposition.

Vosburgh found the time and energy to support M. Grace Jorgensen as they founded, developed, and ran Bellevue through its opening decades. Though she herself never married, Vosburgh was family oriented in every sense of the word, supporting both the overall concept of family and family planning while focusing on, developing, and enhancing women's health care to the very best of her abilities all her working life. More than 2,700 babies owe their entry into this world to Dr. Frances E. Vosburgh.

WARD, AGNES, RN

Agnes Ward came to Bellevue after proudly serving as a nurse in the U.S. Army. She met her husband, Robert, when they were both stationed in Korea. They settled in Schenectady, where Bob became the CEO of Sunnyview Hospital, a regional rehabilitation facility, and Agnes joined the Bellevue nursing staff. Based on her experiences in Korea, Agnes authored a paper in the American Journal of Nursing on frostbite.

At Bellevue, Agnes was OR manager (Operating Room manager), and because of her military background, the OR was always run on time. However, if the surgeon arrived early he could start his case earlier than scheduled, and this allowed the doctors to run efficient offices, which they much appreciated. Professionally, Agnes was an active officer of ACORN (Association of periOperative Registered Nurses). This national organization facilitated teaching, safety and practice dedicated to maintaining the highest OR standards across the country.

A co-worker of Agnes recalled: *"She had the knack of managing all the difficult and diverse personalities, turning them into an effective cooperative OR team for each case."*

This was the time, in the early 1980s, when laparoscopic surgery was in its infancy. It was nicknamed "Band aid surgery." It was of enormous benefit to the patient, who no longer had to undergo exploratory laparotomy/major surgery/big incision. A patient could be diagnosed for pelvic conditions that could be treated medically after the surgeon introduced a tiny instrument to examine the pelvis In those days, before the technology advanced, Agnes spent uncounted hours working with a local Schenectady photo company, Reale's Photo, to adapt a regular 35 mm camera to a scope so pictures of the pelvis could be taken intraoperatively. Dr. J was determined to be able to show her postop patients pictures of the pelvis before and after surgery.

Agnes was well respected by her staff, and tough when the situation warranted. She was a force who came to work first and left last, after the staff members finished their shift. She was always available after hours if you called her with a question or problem. Her ability to appease the staff and the doctors plus her organizational skills maintained a superbly run OR.

Although an enormously hard worker, Agnes could joke about her social life: *"Scrub dress at 5, mink at 7,"* she often laughed when asked what were her evening plans. She also joined the Bellevue Golf League, continuing her patient teaching skills to all newcomers which allowed her to continue playing her beloved golf.

Ward was instrumental in bringing continuing education classes related to *"developing leadership skills: a model for the nurse manager of the OR."* Having attended the first two-week course (1980) and being awarded further credits by the Association of Operating Room Nurses (AORN). Nurse Ward was accredited by the Mount Regional Accrediting Committee of the American Nurses' Association as a provider and approval body for continuing education for nursing. She was a military nurse in

Japan during the Korean War (1950-53) administering infectious control practices.

WAGNER, EDWARD F., PROFESSIONAL

Wagner was named Patients Accounts Manager at Bellevue Maternity Hospital in 1980, coming on staff with twenty years' financial experience having worked at several banks and for the Schenectady Teachers Federal Credit Union. Wagner graduated from Nott Terrace High School and earned a degree from Cobleskill State College in business administration. He is a diplomate of the American Institute of Banking, and a graduate of the New York State Bankers Installment Lending School, Dun & Bradstreet Financial Analysis School, and the Dale Carnegie Institute.

Wagner taught adult education courses in photography and organic gardening at Niskayuna High School, and served as president of the Niskayuna Kiwanis Club.

WEBER, SOPHIE, RN

Nurse Weber worked in the nursery during the evenings. Her daughter was "Miss Diane" who was the emcee of a children's television program Romper Room, which aired on WRGB, Schenectady television.

Diane Weber hosting Romper Room on Albany's WTEN, Channel 10, during the 1950s and early 1960s. Romper Room taught preschool children about reading and moral values. The show was franchised and different versions of Romper Room would appear in most large cities. Photo Museum of Innovation & Science.

WEDRYCHOWICZ, MARY BOURGEOIS, RN

Nicknamed "Bouge," Mary began her employment at Bellevue in 1971 working in the kitchen. She finished her nursing education while staffing labor and delivery, then moved to become the Recover Room Nurse, and ended her career at Bellevue in the position of PCC (Patient Care Coordinator), with responsibility for overseeing nursing throughout the hospital. She ceased her employment at Bellevue in 2006 after 35 years of service.

Mary left Bellevue to take a management position at Albany Medical Center. She became Nurse Manager of Labor and Delivery and Maternal Special Care. She retired in 2018

Bouge (she got the nickname because when she first came to Bellevue there was already one Mary working in the kitchen) and Michael were one of two Bellevue love stories. Michael came to Bellevue to work in the laboratory as a technician under Aram Atashian. For a short time after their marriage, they lived in an apartment on the hospital grounds, becoming neighbors of Dr. J and Dr Westney. Mike was employed at Bellevue for 29 years, ultimately working with Dr. Donhowe and a embryologist to set up an IVF (in vitro fertilization) program which was highly successful throughout the Capital region.

WESTNEY, CLARISSA, MD

One of the founders of the Women's Health Care Group, LLC, Dr. Clarissa Westney graduated from Union College and New York Medical College. Her two-

Dr. Clarissa Westney.

Diana J. Westney (1957-1993), daughter of Grace G. Jorgensen.

year general surgical residency was at Columbia Presbyterian Medical Center; her four-year OB/GYN residency was at Albany Medical Center. Dr. Clarissa Westney was on the medical staff of Bellevue as an obstetrician and gynecologist, and was an active candidate for the American Board of OB/GYN at the time of the founding of the Women's Health Care Group, an affiliate of Bellevue with locations in Niskayuna, Colonie, and Guilderland.

WESTNEY, DIANA

Diana was the daughter of Dr. J. She was diagnosed with Multiple Sclerosis in 1988 and died in 1993.

WESTNEY, HOWARD J, MD

Howard J. Westney, was the husband of Dr. Grace G. Jorgensen. See section in Appendix for his bio and the Atlantic City Shill Rolling Chair Company and his Bellevue Maternity Connection. See page 235.

WESTNEY, JOHN, PROFESSIONAL

John Westney worked as maintenance consultant and then became Chief Operations Officer for Bellevue Maternity Hospital from 1994 until 2001. He also served as a member of the hospital board.

WILTSIE, DORA, RN

In 1979, Nurse Wiltsie was given a special award for thirty-five years of service as a Nursery Nurse in Bellevue's Neonatal Department. She was given a gold chain on which to hang her diamond anniversary pin.

WHITTLESEY, EUNICE B., BOARD

Long-time member of the Bellevue Woman's Hospital Board, Eunice Baird Whittlesey was born in 1922 and passed away in 2009. She graduated from Whitesboro High School as valedictorian, from New York State College for Teachers (now the University at Albany) cum laude in 1944, and became a teacher of English, Speech, and Drama in New Hartford, N.Y., before marrying J. I. Whittelsey in 1947.

Active in both state and national politics, Whittlesey worked for the Republican Party at all levels, a supporter of Nelson Rockefeller as governor and Vice President, and for George H. W. Bush. She served as an enthusiastic campaigner for several Republican candidates from local to national level, including Gerald Ford and Ronald Reagan, having started as the Schenectady County Chair for the Nixon campaign. Rockefeller personally requested that she create the Volunteers' Tie Line as a go-between organization for New York State government and the public: she chaired the group from 1967-1970.

In 1970, Whittlesey chaired the Housewives for Rockefeller Group to publicize and disseminate Rockefeller's political views on women. Through the 1960s and 1970s, Whittlesey joined and supported several groups active in environmental causes from clean water to cleanup programs to beautification.

Never cutting down on her political activities, Whittlesey was extremely active for the Republican Party throughout the 1970s, 1980s, and 1990s. She was a delegate to several national conventions, served as Vice Chair for the New York Republican State Committee, and served on many Party committees from Detroit, Mich. to Elis Island. In 1990, President Bush sent Whittlesey to Bulgaria as part of a six-member group to oversee elections there, having already done so in Taiwan twice in the 1980s.

In 1976, Whittlesey was appointed to the US National Commission for the United National Educational/Scientific/Cultural Organization, and in 1982 to the Commission on Presidential Scholars. Whittlesey served as Captain of the Ellis Hospital Capital Fund Drive in 1986, and became a member of the Bellevue Board in 1987.

Whittlesey's background in education also made her an active supporter of the University at Albany through its Alumni Association and Myskania, a committee for non-academic students. She helped get the Albany Veterans' Wall of Honor, served on the Alumni Board of Directors, was National Chairperson for the Annual Fund, and was a member of SUNY Albany Development Council, the University Foundation, the Benevolent Association Board, and served as a class counselor.

Whittlesey received the Lifetime Achievement Award from SUNY-Albany in 2000. She is listed in *Who's Who in America*, *Who's Who of American Women*, and *Who's Who of Women in World Politics*.

WRIGHT, DOREEN GILLIES, PROFESSIONAL

Doreen Wright came to Bellevue as a professional employee in Public Relations and worked as well in internship and volunteer activities at Temple University from 1985-1988 gave leading seminars and workshops, liaising with parents and students and university staff, assisting in providing information through the weekly news letter, and in interviewing and writing for the North Pennsylvania Reporter.

Wright served as Program Coordinator and Membership Manager for the Greater Philadelphia Chamber of Commerce (1988-1990), Personnel Manager at Brueggers Bagel Bakery in Latham, New York (1990-1992), Youth Coordinator for St. Edward's the Confessor in Clifton Park, New York (1992-1 994), and as Member Services Rep and Teen Coordinator for the Parkside YMCA in Glenville, New York (1994-2002).

Elmer Jorgensen's Lineage

Elmer's lineage is not as well researched as Mary Grace's. However, we do know his father's name was Peter, and the grandfather's name was Christian, and the family originated from the town of Aarhus in Denmark. Peter was born in 1868 and died in 1935.

Elmer's father Peter was married twice and his first wife's name is not known. What is known is that she and their one daughter were in a sledding accident and the mother was killed, but the daughter was not fatally injured and was always part of the family when Peter married Freda Huber. Freda Huber was born in Switzerland in 1881 and died in 1935. Elmer was born in 1903 and was the eldest of four boys: Elmer, Ernest, Oscar and Walter, and one girl, Helga.

Following immigration to the United States, the Christian family appears to have moved to the Capital District of New York and family lore is that the Jorgensens either rented a farm in Charlton whose neighbors were the Norlands, or else the Jorgensen family members were well known to the family that owned that neighboring farm. Either way, that appears to be how Elmer and Mary Grace found each other.

My Management Style
by Grace Jorgensen

Someone, I recall, once asked me about my management style, and when and where did I learn my managing skills? Thinking about it, I had to say that I really had no formal training but I learned my skills by watching my parents and the ways they handled the day-to-day problems of running the hospital and providing at the same time a wonderful and happy family life. In my very early years at Bradt St., the family and the patients were in very close proximity, and even after the moves to Union St. and to the Mansion, the family was only next door and on immediate availability on-call. So my mother's insistence on the welfare of the patients

Dr. Grace Jorgensen during the construction of the new wings of Bellevue in the 1970s.

was engraved in my consciousness almost from the beginning.

Growing up, especially in my teens, I was 'Johnny on the spot,' ready to do any errand required, and in particular, I had the responsibility for the appropriate disposal of the Placenta. Over the years, I have had a continuing interest in the Placenta and I am pleased to say that in the last few years I have continually supported research at the University of Manchester, UK on examining the role of the Placenta in stillbirths. Being around the hospital so much, I saw the effective nursing going on under my mother's leadership. I never had any formal education in Nursing but my early experience has enabled me to recognize when nursing mishaps or mistakes have occurred and to take the appropriate remedies.

My other early mentor was my father, Elmer. He was and acted as a 'True Christian,' and showed respect and acted with respect to anyone, man or woman, with whom he had contact. At GE he was a tool and die craftsman and had the respect of his fellow workers. At the hospital he was his wife's supporter and especially undertook all the cooking and supplies chores. He arose early every morning and went out to transport the nurses of the day to be sure they were on time for their shift, then see about cooking his famous Elmer Breakfast that was so well known that several physicians made sure they were at Bellevue early enough to enjoy his breakfasts.

I should also say, that following our graduation from New York Medical College, my husband Wes and I began our association with Bellevue. As I took over as Medical Director, Wes was a strong supporter of mine and helped considerably especially in the strategic aspects of management and ensuring our growth and the incorporation of new therapeutic techniques as they arose. Even though I was also "on call" when a designated physician was not available, Wes and I made sure we had a happy family life.

Summing up, I would say that my education in management has been predominately experiential, and by successfully recruiting strong and knowledgeable professionals for the various specialities needed in the hospital, I have delegated the responsibilities involved, but, at the same time I kept a constant eye, walking the corridors, and encouraging everyone to do their best for the well-being of the patients.

Paul Jorgensen Biography

Paul Jorgensen, the second child of Mary Grace and Elmer Jorgensen, was born May 16, 1930, a year before the opening of the Bellevue Maternity Home on Bradt St. However, it seems certain that plans for Bellevue must have been well developed at that time. Paul grew up in the Bellevue atmosphere, first at Bradt St., then at Union St. and finally at the home on Troy Road, right next to the Mansion.

One instance he recalls, occurred when he was a teenager; there had been a heavy snow storm overnight and he and his father had to hand shovel a pathway from the roadway, Rt. 7 all the way up to the Mansion so Elmer could drive his truck to pick up the nurses for the day shift and then take home those nurses who had been on the night shift. From that time on, Paul much preferred Florida weather in the wintertime, and later moved his residence to Venice, Florida.

Following his high school education at Schenectady High on Nott Terrace, he graduated with an Associate Degree in Agricultural Engineering at SUNY Cobleskill and then went on to Michigan State where he graduated with a Bachelor's Degree in Agricultural Engineering. For the next twenty plus years he was associated with Bellevue in a variety of operational and management positions, including that of COO, as well as being active in the community. From 1974 to 1980 he served as Vice-President of Carmen Goody Pools and, from 1980 to 1992, he was President of Fantastic Steps and Wood Stoves in Schenectady. Paul was an active and avid Radio Amateur and was awarded the Henry P Broughton Award by the Schenectady Amateur Radio Club for exemplary services to the community. He was a pilot and flew a Piper Cherokee. Paul was a longtime member of Kiwanis International and had a continuing interest in politics, law, curling golf and fishing.

In 1955 he married Judith Nelson and together they raised a family of daughter Julie and son Jens and subsequently had three grandchildren. Paul died on February 28, 2016.

Dr J's "Three "Moms"

"The Mother's heart is the child's schoolroom"
-Henry Ward Beecher (1813-1887)

Dr. J's grandparents Andrew and Theresa Nordlund moved to Charlton, N.Y., in Saratoga County, in upstate New York in 1925 on a small farm on Division St. in West Charlton. In the ensuing years before this, the towns around the Capital District were hotbeds of smart women working for women's rights. Dr J's mother and grandmothers were surrounded by well known local suffragettes such as Lucy Allen, Chloe Sisson, Elizabeth Wakeman Mitchell and Laura Schafer Porter of Easton, Washington County, and Katrina Trask in their own Saratoga County. Growing up in this atmosphere had a profound effect on both Mary Grace and Grace G.

Theresa Wasmer Nordlund and her husband Andrew had eight children, Bellevue founder's Mary Grace was one of them. Her daughter Grace G. was obviously influenced by her mother but both her grandmothers also had a great deal of influence on the young mind of Dr. J. She remembers groups of women and her grandma in sewing groups talking about

Grace Norlund, founder of Bellevue, High School Graduation photo.

women's rights in the living room.

Certainly Dr. J's mother Grace was influenced having no qualms about starting the first woman-run maternity hospital in 1931, a time unheard of for women to be heard let alone start a hospital.

Theresa Wasmer Nordlund

Grandma Freda Huber Jorgensen

Grandma Jorgensen was born blind. Her father was called out to an avalanche and was out in the field when his pregnant wife ran to get him. An ambulance was called and she had a premature delivery and they put the new baby Theresa in an oven to keep her warm. She became blind as a result of that.

She was educated very early as a woman with deficiencies, who had problems and who could not be taught regularly because of her blindness. All the techniques that were used for the famous Helen Keller were applied to Theresa. They had the same kind of education. She was very kind, with the traits of an educated women. Even though she was blind she made blankets during the war. She had a young son who was a prisoner of war and she felt she was making them for her kids.

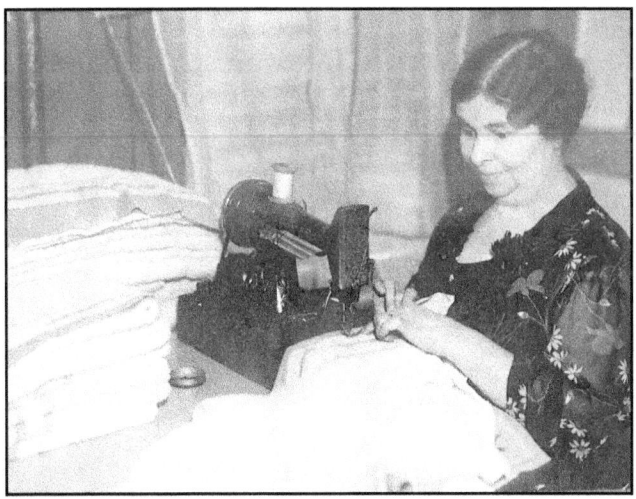

Dr. Grace G. Jorgensen's grandmother Freda, seen here sewing blankets for the war vets.

Grace had a very special event with Grandma Jorgensen. Grace was chosen to select her new artificial eyes. She had her eyes removed and replaced with glass ones. Grace picked out her new eyes when a great big box of eyes were delivered and she picked the eyes that she felt agreed with her.

Grandma Jorgensen was always great at explaining everything to Grace and taught her special cooking techniques with the knowledge that it was a way to make a man happy. She also kept a bird that was constantly singing. Grace spent a lot of time with her and learned a great deal. Grandma Jorgensen lived in an apartment on Henry St. in Schenectady with roommates, and Grace was a frequent visitor. Her Church people were very supportive.

Both of these women were widowed for a long time and had to take care of themselves. They treated Grace G. like a new child and Grace loved them beyond belief. Along with her mother, these women instilled a sense of strong female roles into Grace's consciousness which gave her the strength to compete in an industry that was very much a man's world, and she succeeded.

Westney, Howard J. "Doc" M.D.
1927-2012

According to the following published obituary Howard Jay "Doc" Westney, MD, was known as a man of action in his family, his medical practice, and in the greater community. He was born in Atlantic City, N.J. on March 26, 1927, the only child of Howard Westney, Sr. MD, and Mary Mirswa Westney in their home on Pacific Avenue (of Monopoly fame). He was related to the famous Shill family of Philadelphia, the makers of the famous Atlantic City Rolling Chairs that were used on the Boardwalk.

After losing his father at age 12, he was taken in by his Aunt May and Uncle Rollo Barry in Trenton, N.J. He was embraced by Quaker friends. He received much of the guidance that he needed from his school, the Westtown School, a Quaker school in Pennsylvania. They greatly influenced his life. He believed, and always acted, to contribute more than he was asked. Howard was at Westtown School on December 7, 1941, the 9/11 of his generation.

He enlisted in the Navy, where he was a corpsman, a medic attached to a Marine division. His service and training as a medic inspired him to provide remarkable leadership later in his life. After completing his undergraduate education at Dartmouth, he continued to New York Medical College where he met and married Grace Jorgensen, the love of his life. Together they finished medical school and he followed her back to Schenectady. He started his medical practice in Latham. As it grew, it became the Latham Medical Group in 1960 with partner Dr. Bruce Bagley which grew into eight physicians, two physician assistants and more than 70 employees. Westney retired in 1999. In 2001 the Latham Medical Group combined with Community Care Physicians that had 120 physicians

Harry and Howard Westney.
Courtesy Cindy Lucas.

Howard was raised by Uncle Rollo Barry (left). Family members continue to right, Mr. & Mrs. J. S. Westney Jr., Aunt Ruth, Aunt May. Bottom left to right: Craig Barry, Jack Westney, Marguerite Westney (Bounds). Courtesy Cindy Lucas.

and more than 800 employees. Westney also formed the Regional Emergency Medical Organization which now provides the needs of NYS pre-hospital EMS providers within a six-county region.

As a young doctor in Latham, Howard despaired when he saw how medical emergencies were handled. "Ambulance drivers" would go to grab a patient and drive breakneck to the hospital, where the first medical care would be administered. Often the patient died enroute. This was not good enough for the community that he had adopted as his own.

When not practicing medicine, Howard had his own band.

He did not wait for "someone" to do something about it. He took it upon himself to train firemen, ambulance drivers, and anyone who would learn. The "first responder" was born. He created the first training manual for EMS members.

Howard's long career of volunteer service to this community continued as he collaborated and cooperated with people in the Town of Colonie, fire and police departments, in an expanding circle. Howard began collaborating with like-minded people from around the country who developed training programs, wrote curricula, rallied political support, and wrote TV shows (Jim Page). They were a thousand points of light that, by today, have lit the whole country and beyond. The "paramedic" was born. Howard never sought confrontation, but he did everything necessary to overcome obstacles to progress. For example, in order for paramedics to function, the emergency room doctors had to provide orders by radio. When emergency rooms were unwilling to do so, Howard said, *"Fine. I'll provide the orders (as a volunteer), and we'll take the patients to a different emergency room."* He supervised thousands of emergency calls from his office, from his car, and from his home. He roped his younger medical partners in to doing the same. He did this for several years, until all emergency rooms were dragged in to the modern era. Agencies that should have helped often got in the way. Howard persevered. Howard treasured many lifelong friendships among the people who worked to bring modern emergency medical services to the greater Capital Region.

King of the farm. This pig gave birth to many piglets as Howard studied their diets and lives.

The Westney Farm

Dr. Howard J. Westney (1927-2012)

Even though Howard and Grace had busy lives he made sure they had a fulfilling married life. They purchased a Quaker - built Revolutionary War - era farm in 1965, six miles from the Vermont border between Rupert and Pawlet,

Vermont. The building needed repair and Howard went to work to restore the farm house and worked for a decade to make it a viable farm. It is where their children learned about the birds and bees as they raised pigs, cows, horses, and St Bernards on the farm. The dog was used as therapy and companionship for the kids and Howard. He rebuilt the barn and had one of his sows, Mr Smith, who produced many offspring for them. Howard also analyzed the pigs diet. One amusing story has to do with one of their children had a "Show and Tell" in school and after telling the class and teacher that his job was castrating pigs, Howard and Grace had to go into the school to explain exactly what was happening on the farm. The girls were trying out for the Olympics on the horses. They were awarded a prize for their Maple Syrup. Howard also kept in shape by drumming in a local band in the 60s.

Everyone who knew Howard loved him.

Howard J. Westney, The Atlantic City Shill Rolling Chair Company and Bellevue Maternity Connection

Dr. Howard J. Westney

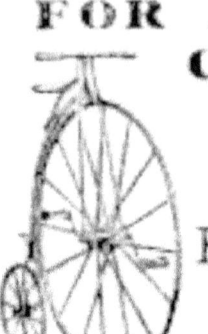

John Westney advertising his wares in 1881.

John Westney advertising his baby carriages on May 29, 1898, in the Philadelphia Inquirer.

Genealogy

Dr. Howard Westney, the late husband of Dr. Grace Jorgensen came from a long distinguished family of

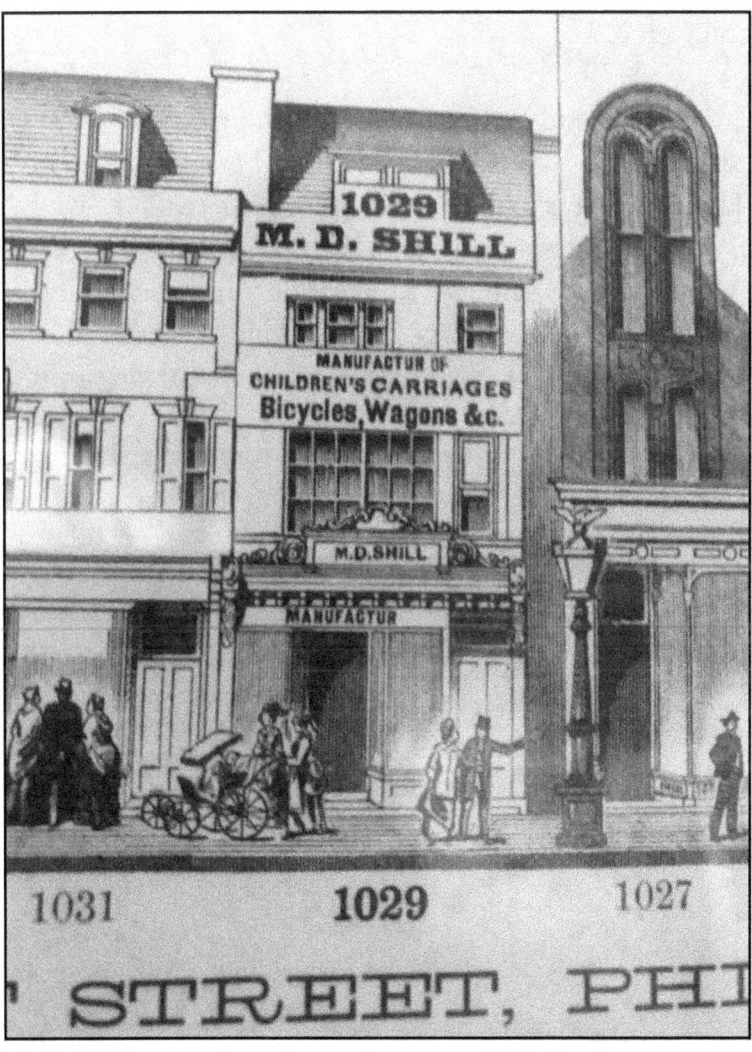

M. D. Shill's manufacturing and store at 1029 Chestnut St. in Philadelphia.

not only doctors but also businessmen from the Dey and Shill families of Philadelphia, including Harry J. Shill, his son Harry J. Shill, Jr., and John Westney. John Westney married Mary Willie Anna Shill in Philadelphia, on July 14, 1874. They had nine children.

James Dey and Isabella Cruickshank came to Montreal in 1834 sailing in from Aberdeen, Scotland. Their children were Charles Dey, four years; Mary Dey, two and one half; and twin babies Margaret and Annie. They came to Montreal but moved to New Glasgow in the county of Montcalm, 40 miles plus from Montreal, and opened a saw mill, turning mill,

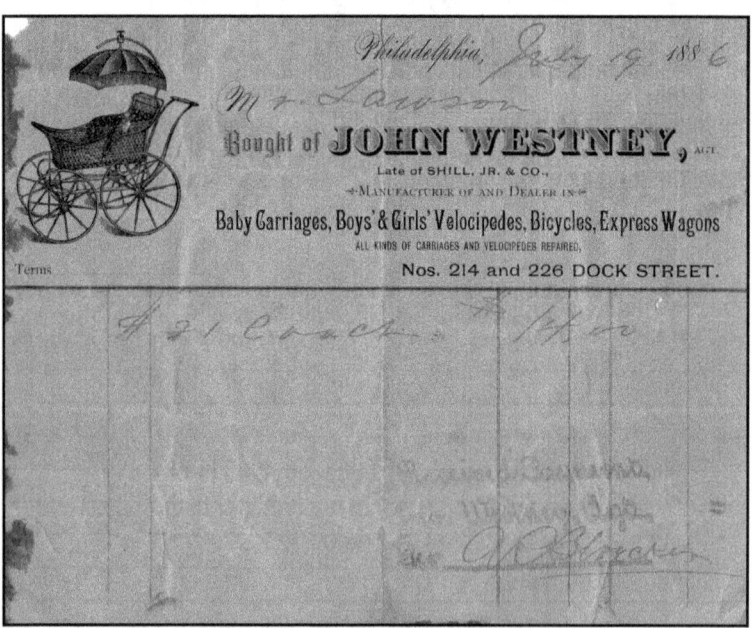

Bill of sale for a number 21 coach for $14.00. John Westney was now on his own in 1886.

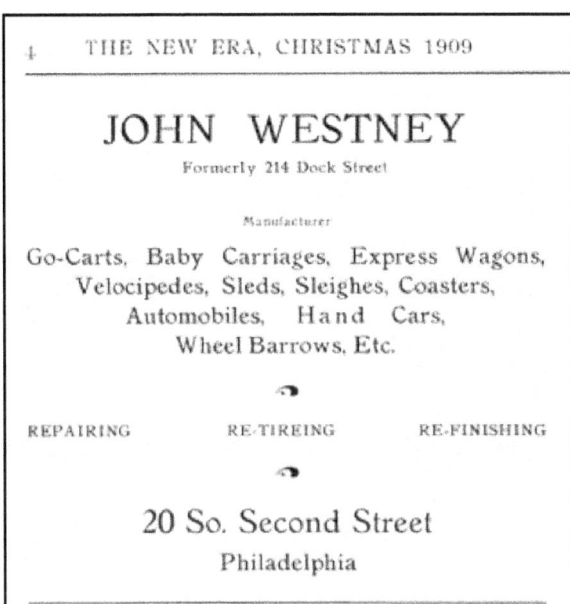

grist mill and a carding mill. While here the Deys had almost a dozen more children.

Children were:

Charles, July 10, 1830; Mary, Dec. 26, 1831; Margaret, Dec. 30 1833; Annie, Dec. 30, 1833; William, Jan. 2, 1836; Elizabeth, Apr 25 1838; Agnes, Dec. 31, 1839. Died in 1842; John Loudon, July 26, 1841. Died in 1842; James, June 26, 1842. Died in 1842; Isabella, July 26, 1844. Died in Philly, June 18, 1868; Ellen, June 25, 1846. Died in 1846; Alexander, May 26, 1847. Died July 26, 1872; Katherine, May 11, 1849.

Three infant sons; James, Dec. 22, 1853.

JAMES DEY. MARY DEY SHILL.

Agnes Cruickshank was the invalid sister of Isabella. She recovered and married John Shill of England, a widower with four children.

Mary Dey visited Agnes in Montreal and met their oldest son Harry, fell in love, and they were married.

> No. 164,107. HARRY J. SHILL, jr., of Philadelphia, Pa., for "Children's carriages."—Application filed 3rd March, 1875.
>
> *Brief.*—"Permits firm adjustment of top in three positions. Top-standards may be withdrawn from sockets, and baby-fastening device substituted."
>
> *Claim.*—" 1, the combination, with the body A and the top B of a juvenile-carriage, of pivot F, standard-sections E, having projections C and G, and standard-sections D, having slots e and sockets H, whereby the sections are rendered capable of extension and vibratory motion, and their right-line position is retained, substantially as set forth. 2, the combination of the body A, sockets I, ring-shanks J, and the strap K, substantially as set forth."

Harry Junior received a patent for his additions to a baby carriage in 1875.

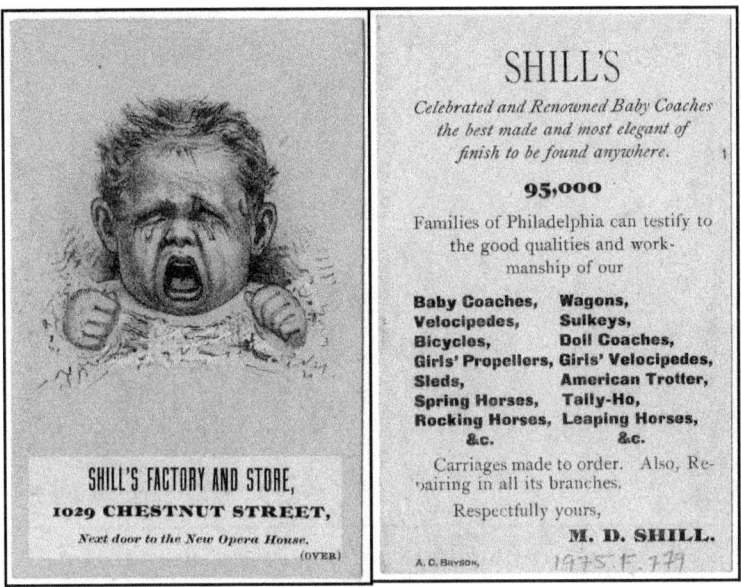

M. D. Shill's Factory and Store. This Victorian Trading Card listed on the back all the products they made. Harry Shill named the company in his wife's name M. D. stood for Mary Dey and she ran the company.

By 1880 John Westney had taken over the Shill Junior company.

J. Westney Victorian trading card advertising his wares on the backside of the card.

Harry J. Shill married Mary Dey at New Glasgow, Canada, on May 8, 1848. (Harry died in Atlantic City, Nov 23, 1902 at 75.)

Harry was born in Gloucestershire in 1828 and was one of the 500 boys who sang greetings for the coronation of Queen Victoria.

Their children were:

Matilda Esther, born New Glasgow, March 13, 1849, and died in Philly, May 26, 1865,; Harry James, born March 4, 1851, (Harry, Jr.,; Louisa Virginia, Oct 4, 1853; Amanda, Feb 23, 1856 and died an infant; Mary Willie Anna, June 15, 1858. Last four born in Philly.

Harry J. Shill, Jr., married Annie Brotherhead in Philly on August 5, 1873. (Harry died in Atlantic City, Nov. 5, 1908)

Their children were Annie Emily, born Aug. 28, 1874 and Mignon Alma, Oct 11, 1876, who died May 21, 1881.

John Westney who was born in England in 1850 married Mary Willie Anna Shill (son of Harry Shill, Sr., she died on Jan. 10, 1920) in Philly on July 14, 1874. (John died on July 25, 1935, in Trenton at his daughter's house, NJ.)

Their children were Alfred W, born in Philly June 9, 1875; Clara, born in Philly on Dec 2, 1877; John Stuart, born in Camden N.J. on May 31, 1880; William Frost, born in Camden on Oct 28 1882; Howard Jay, born in Palmyra NJ on Aug 19, 1885; Harry Leon, Palmyra, Feb 14, 1887; Mary Willie Anna, Palmyra, Jan 22 1890; Ruth Dey, Palmyra, Oct 7, 1893; and Frank Rolf, Palmyra, Nov 19, 1899.

In 1850 Harry Senior and John Shill with their wives Mary and Margaret and Miss Annie Dey moved to Philly. In 1856 Elizabeth joined the group and brought Isabella in 1862. James arrived in 1870.

Harry Senior was a wonderful athlete and musician in Philly during the 1860s. Harry Senior and Junior started the roller chair business.

The Shill Company was carried on by Harry Weisgerber (mother was Louisa Virginia Shill, daughter of Harry Sr.) and Herbert Hemphill (married Annie Emily Shill), daughter of Harry Junior in 1910.

Harry Senior died in 1902 and Harry Junior in 1908. John Westney and his son William were "careful honorable and reliable businessmen." John was an agent for Shill, Jr. & Company makers of baby carriages and other mobile devices.

Harry Shill, Jr., had his own manufacturing company of baby coaches, velocipedes etc, at 226 Dock St. and 1315 Chestnut St. in Philly in 1878. In 1886 the business was located at 214 and 226 Dock St. in Philadelphia where it appears Westney is on his own. In a business directory listing of 1887 Shill Junior is sited at 1719 Bainbridge St. while Westney was at the Dock St. addresses. By 1909, Westney was at 20 South Second St. It appears that when Harry Junior went to Atlantic City with his father, John may have taken over the Shill, Jr., business or was a competitor.

Howard Jay Westney, M.D (son of John Westney and Mary Willie Anna Shill [1858-1910] daughter of

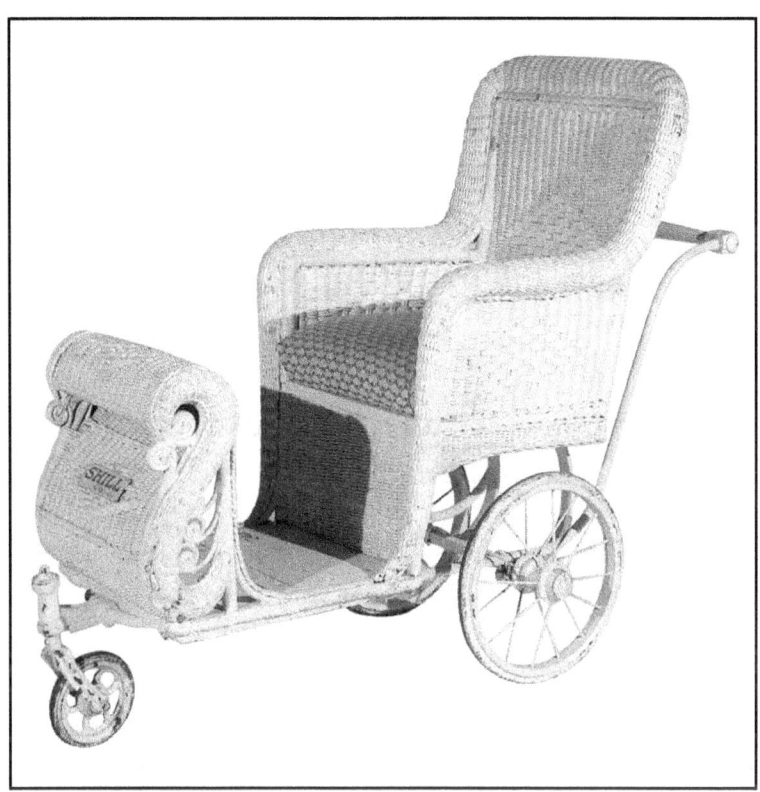

A Shill Rolling Chair for the Atlantic City Boardwalk in 1884 started the ball rolling for Harry J. Shill.

Harry, Jr.), was born on Aug 19, 1885 (died in 1939). He was married to Grace Gibson and then Mary Anna Mirswa (1900-1989).

Howard J. Westney and Mary Anna Mirswa were the parents of Howard J. Westney, Dr. Grace Jorgensen's husband who was born on March 26, 1927, in Atlantic City (died in 2012).

BOARDWALK ROLLING CHAIRS

One newspaper source proclaims that the first Atlantic City Boardwalk rolling chairs, designed by William Hayday in 1887, were modified wooden wheelchairs that allowed people with limited mobility to experience the sea breezes. In an effort to be sure the chairs he rented were returned to his shop and not abandoned at railroad stations or bath houses, he offered the option of hiring a man to push the chairs for the day.

However another source says that the M. D. Shill Company began selling rolling chairs to invalids in 1884. Harry Shill was a Philadelphia wheelchair manufacturer who also made children's carriages, go-carts, and perambulators, and other mobile devices, even winning a silver medal for a children's carriages at the Franklin Institute Exhibition in 1874. One source says he was a "Cripple." He set up a Rolling Chair concession near the Atlantic City Boardwalk and rented out baby carriages to summer families and also rented out invalid chairs for convalescents and handicapped people. His popularity soared when he designed the two-seater with a pusher perfect for lovers or honeymooners, although it was considered for many years improper for a single girl to ride with a companion in one. In 1904 a city ordinance legalized the use of the two passenger rolling chair and required operators to obtain a $15 license to use them. In 1914 the city redesigned sections of the Boardwalk with longitudinal planking to make the ride smoother for the patrons of the rolling chairs.

Triple chairs followed with a charge of 75-cents an hour for one person and $1 for two or more. Shill's chairs became so popular that, well into the 20th century, they became the symbol of carefree luxury for those sitting in the chair. His main addresses at the Boardwalk was Virginia Avenue and Boardwalk, and offices at 1017 Atlantic Avenue, yes, all Monopoly addresses.

In 1887 under children's carriages in the Philadelphia City directory Harry J. Shill, Jr. was listed at 1719 Bainbridge and John Westney at 214 and 1226 Dock.

When Harry J. Shill, Sr., died on Nov 23, 1902 at 75, the paper reported him as known in Atlantic City as "The Rolling Chair Man."

Shill pushers waiting for customers early part of the 20th century. The Shill company became one of the most popular rides on the Boardwalk during the 20th Century.

There was some debate whether Shill or Ezekiel C. Reed invented the rolling chair. Both Reed and Shill carriages were available on the Boardwalk.

On Aug. 1, 1902, the city organized a rolling chair parade, with the chairs adorned with cut flowers and smiling young girls. What was called the Floral Parade became, in 1921, a feature of the Atlantic City Beauty Pageant, known today as the Miss America Competition.

In 1907, Harry J. Shill, Jr, Mary D. S. Shill and R. H. Robertson incorporated the Shill Rolling Chair Company in Atlantic City with capital of $125,000 to

Double chairs rented on right for fifty cents a ride. Rolling chairs in the foreground. Around 1910.

make rolling chairs, go-carts, etc. They had about ten stations and 300 chairs at the time.

Ezekiel C. Reed died in Atlantic City on May 1926 leaving a $250,000 estate. He is given credit by one newspaper as the originator of the world famous Boardwalk rolling chair which came into prominence when the new boardwalk was built in 1896. Reed was a pioneer in bathhouse properties of Atlantic City. At the time of his death, he was the second vice-president of the Shill Rolling Chair Company at 1923 Boardwalk while his son David C. was president (along with being VP of the Equitable Trust Company). Alfred C. Reed also worked at the Shill company. H. E. Weisgerber (the Shill connection) was also listed as vice president and manager. Herbert W. Hemphill was secretary and treasurer, also a Shill connection since Harry Sr. and Jr. had died a few years before.

Reed's Rolling Chairs (upper right) combined with Shill's company in 1912.

A Shill single person rolling chair on the Boardwalk.

Reed and Shill interests were combined in 1912 (both Shills had died in 1902 and 1908) and a large part of the Reed fortune was made up in stock in the Shill Rolling Chair Company of which his son David C. Reed was president. There were over 2000 rolling chairs on the Boardwalk, two-thirds of theses were being operated by Shill Company in 1928.

Shill logo.

During the Reed estate sharing, David C. Reed, Atlantic City banker, received $79,838.04, Alfred C. Reed same amount, third brother Alonzo G. Reed of San Mateo Ca. received $75,405.55. Also a grandson Herman Leubert received $4,990 and Dorothy Reed Schroyer received $2,000.

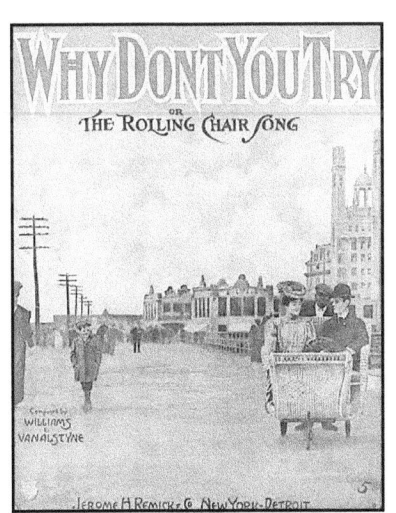

In 1905 you could hear this popular song being sung down the Boardwalk.

In 1916 there was a rate war as operators cut their prices to 30 cents an hour. William Garrett, an independent

Besides the Reed Rolling Company there were others such as the Blue Chair Company that competed with Shill.

A family of single and double Shill rolling chairs.

Getting your photo taken in a Shill Rolling Chair was proof that you were at the Atlantic City Boardwalk. Families, lovers, and even business people would get their photo taken in a Shill rolling chair.

Still popular in the 1940s, Shill's famous rolling chairs were even used by celebrities like the famous comedic duo Abbott & Costello seen below.

was ousted from a stand in front of a large hotel by the Shill Company which controlled thousands of chairs and offered a higher rental and got the concession. Garrett retaliated by lowering his price to 30 cents and the other chair companies followed.

By the 1920s their popularity reached its peak and if one did not want to ride down the Boardwalk, you could rent a chair at night to be placed along the Boardwalk railings for people watching.

A wax figure of President Lyndon Johnson in front of Louis Tussaud's Wax Museum in 1964 sitting in a three seater during the Democratic National Convention in Atlantic City. This was not related to the more reputable Madame Tussauds Wax Museum but owned by Ripley's Believe It or Not and was housed in the old Chalfonte-Hudson Hall Hotel. It was demolished in 1982.

Electric rolling chairs seen here in 1959 were banned later in the 60s.

The first proposal for an electrified chair, using storage batteries, came in 1907. Business declined during World War II and after many attempts, a law permitting 100 electric rolling chairs was finally passed in 1948 (and banned later in the 1960s). Later, a tram joined the rolling chairs on the Boardwalk and in 2015 electric trams that could hold 15 people were rolling on the Boardwalk. Two rolling chair companies sued to stop it.

While the designs of the rolling chairs have changed over the years, the basic look is still in use today and you can still relax, sit back, and enjoy ocean breezes

Wife of attorney John Stuart Westney pushing her grandmother in an early Shill roller chair. Courtesy of Cindy Lucas.

Keep on Smiling on this Shill rolling chair.

A parade of Shills headed down the Boardwalk.

and sunsets while riding along the Boardwalk. Prices today are $5 for a five block push. Twenty dollars will get you a push over 32 blocks.

Two lovers in 1949 on a Shill.

Awards and Recognitions for Bellevue

2016
Schenectady County Legislature. A proclamation honoring Dr. Grace Jorgensen as a nominee for the 2016 Senior Citizen of the Year.

2016
New York State Assembly Certificate of Merit

In recognition of the achievement of Dr. Grace Jorgensen, Nominee. From James Tedesco.

2016
Certificate of Recognition by Senator George A Amedore, Jr.

Nominee 2016 Senior Citizen of the Year.

2016
Certificate of Appreciation awarded to Dr. Grace Jorgensen Nominee for 2016 Senior Citizen of the Year. In recognition of your professional and volunteer services throughout Schenectady County, including the care of women and children served by the Bellevue Women's Hospital. Schenectady County Senior and Long Term Care Services

2014
Leaders in Healthcare Network. Selected as Doctor of Excellence by the Board of the Leaders in Healthcare Network. Spotlighted in Physicians Review: "Doctors of Excellence."

2010-2011
National Association of Professional Women recognizes Grace G. Jorgensen, MD, Woman of the Year.

2005
Niskayuna Community Foundation presents with grateful appreciation from the board of directors to Grace Jorgensen and Howard Westney, MD, members.

2004
Certificate of Meritorious Service presented to Grace Gertrude Jorgensen, MD (1954-2004). From the Medical Society of the County of Schenectady, Inc.

2004
New York Medical College in recognition of fifty years of service.

2003
Grace G. Jorgensen, MD, the Alden March Award on October 16, 2003, from the Albany Medical Center Foundation for a family serving the

healthcare needs of women through Bellevue Woman's Hospital (1931-2001) and Woman's Healthcare Group (1959-present). This award is presented to an individual who demonstrates a sustained leadership involvement in improving health care opportunities and has championed quality health care for citizens of the Capital Region and throughout New York State.

2001
AETNA Foundation Women's Legacy "A work of Heart." 2001 Distinguished Honoree Grace Jorgensen, MD.

2001
Certificate of completion State University of New York Upstate Medical University certifies that Grace Jorgensen, MD, participated in the educational activity "High Risk Obstetrics-Clinical Update."

2001
Union College Appreciation Award presented to Dr. Grace Jorgensen of Bellevue Women's Hospital in appreciation for valuable contributions as a mentor to Union College students.

2000
Bellevue hospital called the finest freestanding women's service in the United States of America at a conference in Snowmass, CO.

1997 (March 4)
Enterprising Women's Leadership Institute 1997 Golden Leadership Award "Going for the Gold" presented to Bellevue Women's Hospital Grace G. Jorgensen, MD, Hospital Board President.

1994
YWCA of Schenectady Academy of Women of Achievement Charter Members.
Dr. Grace Jorgensen

1992
Capital District Masonry Institute. Mark of Excellence awarded to Bellevue Hospital for the ultimate usage of excellent techniques of masonry in construction. Bellevue Hospital Birthing Addition and Alteration, Schenectady N.Y.

1992
The Chamber of Commerce Women's Business Council Women of Excellence to Grace G. Jorgensen, MD, in Business 10+ years.

1992
YWCA of Schenectady County presents this Certificate of Appreciation proclaiming YWCA "Woman of Vision" for distinguishing herself in her career and for outstanding leadership and service to our community.

1992
Woman's Healthcare Plus Service Excellence Award to Dr. Grace G. Jorgensen in recognition of exceptional contributions to the success of Woman's Healthcare Plus., the preservation of its philosophy of care, Your commitment to providing sensitive quality care for women, and your support and encouragement of your colleagues at Woman's Healthcare Plus.

1992
Citation from Senator Hugh T. Farley.

1991
75th Anniversary Celebration. On the occasion of the 75th anniversary of the Sage Colleges, we present you Grace Jorgensen with a 75th anniversary commemorative medal in recognition of your outstanding contributions to the advancement of women's health care and for your dedicated support of Russell Sage College.

1991
Enterprising Women of the Capital Region Special Recognition Award.

Bellevue Hospital Schenectady New York and its founder M. Grace Nordlund Jorgensen for Sixty Years of Service to Women in New York State.

1931-1991. January 25, 1991. Albany Marriott Hotel, Albany N.Y.

1991
Diploma, Clinical Course for Surgical Pelviscopy and Vaginosonography.

1989
Soroptimist International of the Americas. Women of Distinction certificate of honor presented to Grace G. Jorgensen, MD, Soroptimist International of Albany, New York in recognition of her professional/voluntary accomplishments in the program area of Women's Health and Well Being.

1988
Diploma Clinical Course for Surgical Pelviscopy.

1985
The Assembly State of New York Citation to Grace Jorgensen, The World of Well-Being. We have an outstanding citizen, one who is worthy of the esteem of both the Community and the great state of New York. Paul Tonko, Assemblyman.

1984
American Hospital Association Center for Health Promotion. Second National Patient Education Hospital Leader Awards Programs. Award for Outstanding Achievement in the provision of patient education services to a specific target

population. Presented to Bellevue Maternity Hospital, Schenectady, N.Y. Childbirth Reeducation Program.

1982-83
The Alumni Association of New York State Medical College presents this plaque of appreciation to Grace G. Jorgensen, MD, Class of 1954 Benefactor in recognition of generous support to our alumni association goals.

1979
Member the American Academy of Medical Directors Grace G. Jorgensen, MD.

1979
Silver Certificate from New York Medical College for the 25th anniversary of the conferment of the degree of Doctor of Medicine. To Grace Jorgensen, MD.

1977
Bellevue Woman's Hospital

1970
The alumni of Russell Sage College present the Doris L. Crockett Award.

1955
License to practice medicine and surgery in New York State University of the State of New York Education Department to Grace Jorgensen.

1955
National Board of Medical Examiners of the United States of America to Grace Jorgensen awarded Diplomat of the National Board of Medical Examiners.

1955
Hospital Association in City of Schenectady, NY. Ellis Hospital certifies Grace Jorgensen, MD commendably as intern July 1, 1954 - June 30, 1955 at Ellis Hospital

ND
American Fertility Society
Devoted to the promotion of knowledge in fertility and allied fields certifies that Grace Jorgensen has been duly elected to membership.

ND
Sterling Who's Who awarded to Grace G. Jorgensen, MD. Memberships are awarded to those persons who have exhibited excellence and leadership in their chosen fields of endeavor.

ND (No Date)
Phi Kappa Phi
Grace Jorgensen is a member of the Honor Society of Phi Kappa Phi by election of the chapter at Russell Sage College.

ND
The International Women's Leadership Association in recognition of her consistent excellence in Healthcare. Grace Jorgensen is hereby-designated delegate by declaration of the executive Committee of The International Women's Leadership Association.

ND
American Medical Women's Association certificate of membership Grace Jorgensen

ND
Certificate of Membership Grace Jorgensen, MD a member of IPR, Improving Healthcare for the Common Good.

ND
American Medical Women's Association, Inc. Certificate of Membership. Grace Jorgensen, M.D

ND
Certificate of Appreciation. Memorial Sloan-Kettering Cancer Center is proud to recognize Ms. Grace Jorgensen Westney in honor of

outstanding leadership, commitment and support in the battle against cancer.

ND
The Medical Society of the State of New York presents this Citation to Grace Gertrude Jorgensen, MD, of fifty years devoted to the service to the public in the practice of medicine.

Delivery With Grace

History of Childbirth in New York State

Childbirth in America can be divided into three periods. Until the late 18th century giving birth was strictly a relationship between mother and her midwife or attendant and was more of a social affair than a medical one and included friends and relatives at the event. The second period from the late 18th century through the first decades of the 20th century was a transition between social childbirth and medically managed childbirth. Eventually male doctors replaced the midwife and transferred delivery into a medical managed birth system. By the 1920s the medical model became unchallenged and the profession consolidated its control of birthing.

Historians have found that many midwives were very knowledgeable empirically about the birth process. Competent midwives knew the stages, recognized and managed a variety of difficulties such as abnormal presentations, and employed a variety of mechanical and pharmacological means to alleviate pain and to speed up delivery. After the American Revolution many upper-class urban American women started to turn to the new male European trained doctor for delivery taking away what was mostly a women bonding experience with her midwife and family. This male insertion into the female experience came at a price. Social conservatives were against it, as well as health

Delivery With Grace

reformers and feminists. Deliveries became private affairs often in darkened room with female friends and relatives banned from the delivery. However, many middle- and upper-class women continued to use midwives to continue female birth rituals and preserve modesty. Male doctors won over eventually since they promised safer, less painful labor through the use of forceps, drugs, and anesthesia.

Judy Litoff's book *American Midwives, 1860 to the Present* gives a clearer idea of midwives in the 19th century: 19th century midwifery emerges in her study as what she called prototypical "pink-collar" work. Her research found that midwives were usually poor, untrained, immigrant or black women with low social status and little occupational prestige. In fact, they were basically domestic workers with household and child-duties as integral parts of their job. Unlike their European counterparts, American midwives had no professional identity. They worked in isolation, serving small local populations. Unlike doctors, who worked to professionalize medicine by upgrading entry requirements and establishing professional networks, midwives had no way to set or disseminate knowledge. Their exclusion from formal training kept them in ignorance about forceps, anesthesia, and other developments in the field.

In New York City, the "Midwifery Dispensary" was founded as an organization early in 1890 to provide

Delivery With Grace

free attendance in childbirth to impoverished women and to train medical students and young physicians in the techniques of scientific obstetrics. From 1890 through 1893, the dispensary existed independently, but in 1893 it merged with the "Society of the Lying-In Hospital of the City of New York," thereby providing the institutional basis for the New York Lying-In Hospital. From its founding through 1931, the dispensary, called the "Outdoor Department of the Lying-In Hospital" for most of its history, provided obstetrical care to nearly fifty-thousand women on the Lower East Side. Many of its founders and attending physicians, including Asa Davis, achieved national renown in obstetrics.

By 1910 professional doctors lobbied to curtail midwife practices. Some states outlawed it altogether, while some put severe regulatory requirements that most could not meet. Since the midwife industry failed to organize they became the scapegoat for the newly emerging obstetrics industry.

Nurse Midwifery was introduced in the United States in 1920 but most practiced in areas that had no doctors. In the 1920s nearly three-fourths of American births took place in the home. Beginning in 1931, one Schenectady nurse, Mary Grace Jorgensen, was to change all that.

Delivery With Grace

Early Medicine in Schenectady

Seeing to the needs of the sick and injured began in New York from the earliest Dutch period in the early 17th century and continues today. This chapter will review what steps were used to provide medical care of New York's and, in particular, to Schenectady's early inhabitants.

The Capital District region of New York State is one of the oldest continually settled regions in the United States. The first European structure built in America was Fort Nassau, a small Dutch trading fort on Castle Island in 1614, now the Port of Albany. Upon moving over to the mainland in 1624 as Fort Orange, the Dutch were here to stay and eventually formed New Netherland, the first Dutch colony in North America.

New Netherland extended from Albany, New York, in the north to Delaware in the south, and encompassed parts of what are now the states of New York, New Jersey, Pennsylvania, Maryland, Connecticut, and Delaware. The settlement of Schenectady founded in 1661 by Arendt Van Curler, and 15 families from Albany, was the westernmost European settlement in America for the first two hundred years.

New Netherland was sandwiched between the two English colonies of New England to the north and the Virginia Colonies to the south. Populating the region was slow and a series of land grants called

Delivery With Grace

patroonships were allowed by the Dutch government in order to beef up the population. It is estimated that by 1655, 31 years after the founding of Fort Orange (Albany), the population of New Netherland was only between 2000-3500. Even by the time the English took over in 1664 it was estimated to be only around 9,000 people

Along with patroonships, the Dutch government felt that it could help the new colony by importing orphans from the Netherlands to help increase the population

Kiliaen Van Rensselaer, the patroon of Rensselaerswijck (most of the counties of Albany

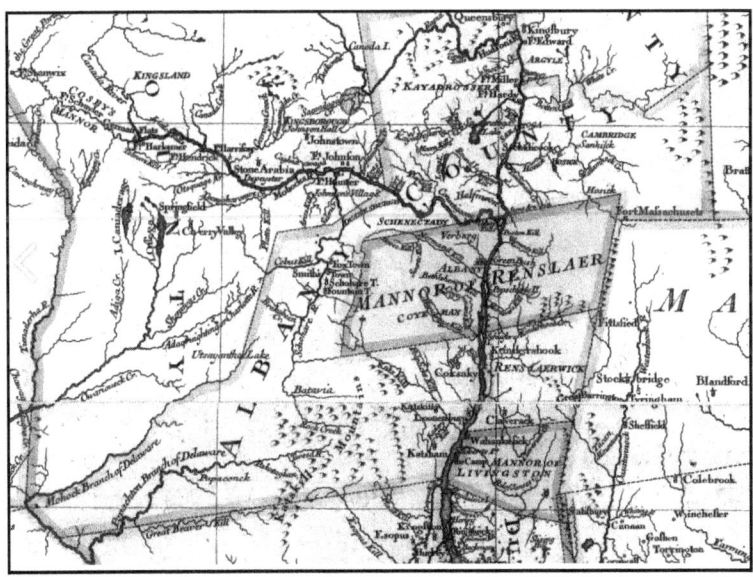

This 18th century map shows the original limits of Rensselaerswijck, today most of the counties of Albany, Rensselaer, and parts of Columbia and Green Counties from 1630-1686.

Delivery With Grace

and Rennselaer and parts of Columbia and Greene Counties from 1630-1686) hoped that his colony would be an ideal place to send settlers to work his land.

During the 17th century, "Comforters of the sick" were some of the earliest arrivals at Fort Ornage and New Amsterdam (New York City). Ther were two class known as *krankenbezoerker* and *ziekentrooster*. The first means a seeker out or visitor of the sick such as those overtaken quickly by an illness, while the latter refered to a comforter to those tha were very sick and particularly nearing the end of life, though the two terms were often used synonymously. Consolers usually came from the humble ranks of society such as carpenters, bankers, bakers, shoemaker, hod-carriers (brick or stone carriers), and even soldiers and tailors applied for the job. One of the earlierst settlers that held the job was Sebastin Jansen Krol. He ended jup becoming commissary of Fort Orange due to his knowledge of Native languages but acted mostly as chief agent for the company at Fort Ornage and helping to purchase the land that became Rennselaerwyck, which makes up the present day Captial District. Peter Minuit's brother-in-law, Jan Huych, was a comforter as early as July 1623. Minuit is famous as the purchaser of Manhattan from the Natives. Harmen Meydertsz van den Bogaert arrived in 1630 and came to Fort Orange. On the same ship was "Tryn" or Catherine Jonas, the official midwife and her two daughters. Hans Kierstede, a

Delivery With Grace

German from Magdeburg was the official surgeon in New Amsterdam for the West India Company in 1638 as well as Gerrit Schutt. Peter van der Linde arrived in New Amsterdam in 1638 and there is a record of him claiming surgeon, fees in Albany on September 17, 1639. In 1640, Jan Pietersen van Essendelft, a ship's surgeon willed his surgical instruments to Master Hans Kierstede, the New Amsterdam surgeon. Jan Pietersen was the first surgeon in the employ of the Dutch on the Delaware for two years and took over from Hanns Janeke who was a barber surgeon in the first Swedish expedition.

There were two types of "doctors" that came to New Netherland. One type is called a *Barbier* (barber-surgeon) who was a professional barber who not only shaved patients but also performed simple surgical procedures. The second was called a *chirurgijn* (surgeon) and the profession involved more rigorous training (usually four years) than a *barbier*.

These "surgeons" took care of many things besides shaving. They operated and performed major and minor surgery, did autopsies, acted as coroners, and took care of the poor that were sick. They also acted as witnesses over domestic fights.

Early Dutch records describe many of these activities early on in New Netherland. Many times the surgeon would have to sue to get paid. Many of the surgeon reports were about fixing up wounds caused by the fighting between the territory's own inhabitants.

For example, on May 17, 1639, the following deposition was recorded:

DECLARATION OF SURGEON HANS KIERSTEDT AS TO THE NATURE OF THE WOUND RECEIVED BY JACOB JURIAENSEN

BEFORE ME, CORNELIS VAN TIENHOVEN, SECRETARY IN NEW NETHERLAND, APPEARED HANS CIRSTEEDE, SURGEON IN FORT AMSTERDAM (NYC), AND IN THE PRESENCE OF THE UNDERSIGNED WITNESSES CERTIFIED AND DECLARED, AS HE DOES HEREBY CERTIFY AND DECLARE, IN PLACE AND WITH PROMISE OF AN OATH IF NECESSARY, THAT IT IS TRUE AND TRUTHFUL THAT, THE DEPONENT HAVING SOME TIME AGO BEEN CALLED TO JACOB JEURLAENSEN FROM DANSICK, WHO WAS WOUNDED BY ONE JOCHEM BEECKMAN, HE, THE DEPONENT, THEN FOUND THE WOUND TO BE BEHIND IN THE BUTTOCK, ABOUT THREE FINGERS-BREADTH FROM HIS FUNDAMENT, GOING DOWNWARD TOWARD THE NECK OF THE BLADDER, THE GREAT ARTERY AND NERVE BEING CUT, WHICH WOUND PROGRESSED FAVORABLY UP TO THE EIGHTH OR NINTH DAY AND ACTED AS IF IT WOULD REACH A PROPER AND SATISFACTORY CURE. BUT AS THE PATIENT DID NOT FOLLOW THE SURGEON'S ORDERS AND DID NOT OBSERVE A PROPER DIET ACCORDING TO THE INSTRUCTIONS OF THE SURGEON, WHO FOUND HIM STANDING UP AND BLEEDING IN FRONT OF HIS BUNK, HE ASKED SAID JACOB JEURLANSEN, "WHY DID YOU COME OUT OF THE BUNK?" HE ANSWERED, "I WANTED TO GET A POT." HE BLED SO PROFUSELY AT THE TIME THAT HE, THE SURGEON, COULD WITH DIFFICULTY STOP THE BLEEDING AND SINCE THEN THE WOUND HAS REPEATEDLY, SOMETIMES TWICE AND SOMETIMES ONCE IN TWENTY-FOUR HOURS, BURST OPEN AND BLED HARD, SO THAT IN CONSEQUENCE OF THE PROFUSE BLEEDING JACOB JEURLAENSEN HAS BECOME SO WEAK AND FEEBLE THAT THE DEPONENT CAN NOT EFFECT A GOOD CURE, AND HE DECLARES THAT THE PATIENT HIMSELF IS THE CAUSE MOVENS OF THE BURSTING OPEN OF THE WOUND. ALL OF WHICH THE DEPONENT DECLARES TO BE TRUE AND TRUTHFUL, BEING READY TO CONFIRM THE SAME BY A SOLEMN OATH; ALSO, THAT HE HAS MADE THIS DECLARATION FOR THE SAKE OF BEARING WITNESS OF THE TRUTH, ESPECIALLY AS HE HAS BEEN CALLED UPON TO DO SO. DONE IN PORT AMSTERDAM, THIS SEVENTEENTH OF

Delivery With Grace

MAY 1639, IN NEW NETHERLAND.
HANS KLERSTEDT
THIS IS THE X MARK OF TOMAS CONLNCK, WITNESS
THIS IS THE X MARK OF JEURLAEN BODOLFF, SERGEANT, WITNESS

On September 17, 1639, a witness testified about a surgeon being owed for services:

DECLARATION OF ARENT VAN LANDEN THAT GREGORY PIETERSEN OWES PIETER VAN DE LINDE FOR SURGEON'S FEES

THE 17TH OF SEPTEMBER, A° 1639, BEFORE ME, CORNELLS VAN TIENHOVEN, SECRETARY OF NEW NETHERLAND, APPEARED ARENT VAN LANDEN AND DECLARED ON HIS CONSCIENCE IN PLACE AND WITH PROMISE OF AN OATH IF NEED BE, AS HE HEREBY TESTIFIES, DECLARES AND CERTIFIES, THAT IT IS TRUE AND TRUTHFUL THAT HE, THE DEPONENT, KNOWS THAT GREGORIS PIETERSEN OWES PIETER VAN DE LINDE THE SUM OF FL. 13*10 FOR SURGEON'S FEES, ARISING FROM A CERTAIN ACCIDENT WHICH THE ABOVE NAMED PIETER VAN DE LINDE CURED ALL OF WHICH THE DEPONENT DECLARES TO BE TRUE AND TRUTHFUL. DONE THIS 17TH OF SEPTEMBER A° 1639, IN FORT AMSTERDAM.
THIS IS THE X MARK OF ARENT VAN LANDEN

On September 1, 1638, surgeon Harmen Meyndertsen van den Boogaert testified as to injuries caused by the misbehaving of one Dutchmen's wife who was beaten by her husband:

TESTIMONY OF SURGEON HARMEN MEYNDERTSEN VAN DEN BOOGAERT RESPECTING MISBEHAVIOR OF THOMAS BEECHE'S WIFE.

BEFORE ME, CORNELLS VAN TIENHOVEN, SECRETARY OF NEW NETHERLAND, APPEARED HARMAN MEYNDERSEN VAN BOGERDT, AGED 26 YEARS, SURGEON, AT THE REQUEST OF MARYN ADRIAENSEN, AND BY TRUE CHRISTIAN WORDS, IN PLACE AND WITH PROMISE OF A SOLEMN OATH IF NEED BE, TESTIFIED AND ATTESTED, AS HE DOES HEREBY, THAT, THE APPEARER BEING LAST THURSDAY, THE 26TH OF AUGUST, WITH OTHERS MERRY AT THE HOUSE OF CLAES CORNELL SEN, * WHEELWRIGHT, WHERE AT THE TIME WERE

Delivery With Grace

PRESENT THOMAS BESCHER'S WIFE AND HER HUSBAND, SHE, NOTWITHSTANDING HER HUSBAND'S PRESENCE, FUMBLED AT THE FRONT OF THE BREECHES OF MOST ALL OF THOSE WHO WERE PRESENT AND PAID FOR A PORTION OF THE WINE THAT HAD BEEN DRUNTC AND, WHEN HER HUSBAND REQUESTED HER TO GO HOME WITH HIM, REFUSED TO DO SO, BUT CONTINUED TO ACT AS BEFORE HER HUSBAND, BECOMING JEALOUS AT THIS, STRUCK HIS WIFE AND MASTER GEERLYN. THE DEPONENT CONCLUDING HIS DECLARATION HEREWITH, PERSISTS THEREIN AND DECLARES IT TO BE TRUE, MAINTAINING THAT EVERY ONE IS BOUND TO GIVE EVIDENCE OF THE TRUTH WHEN REQUIRED SO TO DO. THUS DONE ON THE ISLAND OF MANHATES, THIS FIRST OF SEPTEMBER 1638."

Van der Bogart was the author of the *"Narrative of a Journey into the Mohawk and Oneida Country, 1634-35,"* one of the first publications about Native Americans in what is now New York State. He also died by burning to death in an Indian house in 1648 when he was accused of being a homosexual and attempted to escape punishment of death by the Dutch.

In 1638 two surgeons testified about a murder:

TESTIMONY OF SURGEONS HANS KLERSTEDE AND GERRLT SCHUTT AS TO THE CAUSE OF DEATH OF GERRLT JANSEN

THIS DAY, THE 18TH OF MAY A°- 1638, BEFORE ME, CORNELLS VAN TIENHOVEN, SECRETARY OF NEW NETHERLAND, CAME AND APPEARED MASTER HANS AND MASTER GERRIT, BOTH SURGEONS IN THE SERVICE OF THE WEST INDIA COMPANY HERE IN NEW NETHERLAND, AT THE REQUEST OF THE FISCAL, ULRICH LUPOLT, AND BY TRUE CHRISTIAN WORDS, INSTEAD AND WITH PROMISE OF A SOLEMN OATH IF NECESSARY, TESTIFIED, ATTESTED AND DECLARED THAT IT IS TRUE AND TRUTHFUL THAT ON THE 5TH ULTIMO, IN THE AFTERNOON, THEY, WITH OTHERS, VISITED THE PERSON OF GERRLT JANSEN, GUNNER IN FORT AMSTERDAM, AND FOUND THAT HE HAD BEEN STABBED IN HIS LEFT SIDE, ABOUT TWO FINGERS' BREADTH BELOW THE NIPPLE, IN AN UPWARD DIRECTION, AND THAT IN THEIR

Delivery With Grace

OPINION [THE WEAPON] PENETRATED THROUGH THE LUNG INTO THE HEART, WHEREUPON DEATH 1 FOLLOWED. ALL OF WHICH THEY, THE DEPONENTS, DECLARE TO BE TRUE AND THAT THIS IS DONE BY THEM WITHOUT SIMULATION OR REGARD OF PERSONS, MAINTAINING THAT EVERY ONE IS BOUND TO BEAR TESTIMONY TO THE TRUTH. THUS DONE AT FORT AMSTERDAM* IN NEW NETHERLAND, THE DAY AND YEAR ABOVE WRITTEN.
GERRIT SCHUTT, SURGEON
HANS KIERSTED

Now New York City.

This testimony was given in connection with the prosecution of Jan Gysbertsen originally from Rotterdam, charged with the killing of Gerrit Jansen. See NY Col. MSS:19-20.

One of the earliest surgeons in the Capital District area, then Manor of Rensselaerswijck, was the hiring of Abraham Staas and family by Kiliaen Van Rensselaer. In 1642, surgeon Jan Dircsz Brim recommended Staas as a *"welltrained surgeon"* to Kiliaen van Rensselaer, a director of the Amsterdam Chamber of the Dutch West India Company (WIC). The Dutch West India Company and, in particular, Kiliaen van Rensselaer, was looking to invigorate development in the Fort Orange region of the North (Hudson) River with an infusion of settlers. On February 1, 1642, Van Rensselaer offered Abram a contract with exclusive right to be surgeon at Fort Orange (Albany) for the West India Company for a period of six years, from 1642 to 1648, and allowed him to maintain the right to conduct mercantile activities within the company's rules.

Delivery With Grace

Abraham Staas And Family
February 1, 1642

Extract from the record of Mr. Kiliaen van Rensselaer, lord of Rensselaerswyck, etc., of privileges and contracts granted to and made with his inhabitants and subjects in the said colony, situated in New Netherland, etc.

Abraham Staas van Amsterdam, 24 years of age, for himself as well as for Trijntgen Jochims, his wife, 19 years of age, and a servant or boy whom he must take with him, has gratefully accepted the conditions of freemen of the colony of Rensselaerswyck, after they were read to him, and this for the period of six years commencing on his arrival in the colony, with a view to practicing his profession of surgeon in the colony during the aforesaid time (to the exclusion of all others) on the strength of the good, written testimonial given him by Master Jan Dirck sen Brimmer, 82 surgeon of this city, and shown to the patroon, etc.

Whereupon the aforesaid Abraham, Staas, besides signing these conditions shall take the proper oath of submission and fealty to the lord patroon according to the copy thereof, given him. Done at Amsterdam, the 1st of February 1642, and in witness thereof signed by the said Abraham Staas in the presence of the undersigned notary and witnesses. Was signed: Abram Staas, H: V: Velde, J. Vande Ven, notary public residing in Amsterdam.

Abraham Staas (Staes, Staet, Staets), from Amsterdam, surgeon; entered into a contract with Kiliaen van Rensselaer, Feb. 1, 1642, to sail to the colony with his wife Trijntje Jochims and one servant, and to practice as surgeon for the period of six years from the date of his arrival, to the exclusion of all others. He sailed by den Houttuyn with one servant, but apparently without his wife. In the contract his age- is given as 24; that of his wife as 19 years. Staas is credited in the accounts with various supplies furnished by him between

Delivery With Grace

1642 AND 1648, INDICATING THAT HE WAS ENGAGED IN BUSINESS BESIDES PRACTICING AS A SURGEON; ALSO WITH F30 FOR SALARY AS SURGEON FROM NOV. 16, 1645, TO NOV. 16, 1646; WITH F60 FOR SALARY AS SURGEON AND WORK ON DE VLACKTE TILL NOV. 1647; AND WITH F20 FOR SALARY AS SURGEON TILL MARCH 20, 1648. HE IS FURTHER CREDITED WITH F58:6 FOR SALARY AS RAETSPERSOON (COUNCILOR), FROM FEB. 5, 1643, TO APRIL 10, 1644, AND WITH F400 FOR SALARY AS PRESIDEERONDE (PRESIDING OFFICER OF THE COUNCIL) FROM APRIL 10, 1644, TO APRIL 10, 1648. SEPT. 9, 1649, ABRAHAM STAAS OBTAINED A LOT IN THE BYEENWOONINGE (VILLAGE), NEAR THE FIRST CREEK, ON THE TERMS OF THE FREEMEN. IN 1658, HE OWNED A YACHT AND IS REFERRED
TO AS CAPT. STAES.

Today the family is known as the Staats family and the house and Staats family still occupy Staats Island just south of Albany. *Hooghbergh,* as the family farm was called, was built around 1700 and was the home of Gerrit and Jochem Staats.

On February 22, 1649, two surgeons were called to provide details of the death of a woman:

REPORT OF THE INQUEST ON THE BODY OF ELIZABETH
— ....—?

ON THE 22ND OF FEBRUARY A° 1649, MR. LA MONTAGNE AND FISCAL VAN DYCK, TOGETHER WITH MR. JACOB AND MR. JAN PAU, SURGEONS, WENT TO THE HOUSE OF HERRY PIRS, BY ORDER OF THE HONORABLE DIRECTOR AND COUNCIL, TO EXAMINE THE DEAD BODY OF LYSABET [ ], ON WHICH CORPSE WAS FOUND A SMALL WOUND ON THE FOREHEAD INFLICTED BY AN AXE. THE ABOVE NAMED SURGEONS DECLARE THAT THE SAID WOUND WAS NOT LETHAL, NOR THE CAUSE OF DEATH, AND THAT ELISABET HAD COME TO HER DEATH BY SOME OTHER ACCIDENT. IN TESTIMONY WHEREOF THIS IS SIGNED BY THE SURGEONS IN THE PRESENCE OF THE SAID GENTLEMEN, ON THE DATE ABOVE MENTIONED, IN FORT AMSTERDAM IN NEW NETHERLAND.
JACOB HENDERYCKSZ

Delivery With Grace

JAN PAUITF LA MONTAGNE.

ACKNOWLEDGED BEFORE ME.
COR- VAN TIENHOVEN, SECRETARY

Surgeons were in great demand in New Netherland. In 1650, Secretary Van Tienhoven wrote that, *"A surgeon provided with medicines was required to accompany farmers to New Netherland."* The first educated physician to arrive in New Amsterdam (now New York City) was Dr. Johannes La Montagne, a graduated of Leyden, who came to Rensselaerswijck in 1637.

In 1652 the first ordinance was passed regulating the practice of medicine when a group of barber surgeons petitioned that they were opposed to visiting ship barber surgeons exercising their cutting on land.

"ON THE PETITION OF THE CHIRURGEONS OF NEW AMSTERDAM, NONE BUT THEY ALONE BE ALLOWED TO SHAVE; THE DIRECTOR UNDERSTAND THAT SHAVING DOTH NOT APPERTAIN EXCLUSIVELY TO BUT IS AN APPENDIX THERETO; THAT NO MAN CAN BE PREVENTED ON HIMSELF, NOR TO DO ANOTHER THE FRIENDLY ACT, PROVIDED COURTESY AND NOT FOR GAIN, WHICH IS HEREBY FORBIDDEN. ORDERED THAT SHIP BARBERS SHALL NOT BE ALLOWED TO DRESS NOR ADMINISTER ANY POTIONS ON SHORE WITHOUT THE PREVIOUS AND SPECIAL CONSENT OF THE PETITIONERS, OR AT LEAST OF DR. MONTAGNE."

The names of the petitioning surgeons were : Jan Croon, Van der Bogaert, Aldart Swartout, Hans Kierstede, Jacob Hendrickson Varrevanger and Jacob Hughes.

Delivery With Grace

There are records of settlers coming to the new world suffering from sickness during the long voyage in the ships that brought them to the New World. Vice-Director Alrichs who wrote to the Commander of the Colony on the Delaware River dated New Amstel, October 10, 1658, states:

"William van Rasenberg, who came over as Surgeon, puts forth sundry claims against people whom he attended on the passage, in as much as his wages did not run at the time and on the voyage, and he used his own provisions. There were on board the ship considerable sickness, accidents, and hardship in consequence of a tedious voyage. One hundred souls required at least a hogshead or two of French wine and one of brandy, and a tub of prunes had furnished for refreshment and comfort of those sick of suffering from other troubles, through the protracted from want thereof, the people became so low that death which is a pretty serious matter. Here, on shore, I see the poor, weak, sick, or indigent, sometimes have need this and that to support them, which one cannot easily refuse ; though it be sometimes but a spoonful, frequently it amounts to more than is supposed."

Between 1695 and 1770 some thirty *chirurgeon*s or *barbier chirurgeons* and seven physicians were granted the small burgher rights of the city (New Amsterdam). In 1776, a small infirmary in the west end of the new workhouse and house of correction became the first hospital in New Amsterdam, the present Bellevue Hospital in New York City.

The names of several of the early Dutch midwives have been published. During Van Twiller's administration in 1635, Fort Amsterdam was finished and outside the fort he had a small house erected for the midwife, along with a new bakery and a goat house behind the five large stone houses of the company. On November 26, 1635, the chamber of Amsterdam received *"a letter from Tryntgen Jonas (or Jansen), midwife in New Netherland, requesting an increase in wages and some necessaries."* In a deposition dated July, 1644, Tryntje Jonas was still listed *"midwife of New Netherlands."* On an official list of the employees of the West India Company in New Netherland, dated January 1650, the midwife received 100 guilders per annum. Hellegond Joris, who was appointed city midwife of New Amsterdam in 1655, was granted an annual salary of 100 guilders for her services in attending the poor by Peter Stuyvesant and the council on May 11, 1660. At Esopus (Kingston) in 1655, Mrs. Cornelis Barentsen Slecht was the midwife.

There were several epidemics through the early period. In August 1655 a "general epidemic" occurred in the Dutch period and again in 1659 there was an epidemic of a *"painful and long, lingering sickness."* In 1668, *"an unusual sickness"* was the first English epidemic and was so close to fatal that the new governor Thomas Dongan ordered a fast day. These may have been bouts of yellow fever. In September 1668, Rev. Samuel Megapolensis wrote to a friend that many had died from dysentery and opined that, *"It appears as if God were punishing this land for its sins."* In 1684, Stephanus van Corlandt wrote about the prevalence of fatal sickness stating that,

Delivery With Grace

"Mostly children, the old of (pain) in the side and fever and the young of colds and fever, so that hardly a day passes but someone is buried."

Smallpox hit New York City (formerly New Amsterdam, but changed in 1664 when they English took control over the Dutch) on October 16, 1689, and led to the earliest quarantine. On May 18, 1702, Lord Cornbury wrote that, *"the small pox is very much here, but except that the Province is very healthy."* However on September 17 just four months later, a serious yellow fever broke out. Ten days later Cornbury wrote that, *"sickness has swept away upwards of five hundred people of all ages and sexes."* In December it was over.

The deacons of Beaverwyck (Albany) also gave attention to medical care. As early as 1664 the surgeon Cornells van Dijck was paid an annual fee for *"surgeon's fees for the poor,"* paid for by the deacons. Before this, the deacons paid a surgeon per case, and that could run high. For example in 1660-1661, medical expenses for a Hans Eencluis alone were high.

Alcohol was also part of medicine. The value that was put on the healing and pain relieving powers of alcoholic beverages is shown by the distribution of beer to women in childbed. Another client, in addition to surgeon costs, was provided with two ankers of beer.

Beer, wine, or rum may also have relieved the suffering of Elyas van Ravensteyn or Teunis Tempel during the last weeks of their lives, according to records, revealing the fact that medicine could come in many flavors.

The deacons took great pains to make sure that the sick were well cared for. Baefje Pieters, indigent herself, was paid by the deaconry for boarding the sick Carwaet (Croatian) from October 1664 until February 1665, and the needy wife of Jan Met (with the beard) was given fifty pounds of meat on behalf of Hans Eencluis during his illness.

The deacons exercised a form of preventive medicine for the poor providing an annual retainer for the surgeon and owned animals and land.

Unfortunately, many people who entered the medical profession were unskilled and ignorant and in 1760 the General Assembly of New York recognized the fact and stated that the so-called professionals were *"endangering the lives and limbs of their patients."* The lack of knowledge on the connection between filth and disease was a major cause of lower life expectancy. Slowly the connections were made and even in 1679 the Schenectady "well masters" were told to *"strictly enjoined to see to it that no water is poured out near the wells and that no rinsing is done there, in the space around the wells."* More laws followed.

Delivery With Grace

Epidemics such as yellow fever would send the public into panic since there was no defense known. Every remedy was tried: smoke from cigars, eating garlic, sprinkled vinegar, burned tobacco and people carried their own lances in case they needed to be "bled." Public buildings were closed and those that had to chance it by going out of doors carried vinegar soaked handkerchiefs or sponges pressed against their noses or tarred rope or camphor around the neck. People walked in the middle of the street as not to get too close to a house that might have sick people living there. People stopped shaking hands. Bonfires were set at almost every corner and when that was outlawed for fear of burning down the city, people began firing guns believing that the burning gunpowder might be the cure.

In 1746 Albany had a yellow fever epidemic and lost 45 inhabitants. In 1756 Albany authorities passed a law that all smallpox patients should be sent from the city and a convenient place should be found for their reception.

In 1798, Schenectady had to deal with a yellow fever outbreak and it cut into the population severely. There was no hospital in the city other than a hospital barracks for the soldiers erected during the Revolution near Lafayette St. The Schenectady City Council passed a law to find a house where all people inflicted with the disease were to be sent. After names of inflicted were sent to the Mayor, he

Delivery With Grace

> New-York, November 15
>
> Buried in this City laft Week, viz. *Church of England* 4, *Dutch Church* 4, And *Blacks* 2. In all this Week 10
>
> In the Month of Auguft laft the Small-Pox began to fpread in this City, and for fome Weeks was very favourable, and few died of the Diftemper, but as foon as we obferved the Burials to increafe, which was from the 23d of Auguft, in our Gazette, No. 305. we began to incert weekly, the Number both of Whites and Blacks that were buried this City, by which Account we find, that from the 23d of Auguft to this Inftant, which is two Months and 3 weeks, there was buried in the feveral burying Places of this City, as follows, viz:
>
> | | |
> |---|---|
> | Church of England | 229, |
> | Dutch Church, | 212, |
> | French Church | 15, |
> | Lutheran Church | 1, |
> | Presbyterians | 16, |
> | Quakers | 2, |
> | Baptifts | 1, |
> | Jews | 2. |
> | Whites in all | 478. |
> | Blacks in all | 71, |
> | Whites and blacks, In all | 543. |
>
> From the *New York Gazette*, 1731.

Number of people who died of Smallpox in 1731.

had them examined by a city doctor and if affected they were sent to that very house for treatment. Smallpox was another regular visitor to Schenectady and up until 1800 appeared on a regular basis.

Even though inoculation was introduced first in Boston in 1720 the high cost prevented its ready acceptance. Benjamin Franklin published a pamphlet on how to do it yourself. New York's Cadwallader

Delivery With Grace

Colden opposed inoculation in his writings to Dr. William Douglass who was fighting it in New England. The fight in Boston was so active that a bomb was thrown into the window of Cotton Mather's house, the Boston Reverend, who was supporting it. The bomb did not go off but attached was a note that read *"Cotton Mather, you dog, dam you! I'll inoculate you with this; with a pix to you."* Mather had kept good notes and was able to show that those that did get inoculated only 2 percent died while those that did not get inoculated 14.8 percent died. The New York Gazette in March 1725 quoted a Philadelphia writer as saying that inoculation for smallpox was beginning to be favorably considered and a case was cited to show *"how groundless all those extravagant Reports are, that have been spread through the Province (of New York) to the contrary."*

The Smallpox epidemic of 1731 was severe and some 800 people died. In 1745 the disease was affecting trade and thirteen doctors published a document stating that only a few people still had it in an attempt to get the city (New York) moving forward.

Inoculation did not sit well with New York politicians and on June 6, 1747, Governor Clinton issued the following that inoculation was *"Strictly prohibiting and forbidding all and every of the Doctors, Physicians, Surgeons, and Prectioners of Physic, and all and every person within the Province, to inoculate for the small pox any person or person within the city and County of New York, on pain of being prosecuted to the utmost rigor of the law."* Most people ignored it.

In 1798, Dr. Edward Jenner announced the discovery of vaccination and two years later it was introduced into America. Uproar ensued as it did over small pox inoculation but by 1814 a group of Schenectady doctors was advertising in favor of a Dr. Fancher and his method and ability of giving vaccinations. Vaccinations took place in the Old Dutch Church. Only two years later when smallpox was rearing its head again, the Schenectady City Council published an ad in the paper recommending that everyone get vaccinated.

One medical tradition that seemed accepted by all was "Bleeding." It was thought that taking blood out of the body would remove impurities. This was done by barbers who also did tooth pulling and bone setting/amputation. This carry over is seen in the red and white barber polls. The red signifying blood and white signifying bandages. Leeches were commonly employed as one treatment for a child having croup: *"As soon as the disease is discovered, from three to six leeches....may be applied to the upper and fore part of the neck and the bleeding promoted by the application of clothes wrung out of warm water. As soon as the leeches fall off and before the bleeding has ceased, the patient may be laid between the blankets."*

Delivery With Grace

During colonial times the rise of "patent medicines" became common, as anyone who concocted a "cure" could bottle it, advertise, and sell it. Often these cures "cured" everything from Piles to Dropsy, all swellings, rheumatism, sore throat, crop and whooping cough, all bruises, sprains and burns, and sores and ulcers. In one Schenectady newspaper there was an ad for a *"method of curing disease, From Whatever cause arising (all ending In The Same Effect, I.E., Producing Impure Blood and Fluids With One and Only One Medicine)."*

These patent medicines that became popular had no controls or oversight. John Van Sice in Schenectady in 1797 promised "An Indian Cure" for cancer and sore legs *"From experience found to succeed. No cure, no money."* Van Sice did not do so well with his cure since two years later the city council ordered *"Resolved that the poor master of the first ward produce such clothing for John Van Sice as he may think proper not exceeding in value ten dollars."* John Hetherington, a schoolteacher in Scotia wrote in his diary in 1794, *"Rec. for a Cancer or any Tumor Take half a pint of the juice of Bran leaves when in blossom, of new cream one Pint, and of the best honey half a pound, boil them in an unglazed pipkin very gently till half is consumed — anoint the part affected twice or thrice a day."*

The Schenectady Almanac in 1816 proclaimed *"Speedy Cure For The Cancer which will effect the cure of that diseased in three days. This remedy consists simply in a piece of dough about the size of a small hen's egg, and a lump of hog's lard, the older the better, of the same dimension. These substances thoroughly mixed, so as to form a kind of salved, much be spread on a piece of white leather, and applied to the diseased part." Another cure from the almanac is "Simply the yolk of an egg mixed with salt as long as it will receive it."*

Home recipes were common, followed religiously, and by the ingredients if they did not kill the disease they may have killed the patient. Examples of home recipes in the late Eighteenth and early Nineteenth century illustrate:

BALDNESS: (TO CURE) RUB THE PART MORNING AND EVENING, WITH ONIONS, TILL IT IS RED, AND RUB IT AFTERWARD WITH HONEY...

BITE OF A MAD DOG: PLUNGE INTO COLD WATER DAILY FOR TWENTY DAYS AND KEEP UNDER AS LONG AS POSSIBLE.

COLD: PARE VERY THICK, THE YELLOW RIND OF AN ORANGE. ROLL IT INSIDE OUT, AND THRUST A ROLL INTO EACH NOSTRIL.

CONSUMPTION. EVERY MORNING CUT UP A LITTLE TURF OF FRESH EARTH, AND LYING DOWN BREATHE INTO THE HOLE FOR A QUARTER OF AN HOUR. OR ADVISED HIM TO LOSE SIX OUNCES OF BLOOD EVERY DAY FOR A FORTNIGHT, IF HE LIVED SO LONG AND THEN EVERY OTHER DAY, THEN EVERY THIRD DAY; THEN THE EVERY FIFTH DAY FOR THE SAME TIME, OR IN THE LAST STAGE, SUCK AN HEALTHY WOMAN DAILY. TRIED BY MY FATHER.

Since there was no optometry in Schenectady a person who was having problems with their eyesight could walk into a store such as Porteus, Murdoch & Co. in 1796 and help themselves to a pair of spectacles or goggles, or visit H. H. Ten Eyck's store on State St. at the sign of the Golden Mortar. Teeth problems were no concern for the males in Schenectady as toothbrushes were rare. Women would rub a chalked rag or snuff on their teeth. Men, if they had a tooth problem, would apply a hot iron to the ear, or put hot roasted turnips behind the ear. By 1840, dentistry was a recognized profession and there was a Dr. Chandler on Ferry and Liberty. He carried a variety of porcelain teeth and could insert one or a set and stated they *"cannot be detected from the original."*

As medical knowledge increased it was clear that laws were needed and in 1760 New York City began the practice that anyone who wanted to practice medicine had to be examined and approved by a special board including *"one of His Majesty's Council, the judges of the supreme court, the King's attorney-general and the mayor."* By the end of the century a statewide law required the applicant to prove he attended the practice of some reputable physician for two years if a college graduate, three years if not.

There were a number of educated men in the medical profession during the colonial period. John Nicoll, Cadwallader Colden, Sir James Jay, and Samuel Bard received medical degrees in Edinburgh. John Jones received his from the University of Rheims after training in Edinburgh, London and Paris. Richard Bayley studied under John Hunter in

London and graduates from Leyden included Samuel Staats, John Van Buren, Isaac Dubois, Johannes Kerfbyle, John Van Brugh Tennent, Gerardus Beekman and his son William Beekman. John Dupuy and his son John studied in France. Many of them had the published medical books of the time both of English and Dutch origins. Gerardus Beekman's 1674 copy of the Dutch *Sylvius' Praxcos Medicae*, first published in 1672-74 is in the New York Academy of Medicine library. William Beekman, his father's copy, also there dated 1705. A number of other medical texts were published in New York during the time leading up to the Revolution.

The care given to women in childbirth during this period was mostly in the hands of midwives. In the January 1769 edition of the New York Gazette, a Mrs. Fisher was advertising her services. There were male midwives as well. The December 16, 1751, edition of the New York Gazette stated that Doctor Peter Billings was *"an experienced physician and man-midwife,"* and yet a Doctor William Douglass called him a quack. A Doctor Guischard from Paris in 1760 advertised that, *"he is experienced in women's delivery, and will with the help of the Lord,"* prove himself serviceable. In the obituary of John Dupuy, posted in the New York Post-Boy on August 5, 1745, he was listed as a doctor and midwife. The first professorship in America devoted to obstetrics only was established in 1767 at King's College (now

Delivery With Grace

Columbia College) with J. V. B. Tennent becoming the first professor. If you were poor or homeless there was an official midwife at the Almshouse and if there was a problem a local doctor was called in.

In 1798, the city of Schenectady created the office of the city physician and his job was to take care of the indigent. When the city purchased the Poor House after 1809 many of his patients were tenants there. However there was no effort to separate the strictly poor that could not afford a doctor from those that had tuberculosis, insane, deaf mutes, and indigent children, were commingled. After the creation of the New York State Medical Society, knowledge was spread more systematically and licensing became more stringent. In 1750 a criminal who was executed in New York City was dissected by two doctors for the benefit of students and it was the first to be performed for medical students. Dr. Peter Middleton and Dr. John Bard who were at the time the first private teachers of medicine performed the dissection *"for the instruction of the young men then engaged in the study of medicine."*

Dissection was not accepted by the public for any reason and in 1788 there was the so-called anatomy riot that took place by an angry mob. The doctors locked themselves in the jail but the hospital was ransacked and burned. The following year a law was passed that gave permission to perform dissections that we now call autopsies. In Schenectady at the

Delivery With Grace

same time a sexton for the First Reformed Church was fired when he was caught red-handed body snatching. Gysbert Van Sice had delivered the scull of a corpse to the house of Doctor Anderson and delivered it to a student of medicine named Hagaman. Eventully the public gave in recognizing the need for dissection to advance the state of medicine, and in 1812 New York State opened its first medical college at Fairfield in Herkimer County. In 1829, Dr. Alden March gave a series of lectures in Albany on surgery that included a dissection.

During the 19th century, there was the use of Native American cures (herbs and plants) that were sold as medicine. This dates back to the 17th century when Nicolaes van Wassenaer in his *"Historisch Verhael"* in 1624 noted that:

> "In some places they have abundant means, with herbs and leaves or roots, to cure their ailments. There is not an ailment they have not a remedy for; but in order localities they are altogether devoid of succor, leaving the people to perish like cattle."

> In the Representation of New Netherland, 1650, it states that "The medicinal plants found in New Netherland up to the present time, by little search, as far as they have come to our knowledge, consist principally of Venus' hair, hart's tongue, lingwort, polypody, white mullein, priest's shoe, garden and seabeach orach, water germander, tower-mustard, sweet flag, sassafras, crowfoot, plantain, shepherd's purse, mallows, wild majoram, crane's bill, marsh-mallows, false eglantine, laurel, violet, blue flag, wild indigo, Solomon's seal, dragon's blood, comfrey, milfoil, many sorts of fern, wild lilies of different kinds, agrimony, wild leek, blessed thistle, snakeroot, Spanish figs which grow out of the leaves, tarragon and numerous

Delivery With Grace

OTHER PLANTS AND FLOWERS; BUT AS WE ARE NOT SKILLED IN THOSE THINGS, WE CANNOT SAY MUCH OF THEM; YET IT IS NOT TO BE DOUBTED THAT EXPERTS WOULD BE ABLE TO FIND MANY SIMPLES OF GREAT AND DIFFERENT VIRTUES, IN WHICH WE HAVE CONFIDENCE, PRINCIPALLY BECAUSE THE INDIANS TO CURE VERY DANGEROUS AND PERILOUS WOUNDS LEAVES AND OTHER LITTLE THINGS."

Adriaen van der Donck, the first sheriff in New Netherland in the *"Description of New Netherland,"* 1655, wrote : "NO REASONABLE PERSON WILL DOUBT THAT THERE ARE MANY MEDICINAL AND HEALING PLANTS IN THE NEW NETHERLANDS. A CERTAIN CHIRURGEON, WHO WAS ALSO A BOTANIST, HAD A BEAUTIFUL GARDEN THERE, WHEREIN A GREAT VARIETY OF MEDICINAL WILD PLANTS WERE COLLECTED, BUT THE OWNER HAS REMOVED AND THE GARDEN LIES NEGLECTED. BECAUSE SICKNESS DOES NOT PREVAIL MUCH, I SUPPOSE THE SUBJECT HAS RECEIVED LESS ATTENTION. THE PLANTS WHICH ARE KNOWN TO US ARE THE FOLLOWING : CAPILLI VENERIS, SCHOLOPENDRIA, ANGELICA, POLYPODIUM, VERBASCUM ALBUM, CALTEUS SACERDOTIS, ATRIPLEX HORTENSIS AND MARINA, CHORTIUM, TURRITES, CALAMUS AROMATICUS, SASSAFRAS, ROIS VIRGINIANUM, RANUNCULUS, PLANTAGO, BURSA PASTORIS, MALVA, ORIGAENUM, GERANICUM, ALTHEA, CINOROTON PSEUDO, DAPHNE, VIOLA, IREAS, INDIGO SILVESTRIS, SIGILLUM SALAMONIS, SANGUIS, DRACONUM, CONSOLIDAE, MILLEFOLIUM, NOLI ME TANGERE, CARDO BENEDICTUS, AGRIMONIUM, SERPENTARIAE, CORIANDER, LEEKS, WILD LEEKS, SPANISH FIGS, ELATINE, CAMPERFOLIE, PETUM MALE AND FEMALE, AND MANY OTHER PLANTS. THE LAND IS FULL OF DIFFERENT KINDS OF HERBS AND TREES BESIDES THOSE ENUMERATED, AMONG WHICH THERE UNDOUBTEDLY ARE GOOD SIMPLICIA , WITH WHICH DISCREET PERSONS WOULD DO MUCH GOOD ; FOR WE KNOW THAT THE INDIANS WITH ROOTS, BULBS, LEAVES, ETC., CURE DANGEROUS WOUNDS AND OLD SORES, OF WHICH WE HAVE SEEN MANY INSTANCES."

On June 13, 1810, the Schenectady County Medical Society was formed and met in the Court House on the corner of Union and Ferry Sts. Schenectady had just incorporated twelve years earlier as the fourth city in New York State, although it had

Delivery With Grace

been an important village beginning in 1661. It was the last point of embarkation and debarkation connecting the East to the West in trade and its population had increased to two and one half times the number during the Revolutionary War. The year before in 1809, Schenectady County broke off from its mother Albany County.

There were no medical colleges in the state. If one wanted to pursue a medical career, he would have to apprentice himself to an established doctor. Mr. Darious Coye of Schenectady did that and after a period of time the student would receive a diploma certifying the student had studied the subject and to the best of the doctor's knowledge *"posses a good moral character,"* as stated on Coye's diploma from Dr. J. W. Lay on January 1, 1801.

To be a doctor in Schenectady at this time was considered a luxury. Payment to the doctor was often in the form of produce or services, a pair of shoes mended or sacks of potatoes. Often the doctor would have to publicly announce in the local paper such as the Mohawk Mercury (in 1775, for example) that all persons indebted to the doctor pay up since he was moving out of town. With the formation of the Medical Society however a fee was established of one dollar a visit and not less than fifty cents.

Considering the low fees, many Schenectady doctors took on other jobs. Dr. Joseph Van Ingen managed

Delivery With Grace

The Schenectady Almshouse, formerly in Schenectady's Hamilton Hill area, area bounded by Emmett St., Brandywine Avenue, Duane Avenue, and Steuben St.

several blacksmith shops. Near the Dutch Reformed Church was the drug store of Dr. Van Der Heuval and Dirk Van Ingen, Joseph's father. Van Der Heuval also taught mathematics and philosophy at Union College. One doctor named Anderson operated a medicine, paint and grocery store combined.

During the Nineteenth century in Schenectady James Cuff Swits (c. 1820-1893) was well known for peddling Native American cures. James was a 6-foot 7-inch Mohawk Indian and herb peddler. He was born on the farm of Hendrick Swits, on the south side of State St. opposite Jay St. He took the

Delivery With Grace

> **ASK FOR**
> **"JIM CUFF'S"**
> **SYRUP OF TAR & WILD CHERRY**
> For Coughs and Colds, Asthma, Bronchitis, Whooping Cough and all diseases of Throat and Lungs.
>
> LARGE BOTTLES, - 25 CENTS.
>
> Manufactured by
> **THE ORISENA CO.,**
> Office at "Keller's," 209 State St.,
> LABORATORY, - 105 S. Ferry St.,
> SCHENECTADY, N. Y.
>
> To THE ORISENA CO.
> *Gentlemen*:—For some time I suffered with a severe cold. It was impossible for me to sleep at night. The moment that I laid down I experienced great difficulty in breathing. My friends told me I had consumption. Learning of your preparation known as Jim Cuff's Compound Syrup of Tar and Wild Cherry. I purchased a bottle, which I used with very satisfactory results. I am much better than I have been in some time.
> Yours respectfully,
> GEO. FLANSBURGH,
> 204 Front Street,
> Schenectady, N. Y.
>
> This celebrated Indian's Cough Syrup, which has had the largest sale of any known, one store having sold over 800 bottles through the winter of 1894 and 1895, is made of Tar and Wild Cherry bark together with other barks, herbs and roots. The formula was held for many years by the famous old Indian, "Jim Cuff," known as the "Last of the Mohawk tribe," until a few years ago when he turned it over to THE ORISENA CO.
> This old Indian always lived in Schenectady, N. Y., and made his living by selling this Cough Syrup and in gathering and selling roots, herbs and barks. He died in 1894 at the age of 92 years.
> If your druggist does not sell it send your address and 25 cents, and it will be sent to you.

Medicine label for Jim Cuff's natural medicine.

name James Hartley Swits, but was called James Cuff by almost everyone.

Not much is known about him. Some report that his father was African-American and his mother a full-blooded Mohawk, some report vice versa. He lived alone in a one-room shack outside the city near Albany St. and Brandywine Avenue. He scoured the area for herbs during the spring and summer, and had many customers for his home remedies. He was a regular fixture in downtown Schenectady.

He stopped once a week at Dr. Harman Swits at 218 State St. (replaced by the Carl Building) to deliver his standing order, and later his Jim Cuff's Syrup of

Delivery With Grace

Tar and Wide Cherry was bottled by the Orisean Company at 209 State St. He had no financial interest in the medicine with his name on it. He also collected milkweed that people liked to eat boiled like spinach. He was arrested once on March 19, 1859, for being drunk and threatening to shoot people in a bar, but his weapon was a corncob pipe.

On February 26, 1893, he was removed from his hut and placed in the county almshouse on Steuben St. He died in March of pneumonia. He was buried in Potters Field at Vale Cemetery. A stonecutter friend, Thomas Wallace, made a small stone for him with his likeness in profile and a simple epitaph, *"Admitted to that equal sky."* The headstone was switched when an attempt to rob his grave by students went wrong. They forgot the name of the switched headstone and so his actual burial location is unknown.

His famous cough medicine was sold for many years after he died. One advertisement says the formula was "turned over to The Orisena Co." Since he is buried in Potters Field, one can only assume he didn't make much for giving it up.

19th century Schenectady was also the location of an important medical invention by Robert M. Fuller (1845-1919).

Robert Fuller was born in Schenectady to John Irwin

and Louisa (Gardner) Fuller. His father was a merchant and banker, and later a maker of pianos in New York City. Robert went to Union School, graduating in 1863, and received his MD degree from Albany Medical College (founded in 1839) in 1865. He started his practice in Albany, but in 1866 moved to New York City. He never married. Fuller is credited for inventing the tablet for the taking of medicine. Basically every pill you take can be attributed to his invention.

The Albany Medical Annals, Volume 41 1920, published the following bio:

DR. ROBERT M. FULLER DIED AT HIS HOME IN SCHENECTADY NY, ON SATURDAY MORNING, DECEMBER 27, 1919. DR. FULLER WAS ONE OF THE MOST SUCCESSFUL AND MOST DISTINGUISHED OF THE ALUMNI OF THE ALBANY MEDICAL COLLEGE, PARTICULARLY FROM HIS RESEARCHES IN MICROSCOPY AND PHARMACOLOGY. FOR MANY YEARS AFTER HIS GRADUATION HE WENT QUIETLY AHEAD WITH HIS INVESTIGATIONS AND AVOIDED PUBLICITY, BUT HE HAD QUIETLY AND UNOSTENTATIOUSLY STUDIED OUT THE NOW UNIVERSAL METHOD OF DISPENSING DRUGS IN TABLET FORM. FEW PHYSICIANS ARE ACQUAINTED WITH THE FACT THAT THE SMALL TABLETS, WHICH FORM SO PROMINENT A PART OF THEIR EQUIPMENT, ORIGINATED WITH DR. FULLER. IN 1900 HE RETIRED FROM WORK AND TOOK UP HIS RESIDENCE IN SCHENECTADY, THE CITY OF HIS BIRTH, AND IN 1915 HE JOINED THE THREE OTHER SURVIVING MEMBERS OF HIS MEDICAL CLASS IN A SEMICENTENNIAL ANNIVERSARY OF THEIR CELEBRATION, WHICH WAS HELD IN ALBANY ON MAY 25TH. THE OCCASION WAS A NOTABLE ONE, BECAUSE RARELY HAVE THE CLASS REUNIONS BEEN MARKED BY SUCH A GATHERING OF A REMOTE CLASS. SINCE HIS RETURN TO SCHENECTADY DR. FULLER HAD RENEWED THE INTEREST OF HIS YOUTH IN UNION COLLEGE AND IN THE ALBANY MEDICAL COLLEGE, AND HAS BEEN A FREE CONTRIBUTOR TO THE ACTIVITIES OF THESE INSTITUTIONS, MORE PARTICULAR IN THE ESTABLISHMENT OF A LIBRARY FOR THE CHEMICAL DEPART AT SCHENECTADY. HIS ENTHUSIASM,

Delivery With Grace

James Cuff Swits.

for his Alma Mater has been revealed by the bequests, and he has given for the Medical Department Thirty Thousand dollars, the income of which is to be used to assist needy medical students in obtaining their education.

But apart from all these personal and processional activities of Dr. Fuller, there have been incidents in his life of great moment and

Delivery With Grace

interest. These were described in a biographical sketch provided for the history of the Class of 1863 of Union College, published at Schenectady in June, 1913, as follows:

He is another one of the Class of '63 who has brought great credit to Union College. He was born in Schenectady New York October 27, 1845. He attended the Union School Schenectady, studied pharmacy in New York City, then took a chemistry course of five terms at Union College under Dr. Charles F. Chandler, being entered in the Class of 1863. He received a certificate from Dr. Chandler, dated August 12, 1863, of the work done. He graduated at the Albany Medical College in December, 1865. While there he took a special course in toxicology, and invented the method of using the photographic camera to aid chemical analysis. He made photographs of the octahedral crystals of arsenious acid, which were afterwards used with effect in a notable trial for murder by poisoning.

Dr. Fuller developed this use of the microscope and camera and applied it to the study of bacteria and other microorganisms. He was a pioneer in this field and gained a national reputation. While a student in Dr. James H. Armsby's office in Albany, he was Dr. Armsby's assistant in surgery in the Ira Harris United States Hospital at Albany. Many of the photographs, which he took of wounds, have been used as illustrations in the official Medical and Surgical History of the War. While thus employed he was sent to City Point, VA, to bring home a wounded officer [Lt. John Dempsey]. On his way there he stopped a day in Washington, and, as it happened, he attended Fords' Theater the night President Lincoln was shot. He had seen Lincoln enter the box, followed by Major Rathbone and Miss Harris of Albany. The audience cheered the President. Soon a puff of smoke, a man jumping from Lincoln's box to the stage, tripping and falling to the stage floor, rising and shouting "Sic Semper Tyrannis, Revenge for the South," then turning to the stage entrance, which was filled by actors and actresses coming on the stage, he waved his knife in the air and literally cut a passage for himself and was gone. Meanwhile cries of "The President's shot": rang out, and from the audience cries of "Kill him! Kill him!" Great

Delivery With Grace

CONFUSION ENSUED, WITH FEARS OF OTHER MURDERS AND THROUGH THE NIGHT EXAGGERATED REPORTS ON EVERY SIDE. FULLER SLEPT NONE THAT NIGHT. IT WAS A TRAGIC EXPERIENCE, AND THERE ARE FEW LIVING WHO SAW IT. HIS PASS TO CITY POINT IS DATED APRIL 15, 1865. THERE HE FOUND THE OFFICER HE SOUGHT, TOO SICK TO BE MOVED, SO HE WAS DETAILED IN THE 6TH ARMY CORPS

Swits' headstone in the pauper lot at Schenectady's Vale Cemetery.

Delivery With Grace

Hospital at City Point for nearly a month and had some insight into surgical methods at the front.

In October, 1866, Dr. Fuller settled in New York City, and later on 42ND St., where he practiced for forty years. In 1878 he had invented a new

Delivery With Grace

SYSTEM OF PREPARING DRUGS IN THE FORM OF TABLET TRITURATES TO SECURE ACCURACY OF MEASUREMENT. ON FEBRUARY 21, 1878, HE GAVE THE RESULTS OF HIS INVESTIGATION IN A PAPER READ BEFORE THE NEW YORK ACADEMY OF MEDICINE, ENTITLED, "AN EASY, ECONOMICAL AND ACCURATE METHOD OF DISPENSING MEDICINE IN A COMPACT AND PALATABLE FORM." THIS PAPER WAS PUBLISHED IN THE MEDICAL RECORD OF MARCH 9, 1878. THIS INVENTION HAS BEEN ADOPTED BY ALL THE LEADING PHARMACEUTICS OF TODAY. DR. FULLER'S WORK WAS RECOGNIZED BY HIS APPOINTMENT AS A DELEGATE TO AID IN REVISING THE UNITED STATES PHARMACOPOEIA.

In an editorial in New Remedies, March 1878, the editors say:

DR. FULLER'S METHOD OF SUBDIVIDING REMEDIES SO AS TO ENABLE THEM TO BE ADMINISTERED IN AN AGREEABLE FORM, AND IN UNIFORM AND ADJUSTABLE STRENGTH, WITH THE LEAST EXPENDITURE OF LABOR, APPEARS TO BE A STEP IN ADVANCE OF PREVIOUSLY KNOWN PHARMACEUTICAL METHODS, AND LIKE SOME OTHER INVENTIONS OF PRACTICAL UTILITY, SURPRISES US BY ITS SIMPLICITY AND MAKES US WONDER WHY IT WAS NOT SUGGEST LONG AGO.

Fuller's house at 14 North Ferry, restored in 2015.

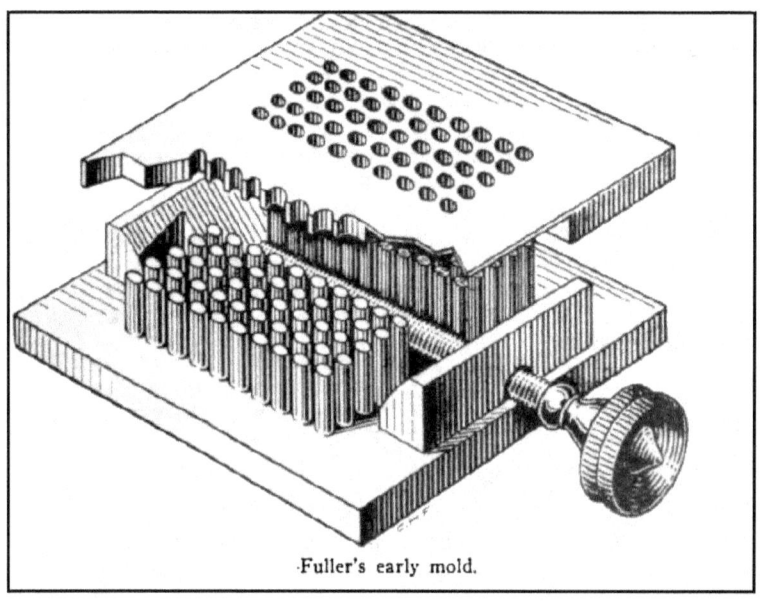
Fuller's early mold.

The American Druggist in January 1887, quotes Dr. Fuller in the Medical Record of March 9, 1878, and March 25, 1882, and says:

THE METHOD OF MAKING TABLET TRITURATES WAS ORIGINAL BY DR. FULLER, WHO HAS VERY GENEROUSLY GIVEN IT TO THE PUBLIC AND VOLUNTARILY DENIED HIMSELF THE VERY CONSIDERABLE INCOME WHICH WOULD HAVE RESULTED FROM A PATENT RIGHT.

In a communication from Sharpe and Dohme, Dr. Fuller is called "The Father of Tablet Triturates." In fact his work has been recognized and adopted by many pharmaceutical associations and manufacturers both here and abroad.

IN REGARD TO HIS FOUNDATION WORK AND STUDY IN THE UNION COLLEGE LABORATORY, DR. FULLER SAID RECENTLY: "IF I LIVE FIFTY YEARS MORE, WHAT I LEARNED

Delivery With Grace

THERE WOULD GIVE ME PLENTY TO DO." IN 1862, HE WAS TREASURER AND LIBRARIAN AND IN 1863 VICE PRESIDENT OF THE CHEMICAL SOCIETY OF UNION COLLEGE. A FEW YEARS AGO HE RETURNED TO SCHENECTADY WHERE HE RESIDED IN THE OLD HOMESTEAD AT 12 NORTH FERRY STREET. HE ATTENDED THE 50TH REUNION OF THE CLASS OF 1863.

The 1921 volume of the Albany Medical Annals, the Journal of the Alumni Association of the Albany Medical College added the following:

ROBERT M. FULLER OF SCHENECTADY BEQUEATHED A FUND TO UNION COLLEGE, THE INCOME OF WHICH IS DIVIDED INTO TEN SCHOLARSHIPS, AWARDED TO STUDENTS IN THE ALBANY MEDICAL COLLEGE WHO HAVE TAKEN THEIR PREMEDICAL COURSES IN UNION COLLEGE. BY THE TERMS OF THE BEQUEST, THE COMMITTEE OF AWARD CONSISTS OF THE PRESIDENT AND THE DEAN OF THE FACULTY OF UNION COLLEGE, AND THE DEAN OF THE ALBANY MEDICAL COLLEGE. THESE SCHOLARSHIPS WILL BE GIVEN ONLY TO THOSE STUDENTS WHO HAVE SHOWN, WHILE IN UNION COLLEGE, GENERAL MENTAL AND PHYSICAL FITNESS FOR THE WORK OF THE MEDICAL PROFESSION, AND WHO HAVE EXCELLED IN THE PREMEDICAL COURSES IN CHEMISTRY. FIVE OF THE SCHOLARSHIPS ARE RESERVED FOR THOSE STUDENTS WHO, AT THE TIME OF ENTERING THE MEDICAL COLLEGE, HAVE RECEIVED OR ARE CANDIDATES FOR A BACHELOR'S DEGREE FROM UNION COLLEGE. THE OTHER FIVE MAY BE AWARDED TO STUDENTS WHO HAVE COMPLETED THE TWO YEARS PREMEDICAL COURSE.

Thirty-thousand dollars was given to the college for the scholarships and they are still available to Union College students.

Dr. Fuller developed a method of used medicated milk sugar to fill pill molds with medicine and proposed the concept in a paper read at the American Medical Society on February 21, 1878, titled: *"Dose Dispensing Simplified, an Easy, Economical,*

Delivery With Grace

and Accurate Method of Dispensing Medicines in a Compact and Palatable Form." He and Horatio N. Frasier, a New York pharmacist, went into business in 1893 to make them and with the public statement that the process will not and should not be patented so that all pharmacists could make them. When he died at his house on 14 North Ferry St., the *New York Times* said he was a millionaire.

In a book published about the first century of the Philadelphia College of Pharmacy, this passage refers to the importance of Fuller.

"DR. ROBERT M. FULLER OF SCHENECTADY, NY, IS UNDOUBTEDLY THE ORIGINATOR (IN 1861) OF TABLE TRITURATES (MOULDED TABLETS), AND THE MOVING SPIRIT IN PLACING THE INDUSTRY ON A SUBSTANTIAL BASIS... COMPRESSED TABLETS AND TABLET TRITURATES, FROM WHICH ALL OTHER VARIETIES ORIGINATE, HAVE HAD DIFFERENT LINES OF EVOLUTION. IN POINT OF TIME, HOWEVER, THE IMPROVEMENTS PROCEEDED ALMOST SIMULTANEOUSLY. TABLET TRITURATES ARE EITHER COMPRESSED OR MOULDED. THEIR UPPER AND LOWER SURFACES ARE FLAT. IN THE CASE OF COMPRESSED TABLETS, THE UPPER AND LOWER SURFACES MAY BE CONVEX OR FLAT. THE THREE WORKERS WHO STAND OUT IN THE EARLY HISTORY OF THE INDUSTRY ARE BROKEDON, DUNBTON AND FULLER."

A Schenectadian who took full advantage of the compressed pill as well as other remedies was Willis T. Hanson (1858-1933). During the 19th and early 20th century there were few laws governing patent medicines and there were hundreds of different remedies that could be purchased without any real knowledge if they were beneficial at all. One Schenectady man, Willis T. Hanson, became

Delivery With Grace

wealthy selling "Dr. William's Pink Pills for Pale People" in the late 1800s, a very popular cure-all pill at the time.

The pills originated with a Dr. William Jackson in Brockville, Ontario, Canada, who patented his pill in 1886 and sold the rights for $100 in 1891 to Canadian Senator George Fulford in Brockville. He formed the G. T. Fulford & Company in 1887 to manufacture and distribute patent medicines. He formed the Dr. Williams Medicine Company and sold Pink Pills for Pale People (the trading arm of Fulford). He did so well he expanded through North America, Europe and the British Empire. The pills were advertised in 82 countries. The claims ranged from curing digestive problems for Civil War vets to curing all disease resulting from the "vitiated humors in the blood." The publication of testimonials from satisfied users of Pink Pills was his principal advertising technique. Designed to appeal to the average person's trust in other human beings, they provided a gripping, first-hand account of a "miraculous" cure. An early one claimed that Pink Pills had cured him of *locomotor ataxia*, a disorder affecting coordination. Testimonials were customized to fit the locality of business. One produced for the American market in the mid-1890s, for example, drew notice to the health problems of Civil War veterans. When Fulford expanded his enterprise to England, he attracted attention to Pink Pills by offering bicycles as prizes in different areas to those who collected the best testimonials.

Ads for the pills were cleverly made. They often read like a newspaper article or feature only for the reader at the end to see that the person was cured when they took Dr. Williams' Pink Pills for Pale People. The person cured was usually a local person and would sometimes have local or regional connections to it.

Fulford became very wealthy and built a Beaux Arts style mansion called Fulford Place in Ontario, Canada, designed by Albany architect Albert W. Fuller.

After Fulford's death in 1905, the company was run by his partner William T. Hanson of Schenectady until 1929, when George Taylor Fulford, Jr., took over.

Hanson acquired the rights in 1892 to market the pills in the US with his company, the Dr. Williams' Medicine Company at 147 Centre St. (Broadway). It was also listed as 195 State St. in 1887, where he is listed as an agent for the American Pharmaceutical Association. It was the location of his pharmacy.

Hanson lived at 821 Union and had a summer house at The Knolls where the General Electric Global Research Center now sits. He was the first President

Delivery With Grace

of the Union National Bank, President of the Board of Managers of Ellis Hospital, the Board of Trade, and a Trustee of Union College.

The tax laws of 1863 until 1883, and from 1898 to 1902, were passed to help pay for the Civil War and later, the Spanish American War. Companies that were taxed were allowed to make a special tax stamp that they could put on their product. The products included medicine, perfumes and cosmetics, chewing gum and sparkling wines. A few companies such as Hanson's used the stamps. He had his own private die stamp beginning in 1899. 480,000 of them were printed. Hanson's tax was for the Spanish American War.

Most companies used general issue stamps bearing the picture of a battleship, but a handful chose to have their own made to give them some additional advertising and to set them apart from competitors. These private die stamps were approved by the IRS before they could be used, so they are considered to be federal revenue stamps.

Hanson did well until the passage of the Pure Food and Drug Act in 1906 and articles began to be published about the fraudulence of these claims from patented medicines. A scientific analysis of his product revealed they were mostly iron sulphate, starch and sugar, but also had some strychnine in it (in Australia the pills had arsenic in it). The company

Delivery With Grace

was sued and found guilty of mislabeling. By the 1930s the boon was over. Hanson died in 1933.

The label on this package shown of Dr. Williams' Pink Pills for Pale People reads:

SAFE AND EFFECTIVE TONIC FOR THE BLOOD AND NERVES. ANEMIC CONDITIONS, DISEASES CAUSED BY OR DEPENDENT THIN, IMPOVERISHED BLOOD AND FOR NERVOUS DISORDERS RESULTING FROM MALNUTRITION. USEFUL WHEREVER A NERVINE OR DIGESTIVE TONIC IS REQUIRED. THESE PILLS ARE GUARANTEED TO CONTAIN NO OPIATES OR NARCOTICS. CONTENTS 40 PILLS.

PRICE 50 CENTS. 6 BOXES FOR $2.50.

THE DR. WILLIAMS MEDICAL COMPANY. SCHENECTADY,

Hanson's mansion at 821 Union Street.

Delivery With Grace

N.Y. AND BROCKVILLE, ONTARIO.

W. T. HANSON COMPANY, SCHENECTADY, N.Y. U.S. DISTRIBUTORS.

DIRECTIONS INSIDE IN ENGLISH, FRENCH, GERMAN, SPANISH, ITALIAN.

Dr. William's Medicine Company continued as a business until 1989. Hanson's monument at Vale Cemetery is pink.

A sample of William's advertisements appeared in the African American Philadelphia newspaper The *Christian Recorder* on January 9, 1896:

FOR COUNTRY'S SAKE.

AN INDIAN FIGHTER SUFFERS AGONIES FROM DISEASE.

HE WAS IN THE BATTLE WITH THE APACHES WHEN GERONIMO WAS CAPTURED.

FROM THE "PRESS," NEW YORK CITY.

WORN WITH THE EXPOSURE OF ARMY LIFE ON THE FRONTIER, AND POISONED BY THE CONTINUAL DRINKING OF ALKALI WATER, JOSEPH FLEGAUF RETURNED TO PHILADELPHIA EIGHT YEARS AGO, BROKEN DOWN IN HEALTH AND UNABLE TO DO ANY WORK.

HE HAD SERVED FIVE YEARS WITH THE NINTH UNITED STATES INFANTRY IN MANY A DESPERATE FIGHT WITH THE INDIANS IN ARIZONA AND OTHER FRONTIER STATES AND HAD WON AN ENVIABLE RECORD. IN THE FIERCE CONFLICT WHEN GERONIMO, THE FAMOUS CALLED OF THE APACHES, WAS CAPTURED, MR. FLEGAUF WAS AMONG THE BRAVE SOLDIERS WHO, FORGETFUL OF EVERYTHING BUT DUTY, CHARGED UPON THEM STILE INDIANS.

LIFE ON THE PLAINS SENT TO AN UNTIMELY DEATH MANY SOLDIERS WHO WERE NEVER TOUCHED BY A REDSKINS' BULLET OR ARROW, AND MR. FLEGAUF CAME NEAR SUCH A

Delivery With Grace

fate as that. A long time before his time was out he was taken seriously ill, but he stuck to his post until an honorable discharge was finally given to him.

When he reached Philadelphia the Indian fighter was scarcely more than skin and bones, and for three weeks he lay desperately ill in a hospital. He felt dizzy and his stomach felt as if it had been dried up. These symptoms were accompanied by bloody dysentery, which no medicine seem to relieve.

After two years of suffering Mr. Flegauf came to New York and was treated by several physicians. These did not agree, some calling his disease catarrh of the stomach, and others chronic diarrhea.

In speaking to a reporter about his illness Mr. Flegauf said the doctors helped him, but, with all the money he spent for advice and medicine , he was able to work only a small part of the time. Since moving to his present home, No. 517 West Forty second Street, in New York, about a year ago, Mr. Flegauf has been so ill that his voice and hearing almost left him.

Then all medicines failed, and the sick man had little hope of recovery. At this critical time Dr. Williams' Pink Pills for Pale People were recommended to Mr. Flegauf, and, almost as a last hope, he began taking them.

"The beneficial effect of the medicine was felt at once," Mr. Flegauf told the reporter, "and before I had taken a box I began to eat with relish. Three boxes made me so much better that I began work and have been able to keep at it since for five months."

Dr. Williams' Pink Pills for Pale People are not a patent medicine in the sense that HAMI implies. They were first compounded as a prescription and used as such in general practice by an eminent physician. So great was their efficacy that it was deemed wise to place them within the reach of all. They are now manufactured by the

Delivery With Grace

Dr. Williams' Pink Pill 1898 Brochure front cover.

DR. WILLIAMS' MEDICINE CO., SCHENECTADY, N.Y. AND ARE SOLD IN BOXES (NEVER IN LOOSE FORM BY THE DOZEN OR HUNDRED, AND THE PUBLIC ARE CAUTIONED AGAINST NUMEROUS IMITATIONS SOLD IN THIS SHAPE) AT 50 CENTS A BOX, OR SIX BOXES FOR $2.50, AND MAY BE HAD OF ALL DRUGGISTS OR DIRECT BY MAIL FROM DR. WILLIAMS' MEDICINE COMPANY.

BY 1892 (1890-91) ANOTHER DISEASE HIT SCHENECTADY. THIS TIME CHOLERA TOOK ITS TOLL ON YOUNG AND OLD AND FUNERALS WERE SEEN ALMOST EVERY HOUR FOR A TIME. IT LASTED FROM JULY 1890 TO APRIL 1891 AND SOME 300 CASES WERE REPORTED. THIS WAS CAUSED MOSTLY BY AN INADEQUATE WATER SUPPLY THAT TOOK WATER FROM THE MOHAWK RIVER FOR ITS FRESH WATER SUPPLY, THE SAME RIVER THAT SEWAGE WAS DUMPED INTO. IT ALSO CAUSED AN EPIDEMIC DOWNRIVER IN COHOES (1000 CASES) AND WEST TROY (WATERVLIET) WITH OVER 100 CASES. THE CITY BOARD OF HEALTH RESOLVED THAT, "ALL THE PHYSICIANS OF THIS CITY ARE EMPLOYED BY THE BOARD OF HEALTH TO ATTEND UPON THOSE WHO DO NOT FEEL ABLE TO PAY FOR MEDICAL ADVICE." THE OLD COLLEGE BUILDING IN THE STOCKADE AREA WAS FITTED UP TO BECOME A TEMPORARY ISOLATION HOSPITAL. YEARS LATER, A STATE LAW IN 1868 MANDATED A WATER SUPPLY FOR THE CITY OF

SCHENECTADY BUT INSTEAD THE CITY CONTRACTED FOR ITS WATER WITH CHARLES STANFORD, BROTHER OR RAILROAD MAGNATE LELAND STANFORD, AND ALSO NEW YORK SENATOR AND OWNER OF A SCHENECTADY NEWSPAPER. HIS COMPANY DURING THE SUMMER OF 1871 WAS LAYING WATER MAINS FROM POLLUTED MOHAWK RIVER WATER INTO SCHENECTADY HOMES. IN THE SPRING OF 1920 AN EPIDEMIC OF GASTROENTERITIS FOLLOWED BY AN OUTBREAK OF TYPHOID FEVER WAS CAUSED BY THIS WATER SUPPLY.

Elizabeth Gillette

Women also played a major role in the early medical history of Schenectady. Dr. Elizabeth Van Rensselaer Gillette (1874-1965), who was born in 1874 at Granby, Conn., is considered to be the first women surgeon in Schenectady County. She began her practice on June 1, 1900, and it lasted almost six decades. She retired in 1959 at age 85.

Gillette lived and died in her home at the corner of Union and College Sts. at the entrance to Schenectady's historic stockade district. Her home was renovated and now is a commercial structure.

For a woman to become a medical doctor during the 19th century was no small accomplishment. It took the 26-year-old Elizabeth Blackwell (1821-1910) to become the first woman to earn an MD degree from Geneva (N.Y.) Medical College, on January 23, 1849. She went on blazing the trail for women and in 1857 she opened the New York Infirmary to serve poor women and children, and provided women opportunities to study medicine and nursing. Blackwell's medical degree did not go over well in medical circles and a letter in the February 21, 1849, Boston Medical and Surgical Journal condemned "*the farce, enacted at the Geneva Medical College.*" The writer hoped that, "*as this is the first case of the kind that has been perpetrated either in Europe or America, I hope, for the honor of humanity, that it will be the last.*" Most medical colleges agreed — many women like Elizabeth Gillette did not. Gillette studied medicine at the New York Medical College and Hospital for Women, and received her license to practice in 1899, the year before moving to Schenectady.

Gillette also had politics in her blood. As a descendant of Thomas Rogers, a Mayflower passenger, and Connecticut's Jewett family, doctors and politicians were part of life. One of Gillette's relatives was General Chauncey Pettibone (1762-1814), a legislator in Connecticut who served 13 consecutive terms. Another was Governor (and preacher) Jonathan Trumbull, the only colonial governor to support the War for Independence. Trumbull was a close confidant of George Washington, and before making major decisions, Washington would often comment, "*Let us consult Brother Jonathan.*"

"Brother Jon" became the symbol for the fledgling unified colonies that became the United States, and for years, "Brother Jonathan" was usually depicted in cartoons as an American revolutionary with tri-

Delivery With Grace

cornered hat and long military jacket. Our own Troy-based "Uncle Sam" Wilson later replaced this American icon during the early 19th century after the War of 1812.

Under the influence of Dr. George R. Lunn, preacher and Socialist mayor of Schenectady, Dr. Gillette ran in 1919 for the New York State Assembly as a Democrat. She won by only 247 votes. She was the first woman in upstate New York to get elected to the legislature and considering that from 1920 to 1964 was the only Democrat elected from Schenectady County, it was quite a rare victory.

Gillette's one-year tenure in the Assembly came at a time of political turmoil. While she focused on legislation dealing with medical issues such as regulating certain drugs, or mandating physicals for children who work in factories, she could write laws, but as a woman could not actually vote for them in a general election. Women were not given the right to vote until the Nineteenth Amendment was passed on August 26, 1920.

Gillette also served during the period known as "The Red Scare." In March 1919, the NY Legislature established the Joint Legislative Committee to Investigate Seditious Activities (Lusk Committee) at the height of the Red Scare to investigate individuals and organizations deemed radical or subversive.

The Committee operated until May 1920, and watched closely the activities of suspected "radicals," as well as attended mass meetings, subpoenaed

Delivery With Grace

individuals and records, and even raided organizations and seized their files.

Women also played important roles on both sides of the investigation serving as "operators" or investigators for the Committee. They filed frequent reports on their clandestine observations. Investigations were conducted on feminists such as Emma Goldman, and women's organizations such as the Women's Trade Union League, and Women's Peace Party. Goldman was an influential and well-known anarchist and an early advocate of free speech, birth control, women's equality and independence, and union organization. She spent two years in prison for her criticism of mandatory conscription of young men into the military during World War I and was deported in 1919. The Committee also compiled files dealing with birth control, collected leftist pamphlets, broadsides, and other literature, some of it by women.

During Gillette's tenure, five Socialist Party Assemblymen were expelled from the legislative body on the grounds that membership in the Socialist Party constituted disloyalty to the United States. Ironic, since a few years earlier, Lunn was Schenectady's socialist mayor and General Electric scientist Charles Steinmetz who was also a socialist was the city's head of the common council.

The socialist assemblymen: August Claessens, Samuel A. De Witt, Samuel Orr, Charles Solomon, and Louis Waldman, along with the Socialist Party, tried to overturn the Assembly action and be seated as legally elected representatives of their respective assembly districts. The Socialist Party organized a special committee to raise funds and hold meetings on the case. The New York State Bar Association also appointed a special committee to plead for the seating of the disposed assemblymen. It was composed of Charles Evans Hughes, Ogden Mills, and Joseph Proskauer. These efforts were unsuccessful, however, as the Assembly refused to reverse its earlier decision.

Gillette was defeated in the next election by 4,585 votes to William W. Campbell, who ran on the Republican and Prohibition line. It was a Republican sweep in the legislature, and she went back to practicing medicine at her home at 254 Union,

Dr. Gillette in her automobile in Schenectady.

although she continued to practice while serving in the legislature.

Dr. Gillette spent her final years working on her favorite causes including the Schenectady Humane Society, the Schenectady County Historical Society, and the DAR. She died at her home on June 26, 1965.

Gillette's simple philosophy can be summed up by one of her quotes from a newspaper interview where she advised women to: *"Vote in every election, go to every political meeting possible, learn all you can about political affairs — and always be a lady."*

Janet Murray

Another important women doctor was Janet Murray (1856-1940). Born in Peebles, Scotland, in 1856 to Ralph and Isabella (Kerr) Murray and educated in England, Murray moved to Ontario, Canada in 1866 at age 10, with her family. Her father was a mining engineer (also listed as a minister) when in Peebles. After nursing her father back to health after an accident, nursing her mother who was a invalid, and dressing wounds of neighbors before the doctor arrived, her family began telling her she should become a doctor.

In 1891 she graduated from the Medical College of Queen's University, being one of the first females to attend there, and began working for doctors in

Dr. Janet Murray.

Canada. After a quick stop in Schenectady on her way to Boston for an interview, she returned to Schenectady in 1893 when the job didn't materialize and opened her practice above a Jay St. tailor shop (although listed 242-230-1/2 State St.) and then to 14 Mynderse St., where she practiced for the next forty years. There was no hospital in Schenectady when she began. If someone needed an operation, they had to be taken by wagon to the railroad station, be put in a baggage car, and ride to Albany. She always made time to take care of the poor.

She quickly integrated into the medical societies and clubs in the area. In 1935 she was elected to become Vice President of the Queens University Alumni Association and also a member of the Board of Councilors of the Women's Medical Society of New York. Her entrance to the county medical society was met with skepticism. By 1905 she was Vice President of the society.

Delivery With Grace

She made the news on August 19, 1921, when she was involved in a car accident, ironically in front of a doctor's office. Janet and a woman companion were bruised and cut when she crashed her Kissel Coupe car into a telephone pole in front of Dr. William H. Seward's on West Main St. They were coming home from a trip in Utica. It was raining hard and the lights of an approaching car blinded her. They were taken care of by Dr. Seward and the Kissel car was taken to the L. R. Mack garage. She retired to the Old Ladies Home (Heritage Home for Women) in March 1937 and died there on February 20, 1940, at age 83 after a ten day illness. While there she volunteered her services. She had practiced medicine for 64 years in Schenectady.

Russell Sage College's M. Grace Jorgensen Nursing Achievement Award and the Bellevue Hospital Nursing Achievement Award goes to two third-year Sage students majoring in nursing who display academic and personal excellence, who demonstrate interest in women's health, who show promise of making significant contributions to the health-related professions, and who show interest in working in cooperation with others rather than in competition with others. The awards are given to RSC students by Dr. Grace G. Jorgensen (daughter of founder) on the left and continues each year. The 2021 winners were Mia Flanagan (left) and Evelyn Welch (right).

Delivery With Grace

A Birthing at Bellevue in the 1980's
Grace Jorgensen

First a little history: Schenectady during World War II was a very busy place. General Electric had 40,000 workers engaged in making all kinds of electrical and electronic equipment and vacuum tubes for the war effort. Schenectady Locomotive (ALCO) also had a major workforce of over a thousand engaged in making tanks and anti-tank guns. In the years immediately following the war, General Electric expanded its Research Laboratory and with the formation of the Knolls Atomic Laboratory there was a large influx of highly paid scientists, engineers and technicians into the Capital District, all with good family health insurance. Thus the area became attractive to all specialties of physicians and surgeons, especially OBYGYN. Prenatal observation and care became more widespread and one of the results was the building of the addition to Bellevue in the early 70's. There were three birthing institutions operating in Schenectady, St. Clare's Hospital, Ellis Hospital and Bellevue.

Prenatal Visits

If during a normal prenatal office visit, a problem was encountered, the patient would be sent to Bellevue for consultation and if necessary tests, and generally on that same day, she would be taken to the appropriate section of the hospital; for genetic issues the patient would see Dr. Kris Amyott; for a laboratory problem she would see Dr. Donohowe; and for diet she would see the hospital dietician, June Causey. By providing these consultations on the same day, the patient was saved the worry of a long period of waiting to find out the problem and the procedures that may be needed to have it rectified. In

Delivery With Grace

many cases when Bellevue was indicated as the preferred birthing location, at 36 weeks a copy of the patient record would be sent from the doctor's office to the laboratory at Bellevue. The OB doctors considered this transfer so crucial, that if a patient showed up at Bellevue without a record on file, the Doctor involved would often make a personal visit to Bellevue to rectify the error.

Signs of Impending Birth

Patients were usually instructed by their obstetrician that if contractions began and it was during the week, they should get in touch with the office and at weekends, with Bellevue. Many physicians kept their patients in early labor at home, usually by telephone contact; thus most of the patients were in active labor when they arrived at Bellevue. The Labor and Delivery (L&D) section had a designated Reception Room where the status of the patient could be assessed and if the patient was not in true labor they could be sent home. Sometimes, to differentiate false labor, the physician would instruct the patient to take a hot bath. If contractions stopped, the patient stayed in the comfort of their own home. The physician would then call for an office visit and a situation review the following day.

Premature Labor now is called "pre-term"

In cases where contractions were commencing at times ahead of the predicted birthing date, patients would be instructed to go to the hospital immediately and the physician always met with the patient on admission. If pre-term delivery was immediate, the neonatologist was called to attend the delivery, so if baby problems occurred, then they could be identified early and the

Delivery With Grace

SCN (Special Care Nursery) would be notified to prepare for intensive care for the baby.

Normal Birth

For most patients, the arrival at Bellevue was documented in the Admissions Room, and a status assessment made by an Admissions Nurse. The assessment tests usually included a blood analysis, blood pressure, etc. The appropriate physician was called and given a report on the patient status. The patient was then transferred to the Labor Room. Before 1974, when extended facilities were added, all the activities took place in the Mansion. Patients labored in a two bed room and the delivery rooms were on the second floor. Then only fathers were allowed to visit. Now, with the Birthing Suite added, a few family members are allowed to attend. In pre-1974 days, patients were transferred between floors by a unique gurney that just fitted into the available elevator, as shown on page 46.

When the patient was 10 cm. dilated they were transferred to the Delivery Room, accompanied by the father, to begin pushing. Each physician had their own special labor orders; some ordered enemas, others prescribed perinatal shaves. Fetal monitors, used rarely, were reserved for high-end risk patients or an abnormal fetal heart rate and were usually there at birthing time. In addition to the physician, the staff in attendance was one L&D nurse, the laboratory technician, on duty around the clock, an anesthetist to administer regional anesthesia, which is now accepted as 'State of the Art.' If for some reason the physician was unable to be there, there was always Dr. J., or her husband Dr. Westney available, since their home was located adjacent to the hospital.

Delivery With Grace

Post Delivery

Mom, Dad & Baby remained in the delivery room for approximately one hour after birth. Dad took pictures and called the family from the hallway phones. Dr. J. recognized the importance of a quiet, calm atmosphere in the delivery room along with early skin-to-skin mother baby contact, now given the term "bonding." After one hour or the effects of the anesthetic had worn off for the mother, the baby was taken to the nursery for a two-hour observation period. This included an assessment using the APGAR scale. The mother was given a bath and then transferred to the PPU, the Post Partum Unit. After approximately two hours, the baby was returned to the mother for the first feeding. In the 1980's, breast-feeding had gone out of style and bottle-feeding was the vogue. From then on, the baby was kept in the nursery and brought to the mother for feeding on a four-hour schedule. Moms could request their babies at any time and have them brought from the nursery. Otherwise, the conventional wisdom was that the separation allowed the mother as much rest as possible. Nowadays, cost cutting measures have eliminated the nursery and the baby stays with the mother around the clock. Also the actual time of stay in the hospital is now as short as two days, whereas when Bellevue started, mothers stayed usually for ten days. By the 1980's it had decreased to four days.

Visiting hours were from 11 a.m. to 7 p.m. and were usually limited to four people at a time. Post-partum patients usually occupied 2-bedded rooms with a divider curtain between the beds, which could be drawn when privacy was needed. Three days after birth, baby pictures were taken by the nursery staff, since this time was

Delivery With Grace

believed to be a baby's prettiest day. Parents could purchase the pictures for a fee.

The result of the elimination of the Nursery is that the number of bunk-dropped babies has increased nationwide and the time that babies are under direct observation by an experienced nursery nurse is seriously decreased. The latter consequence is that early neonatal medical problems are not as quickly detected. However, from the insurance point of view, the elimination of the nursery has been a cost-saving measure.

Nutrition

Nutrition was always a major focus at Bellevue. In the beginning, husband Elmer was the chef, cooking breakfast, lunch and dinner for both patients and staff. He emphasized the importance of healthy foods as a crucial part of the mother's recovery process. As the hospital grew in size, the kitchen staff prided themselves on the food that was served. Dr. J. often looked over the patient trays to be sure the food met her standards. In the period we are recounting, if a patient tray was returned with food not eaten, then the incident was recorded, and a kitchen representative would visit with the patient to become aware of their preferences and future trays would reflect the encounter. There was a personal touch too: if the patient's record indicated a birthday during her time of hospitalization, then the kitchen was notified and a special dinner was arranged, including the father, and a birthday cake would be prepared. This strong interest in nutrition also extended to the employees, who generally were served the same foods as the patients. Nowadays, patients are served dishes prepared from frozen foods, whereas in those days the food was always freshly prepared.

Delivery With Grace

Discharge

Patients with uncomplicated deliveries were usually discharged after four days, and C-section patients after five days. This is in contrast to nowadays where insurance companies promote early discharge as soon as two days, and pediatricians expect to see the babies in the office at two days old. As late as the 1980's, at four days, moms went home in good shape; as well rested as possible and past the 3rd. day of breast-feeding, when milk comes in. Circumcisions were fairly healed by this time. Discharge time was mandated at 11 a.m., and this was enforced to ensure that there were enough beds available for L&D and post-op patients later in the day. In this regard, the physicians liked to work early in the morning at Bellevue, attracted by the renowned breakfasts, so they cooperated about making early morning rounds and signing out their patients for discharge. In the 80's, when circumcision occurred, the Nursery nurses had three days for observation of any subsequent complications. Nowadays, baby boys can be discharged a mere four hours after the procedure. For breast-feeding mothers, on discharge they were given a large basket of supplies, compliments of a formula company. The basket usually consisted of diapers, baby soap, a toy, formula, a pacifier and one baby blanket. As a safety issue, patients and babies were escorted out the front door to their automobile, so that the Nursery Nurse could confirm that the baby car seat was compliant with regulations.

Birthing Suite Layout

The Birthing Suite at this time had become located on one floor. The eight rooms were arranged in a ring with the Nurses Station located along the western wall, and situated so that a nurse at the station could easily see any signal given by another nurse at any of the doorways. There were phone extensions inside and outside every room. The nursery was located a short distance away on the floor below. There were six Delivery and Labor Rooms, two rooms for PPU and one operating room that also could serve as a Delivery and Labor room, and one 4-bed room for recovery. The fact that all the rooms were under easy surveillance was extremely important from a safety point of view. After each use of any of the rooms, the cleaning squad was immediately notified and the room returned to a pristine condition. With as many as 20 or even 30 deliveries and operations in any eight-hour shift, the cleaning squad was kept very busy.

The Nursery Unit

The Nursery Unit consisted of a large rectangular room with an adjacent separate room for the nurses' station. One side of the large room consisted of a full-length observation window for visitor viewing and a draw curtain to provide isolation at non-viewing times. The wall to the Nursing Station included a viewing window so that a nurse was always observing the instrumentation associated with any incubators. For normal-birth babies, each was in its own crib with its name prominently displayed at the end of each crib. For preemie babies and others with special problems, the cribs were highly instrumented incubators. The Nursery was manned around the clock and the night nurse covering the Nursery was in a very responsible position. For many years, the night nurse covering the Nursery was Nurse Mabel Fan.

Delivery With Grace

Recruiting
Grace Jorgensen, MD

As Medical Director of Bellevue, one of my principal responsibilities was to make sure that the hospital had the best available equipment, was using the most up-to-date protocols and was staffed by the best physicians, technicians and other personnel as it was possible to draw to Bellevue. You may recall that Bellevue was a privately owned solely Female Healthcare facility and was certainly unique in New York and perhaps in the whole of the U.S. I therefore made an effort to attend national and international scientific meetings, covering all the medical specialties involved in the hospital, both for the content but also to meet and attempt to recruit top-notch physicians. A principal helper in identifying prospective recruits was my husband, Dr. Howard Westney. He networked his associates and colleagues as well as covering the relevant literature. For example, Dr. Wood was a fellow student who was persuaded to join Bellevue several years after college. It was through Dr. Wood that Aram Atashian was recruited as Laboratory Director. As indicated elsewhere, Dr. Albright was renowned for his ideas in the field of birthing anesthesia and was recruited to implement his ideas at Bellevue. Other significant recruits include Dr. Frede for Ultrasound Imaging, Dr. Lim for the new field of Neonatology and Dr. Macpherson as Senior Vice President and Medical Director. Other experts in their respective professional fields were recruited as consultants, such as Dr. Apgar, for post-birth assessment, Dr. Grover for unusual diagnoses, or as speakers at Bellevue such as Dr. Stephen B. Levine, author of the book *Sex is not Simple*, who in his talk at Bellevue interpreted the findings of Kinsey for the medical and nursing audience. Looking back, though specific recruiting trips were occasionally draining and took me out of town away from family, they certainly enabled Bellevue to remain at the forefront and ensured that our patients were receiving the best medical treatments that were available in the profession.

GRACE G. JORGENSEN, M.D.
2110 Troy Schenectady Road
Niskayuna, NY 12309

PROFESSIONAL AND COMMUNITY ACTIVITIES:

Director, Owner and Major Shareholder	Bellevue Woman's Hospital (1959 - October 2001); (served with no compensation and with no retirement benefits upon transfer of Hospital to non-profit status 2001; 42 years of voluntary service and leadership *as did my Mother, a nurse, who founded the Hospital for Women 28 years before*)
Founder	A medical health service for women which evolved into the present Woman's HealthCare Group, LLC.
Founder	Bellevue Woman's Health
Established (1991)	The Bellevue Research Foundation, Inc..
1979	Member, American Academy of Medical Directors
Member	Board of Directors, HSBC Bank (formerly Marine Midland)
Past President	American Medical Woman's Association (AMWA)
2000	Civic Leaders Council, 190th Air National Guard
Member	Distribution Committee, The Schenectady Foundation for non-profit corporations
Member	Schenectady 2000, Economic and Civic Development
Member	Center for Economic Growth, Capital Region
Member	Inducted into the "50 Group" of Capital Region Civic Leaders by invitation

PROFESSIONAL ORGANIZATION MEMBERSHIPS:

American Medical Association
American Medical Women's Association
Medical Society of the State of New York
Medical Society of Schenectady
American Society for Reproductive Medicine
American Association of Gynecologic Laparoscopy
North American Menopause Society
New York State Society of OB-GYN Physicians

BENEFACTOR TO:

Russell Sage College
Union College
State University of New York at Albany (SUNY)
Rensselaer Polytechnic Institute (RPI)
New York Medical College
Schaffer Library Albany Medical College -Lifetime Member

GRACE G. JORGENSEN, M.D, continued

HONORS, AWARDS AND ACHIEVEMENTS:

- 1957 -Present   Fully Accredited by the Joint Commission of Accreditation of Health care Organizations since the hospital's first inspection

- 1992-94,1997-98   "Top 10 Employer in the Capital Region Award by the Capital Region Human Resource Management, affiliate of National Society for Human Resource Management

- May 17,1989   Soroptimist International of the Americas Women of Distinction by Soroptimist International of New York for professional and voluntary accomplishment in Women's Health and well being

- April 25,1991   75th Anniversary Celebration of the Sage Colleges for Outstanding Contributions to the Advancement of Women's Health Care and Dedicated Support of Russell Sage College

- 1991   Recognition by Quirks Marketing Research Review -1991 Source Book Supplement, *"Patients Tell a New York Hospital That Services Match Its Strong Reputation."*

- June, 1992   Excellence in Business, 10+ years by the Woman's Business Council of the Albany-Colonie Regional of Commerce

- 1992   "Quality Commitment Award" -American Society for Training & Development…Results of Patient Satisfaction Surveys conducted by Gallup indicated that 99% of Bellevue's patients rated quality of service as "Excellent" and "Very Good"

- May, 1997   Bellevue named in *"Self"* magazine as one of the Top 10 Women's Health Centers/Hospitals in the United States

- March 4,1997   "Going for Gold'-Golden Leadership Award by Enterprising Women's Leadership Institute

- May 7, 1997   Vision, Leadership, Encouragement, Compassion and Sensitivity & Belief that Health Care Encompasses the Whole Person, Body, Mind and Spirit by Bellevue Woman's Hospital and Woman's HealthCare Plus

- May 30,2001   Appreciation Award by Union College for mentoring Union College students

- 2001   Distinguished Honoree for Women's Legacy: awarded a of a work of art presented by AETNA and the American Heart Association

- 2001   "Success of the Year" - Recognition of Bellevue Woman's Hospital as a National Model by the "Ireland Report," Snowmass Institute

- June 2001   100 Women of Excellence - Lifetime Achievement Award by the Women's Business Council of the Albany-Colonie Regional Chamber of Commerce

- June 2001   ..Doris L. Crockett Award by the Alumni Association of Russell Sage College
..Phi Kappa Phi Honor Society
..Benefactor Award by the Medical Society of the State of New York
..Girl Scout's Leadership Award by the Hudson Valley Girl Scout's Council
..Leadership Award by the Young Women's Christian Association (YWCA)
..Lifetime Achievement Award: NYS Federation of Business & Professional Women
Soroptimists' Achievement Award

- October 2003   Albany Medical Center's periodic Alden March Award presented to an individual who demonstrates a sustained leadership involvement in improving health care opportunities and has championed quality health care for the citizens of the Capital Region and throughout the State of New York, (first time award to a woman)

ESTABLISHED SCHOLARHIPS for Nursing Students:
M. Grace Jorgensen Nursing Scholarship at Russell Sage College (in honor of Mother who founded Bellevue Hospital)
Bellevue Woman's Hospital Scholarship

EDUCATION:
1946-47 Union College, Schenectady, NY
1950   Russell Sage College, Troy, NY
        Bachelor of Arts in General Science degree, Science Award
1954   New York Medical School, New York City, NY
        Flower & Fifth Avenue Medical School
        Doctorate of Medicine

RESIDENCY PROGRAMS:
Ellis Hospital, Schenectady, NY
Bellevue Hospital, Schenectady, NY

BELLEVUE WOMAN'S HOSPITAL ACTIVE MEDICAL STAFF - 5-19-1999- TO -09-2001
AAGL- AMERICAN ASSOCIATION GYNECOLOGIC LAPAROSCOPISTS
HONORS SOCEITY PHI KAPPA PHI
DORIS CROCKETT AWARD - RUSSELL SAGE COLLEGE
SCHOLARSHIP ESTABLISHED -RSC NURSING - M.G. JORGENSEN R.N.
50 GROUP MEMBER
FOUNDING MEMBER BELLEVUE RESEARCH FOUNDATION
LEADERSHIP AWARD -Y.M.C.A.
ACHIEVEMENT AWARD: SOROPTOMISTS
MEMBER - SCHENECTADY 2000
CENTER FOR ECOMONIC GROWTH - MEMBER
MAY 17, 1989 - AWARD - SOROPTIMIST INTERNATIONAL OF THE AMERICAS WOMEN DISTINCTION. BY SOROPTIMIST INTERNATIONAL OF NEW YORK FOR PROFESSIONAL AND VOLUNTARY ACCOMPLISHMENTS IN THE AREA OF WOMEN'S HEALTH AND WELL BEING
AMA
NYS MEDICAL SOCIETY
SCHENECTADY COUNTY MEDICAL SOCIETY
AMERICAN FERTILITY SOCIETY
AMERICAN SOCIETY OF REPRODUCTIVE MEDICINE
NORTH AMERICAN MENOPAUSE SOCIETY
NYS SOCIETY OF OB/GYN PHYSICIANS
AMERICAN ACADEMY OF MEDICAL DIRECTORS
SCIENCE AWARD RSC 1950
BENEFACTOR - SCHAEFIFER LIBRARY
LIFETIME MEMBER BENEFACTOR AWARD - NY MED COLLEGE
SCHOLARSHIP ESTABLISHED - RSC NURSING - BELLEVUE WOMAN'S HOSPITAL
UNION COLLEGE APPRECIATION AWARD FOR VALUABLE CONTRIBUTIONS AS A MENTOR TO UNION COLLEGE STUDENTS
CIVIC LEADERS COUNCIL - 190TH AIR NATIONAL GUARD
DISTRIBUTION COMM. - THE SCHENECTADY FOUNDATION
APRIL 25, 1991 - AWARD - 75TH ANNIVERSARY CELEBRATION OF THE SAGE COLLEGES FOR OUTSTANDING CONTRIBUTIONS TO THE ADVANCEMENT OF WOMEN'S HEALTH CARE AND DEDICATED SUPPORT OF RUSSELL SAGE COLLEGE
1992 - AWARD - WOMEN OF EXCELLENCE, 10+ YEARS. BY THE CHAMBER WOMEN'S BUSINESS COUNCIL.
MARCH 4, 1997 AWARD - GOLDEN LEADERSHIP AWARD. BY ENTERPRISING WOMEN'S LEADERSHIP INSTITUTE FOR GOING FOR THE GOLD
MAY 7, 1997 - AWARD - VISION, LEADERSHIP, ENCOURAGEMENT, COMPASSION AND SENSITIVITY & BELIEF THAT HEALTH CARE ENCOMPASSES THE WHOLE PERSON, BODY, MIND AND SPIRIT BY BELLEVUE WOMAN'S HOSPITAL AND WOMAN'S HEALTHCARE PLUS
MAY 30, 2001 - AWARD - APPRECIATION AWARD BY UNION COLLEGE FOR VALUABLE CONTRIBUTIONS AS A MENTOR TO UNION COLLEGE STUDENTS
2001 - AWARD - DISTINGUISHED HONOREE FOR WOMEN'S LEGACY. A WORK OF ART BY AETNA AND AMERICAN HEART ASSOC.
2001 - AWARD - 100 WOMEN OF EXCELLENCE3 BY THE CHAMBER - ALBANY - COLONIE REGIONAL CHAMBER OF COMMERCE

Sources

A Description of New Netherland By Adriaen van der Donck. Syracuse University Press, 1968

Historisch verhael aller gedencwaerdiger gheschiedenissen die in Europa: als Duytslant Vrackrijck,etc.,deses jaers 1623 [-24] voorgevallen sÿn. Deel 5 & 6. Nicolaes van Wassenaer bij I. Hondium, 1624

Memories of Bellevue, 1931-1991. Published by Bellevue. Pat Roslund. 32 pages.

Newspaper Sources Consulted: The New York Times, New York Tribune, Albany Times Union, Knickerbocker News, Ballston Spa Daily Journal, Saratogian, Schenectady Cabinet, Schenectady Democrat, Schenectady Reflector, Daily Gazette.

New York Colonial Manuscripts, 1664-1691. New York State Library.

Review of Reviews. Medical Review of Reviews, Volume 21, No. 4. April 1915. Page 193.

Schenectady Almanac, 1816.

Schenectady's Stockade: New York's First Historic District, Don Rittner, Arcadia Press. Pages 86-87. 2008

The Albany Medical Annals, Volume 41 1920, page 70. Journal of the Alumni Association of the Albany Medical College.

The American Druggist, 1887. Volume 17.

Two Centuries: Caring for a community. The Medical Society of the County of Schenectady Bicentennial 1810-2010. James S. Strosburg, 2010. Pages 61; 63; 92-93.

Unites States Patent search

Weekly Heath Index, Dept. of Commerce, Bureau of Census. September 12, 1936, page 2.

Original Sources

Bellevue Maternity Hospital private papers.

Personal Communication

Grace G. Jorgensen, Walter Grattidge, Mary Printsky, Sanford Roth, Bill Hammond, Dominick Mele, Maria Fort, Doris Lane Wood, Rita Glavin, Cindy Lucas.

INDEX

Index

A
AAHPM 205
AAPM 205
Aarhus 226
Abbe 151–152
ABBE 151
Abbott 260
Aberdeen 244
ABO 71
Abortion 73
Abraham 287–289
Abram 287–288
Academic 201
Academic-related 201
Academy 171, 176, 180, 186, 190, 197, 270, 273, 302, 315
Accountant 143
Accounts 218
Accreditation 67, 175
Accrediting 217
Accurate 315, 318
Achievement 53, 54, 136, 225, 270, 272
Ackerknecht 25, 42, 53, 62-64, 125, 127–129, 169, 188
Ackerknecht's 125
Acknowledgements V, 1–2
ACLS 164
ACORN 216
Adinolfi 136–137
Administration 160, 167, 176, 181
Administration's 75
Administrative 58, 167, 181, 191, 213
Administrator 168, 178, 191
Admissions 337
Admitted 309
Adriaen 305
Adriaensen 285
Ads 320
Advisory 152, 164, 172
Aerial 35, 80
AETNA 269
Affair V, 5
Affairs 162, 201
Affected 210
Affiliated VI, 151
Africa 180–181
African 323 African-American 101, 308 After 14, 39, 83, 135, 141, 144, Agencies 239
Agent 151
Agnes 215–217, 245–246
AGNES 215
AGONIES 323
Agricultural 230
A birthing at Bellevue in the 1980s 335

AHA 41
Aiden 136
AIUM 82
Albany 8, 51, 64–65, 70, 73–75, 78, 82, 86, 90, 92, 105, 126–127, 132, 136, 144, 162–163, 173, 176–179, 188, 190, 195, 200–201, 206, 213–214, 219–221, 223–224, 268, 272, 280–283, 287, 289, 293, 295, 304, 306, 308, 310, 312, 317, 320, 332
Albert 57, 193, 199, 320
Albright VI, 87, 152–155, 342
Alcohol 293
Aldart 290
Alden 268, 304
Alexander 245
Alexanderson 11

Alfo 129
Alfred 37, 249, 255, 257
Allen 160, 231
Allied 144
Alma 154, 249, 311
Almanac 299
Almshouse 303, 307
Alonzo 257
Alrichs 291
Alteration 270
Although 140, 204, 217
Altos 153
Alumni 177, 224, 273, 317, 332
AMA 170
Amanda 248
Amateur 230
Ambrose 162
Ambulance 237
Amedore 267
Amendment 328
America 11, 13, 132, 225, 254, 269, 274, 277, 280, 298, 302, 319, 327
American 7, 37, 41, 66–67, 78, 82, 100, 127, 137, 145, 148–149, 153, 161–163, 165–166, 169–171, 176–177, 179, 182, 186, 190, 197, 200, 204, 213, 215, 217–218, 222, 225, 272–275, 277–279, 304, 307, 316–317, 319–321, 323, 327–328
Americans 210, 286
Americas 272
Ames 214
Among 141
Amstel 291
Amsterdam 7, 13, 17, 105, 212, 282–293
Amyott 335
Analysis 218
Anatomic 166, 176
Anderson 163, 304, 307
Andrew 11–13, 231

Anemic 322
Anesthesia 87, 152, 154–155, 189
Anesthesiologists 87, 170
Anesthesiology 153, 169, 190
Anesthetist 87
Ann 1, 46, 90
Anna 13, 37, 145, 244, 248–250, 252
Annals 310, 317
Annandale-on-Hudson 211
Anne 102
Annie 244–245, 249–250
Anniversary 271
Annual 224
Anthology 37
Antonio 203
AOA 186
AORN 217
Apaches 323
Apgar 44, 338, 342
Apollo 153
Appendix V, 222
Apperson 156
Apple 157
Appointed 160, 173
Appreciation 136, 267, 269–270, 275
Approbation 211
Apr 245
April 15, 64, 75, 132, 134, 144, 156, 169, 180, 289, 313, 325
Aram 47–49, 57–58, 71, 157, 195, 200, 220, 342
Arendt 280
Arent 285
Arizona 323
Armsby's 312
Army 51, 167, 190, 213, 215, 313
Art 337
Arthritis 208
Arthur 13
Arts 126, 179, 189, 320

Arzt 211
Asa 279
ASAP 207
Ashaff 163
Asia 137–138
Asiatic 132
Asma 192
ASMA 192
Asof 93
Aspen 155
Assembly 11, 267, 272, 294, 328, 330
Assemblyman 272
Assemblymen 329
Assessor 79
Assist 164
Assistant 165, 167–168, 178–179, 190, 199, 213
Associate 168, 173, 177, 202, 230
Associates 68, 87
Association 21, 41–42, 78, 100, 127, 136, 145, 152, 161–163, 169, 177, 186, 197, 204, 213–214, 216–217, 224, 268, 272–275, 317, 320, 330, 332
Assumption 18
Atashian 47–49, 57–58, 71, 157–158, 195, 200, 220, 342
Atlanta 50
Atlantic 3, 222, 235, 241, 248–255, 257, 259, 261
Atomic 68, 213, 335
Aug 249, 252, 254
August 14, 72, 75–76, 128, 131, 249, 292, 302, 312, 328–329, 333
August-November 75
Aunt 235, 237
Aurelian 186
Australia 152, 321
Austria 84
Austrian 82

Auxiliary 213
Ave 32
Avenue 36, 38, 79, 90, 235, 253, 307–308
Aviation 153
Award 53-54, 136, 169, 175, 225, 230, 268–273
Awards VI, 164, 175, 267, 272

B
B-scanner 82
Babies 174
Baby 85, 180, 338
Bachelor 126
Bachelor's 146, 230
Back II, 177
Bacteriology 50
Baefje 294
Bagel 225
Bagley 236
Bailey 158–159
Bainbridge 250, 253
Baird 223
Bakery 225
Baldness 300
Ball 137
Baltimore 76, 166, 211
Band 216
Bank 7, 136–137, 321
Bankers 218
Banking 218
Baptist 31, 145
Bar 78, 330
BARBARA 204
Barbier 283
Bard 211, 301, 303
Barentsen 292
Barry 235, 237
Based 86, 95, 165, 215
Basic 153, 190
Basically 310
Bassett 193

Battle 323
Baum 158–159, 185, 195
Bayley 301
Bazaar 53
Beaufort 132, 134
Beaumont 205
Beauty 254
Beaux 320
Beaverwyck 293
Because 106, 305
Beeche's 285
Beecher 231
Beeckman 284
Beekman 302
Beekman's 302
Beer 294
Before 41, 75, 160, 162, 165, 169, 189, 191–192, 199, 284–285, 293, 337
Beginning 59, 279
Being 228, 272
Believe 261
Bellevue I–V, V–5, 7–8, 11, 14, 16, 18–25, 27, 31–33, 35, 39–43, 45–47, 50–51, 53–54, 58–65, 67–88, 90–94, 101–107, 125, 128–129, 134–137, 143–144, 146–147, 149, 151–176, 178–180, 182, 184–193, 195–200, 202–225, 227–231, 241, 267, 269–271, 273, 291, 335–340, 342
Bellevue's V, 2–3, 40, 53, 62, 67, 71–72, 83, 87-88, 91–92, 104, 107, 154–155, 158, 164, 174, 182, 185-186, 198, 212, 222
Bellows 160
Bendall 80
Benefactor 273
Benevolent 145, 224
Benjamin 296
Berdon 189

Berger V, 8, 88–89, 93, 102–103, 136
Berlin 211
Bernard 47, 241
Bernhart 49
Bescher's 286
Beta 145
Beth 177
Bethlehem 86, 173
Betty 173
Between 291
Betz 19
Bill 1, 93, 101, 244
Billings 302
Biographies VI, 125
Biography 229
Biology 49, 179
Birth 16, 66, 214, 336–337
Birthing 161, 270, 335, 337, 340
Births 68
Bite 300
Blackwell 326-327
Blake 160
Bleeding 298
Blood 299, 322
Blue 162, 258
Board 7, 87, 148–149, 152–153, 155, 160, 162–166, 171–173, 176–177, 182, 185, 187, 190, 200, 204, 211, 222–224, 268, 270, 274, 321, 325, 332
Board-certified 176
Boards 205
Boardwalk 235, 251–257, 259, 261–262, 264–265
Bob 215
Bobbi 205
Bocce 86
Bodi 52
Bodolff 285
Bogaert 282, 285, 290
Bogart 286

Bogerdt 285
Bohm 1, 4
Bon 295
Bond 85
Bonnie 202–203
Borghardt 71, 160
Borghart 45
Borichevsky 160
Born V, 14, 146, 167, 180, 331
Boston 160, 176, 205–206, 296–297, 327, 332
Bouge 219–220
Boule 71, 161
Bounds 237
BOURGEOIS 219
Bowden 161
Boyagian 76
Bradstreet 218
Bradt 5, 18–20, 135, 191, 227, 229
Bran 299
Branch 78
Brandywine 307–308
Braxton 12
Breakfast 40, 208, 228
Breast 175
Bridge 198
Bridgeport 213
Brigham 176
Brim 287
British 319
British-trained 169, 196
Broadway 22, 145, 320
Brochure 325
Brockville 319, 323
Brockwayville 145
Brokedon 318
Bronx-born 177
Brooklyn 182
Brother 143, 327
Brotherhead 249
Broughton 230
Bruce 236

Brueggers 225
Brugh 302
Brunswick 150, 170, 201
BSN 158, 202
Bud 36
Buffalo 176–179
Building 308
Built 27
Bulgaria 224
Bunsen 157
Bureau 14, 16
Buren 302
Burke 191
Bush 223–224
Business 7, 21, 72, 77–78, 160, 162, 190, 204, 262, 270
But 102, 135, 284, 311
Butler 162
Byrnes 144

C
C-section 207–209, 340
Cadwallader 296, 301
Cafeteria 208
Caitlin 54
Cal 257
California 86, 152–153, 188, 199
California-San 173
Camden 249
Camp 129
Campbell 330
Campus 106
Canada 152, 248, 319–320, 331–332
Canadian 319
Cancer 175, 179, 275, 299
Canistahejoene 26, 32, 35
Canton-born 166
Cape 180–181
Capilli 305
Capital 2–3, 46, 73, 77, 82, 87, 105–106, 145, 157, 169, 172,

178, 183, 188, 190, 206, 208, 220, 224, 226, 231, 239, 269–271, 280, 282, 287, 335
Capt 289
Captain 224
Carcinoma 163
Cardiac 153
Care 8, 70, 87, 89, 161–162, 167–168, 172, 193, 199, 219–220, 222, 236, 267, 336
Carl 86, 197, 308
Carmen 230
Carnegie 218
Carol 127
Carpet 6
Carwaet 294
Casey 162
Castle 280
Castleton 160
Catherine 144, 282
Catholic 18, 24, 106
Causey 335
CDC 14, 58
CDHPC 88
Celebration 271
Cemetery 146, 309, 313, 323
Census 13, 16
Century 11, 89, 254
CEO 77, 98, 102, 182, 185, 194, 215
Certi 143
Certificate 136, 267–270, 273, 275
Certification 204
Certified 87, 149
Ceylon 130–132
CFO 103, 197, 200
Chair 174, 178, 191, 222–224, 235, 241, 251–256, 257–259, 262
Chairman 7, 164
Chairperson 224
Chalfonte 261
Chamber 136, 225, 270, 287

Chambers 86
Chandler 301, 312
Channel 219
Chapter 145, 162
Charles 12–13, 25, 27, 37, 127, 244–245, 312, 326, 329–330
Charlton 13, 105, 226, 231
Charter 270
Chaudhry 162–163
Chauncey 70, 327
ChB 181
Checking 56
Chef 208
Chemical 310, 317
Chemistry 49, 135, 139, 165
Cheon 163, 197
Chernobyl 137
Cherokee 230
Cherry 309
Chesky 163
Chestnut 243, 250
Chicago 105, 154, 162, 188, 191
Chief 85, 87, 146, 149, 152, 158, 168–169, 171–173, 180–182, 186, 189, 197, 200, 202, 204, 212, 222
Childbirth VI, 161, 204, 273, 277
China 169, 196, 202
Chips 191
Chirurgeons 290
Chlamydia 49
Chloe 231
Chopper 102
Christian 203, 226, 228, 285–286, 323
Christian-Albrechts 212
Christmas 67, 184, 206
Christopher 190
Chronobiology 177
Chuda 87
Church 18, 24, 127, 145, 234, 298, 304, 307

355

Cincinnati 171
Cindy 1, 236–237, 263
Circumcisions 340
Cirsteede 284
Citation 271–272, 276
Citizen 267
Citizens 19, 137
City 3, 16, 25, 32, 64, 88, 125, 132, 135, 144, 180, 183, 222, 235, 241, 248–255, 257, 259, 261, 274, 278–279, 282, 287, 290–291, 293, 295, 298, 301, 303, 310, 312–314, 323
City-born 192
Civil 125, 319, 321
Claes 285
Claessens 329
Clara 249
Clare's 149
Clare's 64, 68, 90, 92, 145, 147, 163, 170, 186, 198
Clarence 25, 42, 53, 125
Clares 106, 335
Clarissa 1, 3, 7, 77, 86, 141, 162, 220–221
Class 273, 312
Claus 206
Cleaning 341
Clifford 51, 167
Clifton 172, 225
Clinic 153, 167
Clinical 157, 165, 169, 171, 176, 272
Clinton 297
Club 39–40, 47, 127, 148, 186, 191, 218, 230
Clute's 31
CMO 181
Cobleskill 218, 230
Coffin 51
Cohoes 74, 325
Col 287

Cold 300
Colden 297, 301
Collectively 89
College 2, 7, 44, 49, 54, 58, 127, 132–133, 135–136, 138–139, 142, 144, 146, 148–152, 154, 160–162, 165, 168, 174, 176–179, 182, 188–190, 192–193, 195, 199–201, 203–205, 211, 213, 218, 220, 223, 229, 236, 268–269, 271, 273, 275, 302–303, 307, 310, 312, 316–318, 321, 326–327, 331
Colleges 102, 271
Colonie 134, 136, 161, 167, 222, 238
Colonies 280
Colony 291
Colorado 155
Columbia 44, 161, 193, 199–200, 221, 281–282, 303
Columbus 186
Comforters 282
Commander 186, 291
Commerce 16, 136, 225, 270
Commission V, 8, 67, 88–89, 93, 102–103, 106, 136, 171, 224
Committee 175, 217, 224, 275, 328–329
Common 211, 275
Communications 191
Community 58, 160, 162, 197, 201, 213, 230, 236, 268, 272
Compact 315, 318
Company 6, 21, 37, 39, 46, 153, 160, 189, 214, 222, 241, 250, 252, 254–255, 257–258, 261, 283, 286–287, 292, 309, 319–32321, 322–323, 325
Competent 277
Competition 254
Comprehensive 81

Compressed 318
Comptroller 213
Conception 18, 24
Conference 7, 155
Confessor 225
Confidential 210
Congress 44
Congressional 75
Conlnck 285
Conn 149–150
Connecticut 156, 280, 326–327
Connection 222, 241
Connie 72, 172
Consequently 32
Considering 306
Consolers 282
Consolidating 92
Consolidation 92
Consortium 178
Constance 202, 204
Consultant 201
Consulting 206
Consumer 142
Consumption 300
Contents V, 322
Contest 169
Control 14, 50, 58, 143
Convent 205
Convention 261
Conversion 99
COO 230
Coordinator 168, 219, 225
Cor 290
Corlandt 292
Cornbury 293
Cornelis 284, 292
Cornell 126–127, 177, 214, 285
Cornells 285–286, 293
Cornerstone 32
Coroner 137
Corporate 151, 213
Corporation 172, 204

Corps 102, 190, 313
Cosico 164
Costello 260
Costs 61
Cotton 297
Council 77–78, 97, 224, 270, 298, 301
Councilors 332
Counties 281–282
County V, 11, 13, 18, 53, 78, 90, 92, 127, 145, 148, 170, 186, 204, 214, 223, 231, 267–268, 270, 298, 304–306, 326, 328, 331
Coupe 333
Courage 36, 56
Course 170, 272
Court 305
Courtesy 236–237, 263
Cove 197
Cover II
Coye 306
Coye's 306
CPA's 143
CPAP 170
CPR 179
Craig 237
Credit 218
Cripple 252
Croatian 294
Crockett 136, 273
Croon 290
Cross 162, 179
Crossroads 145
Croup 298
Cruickshank 244, 246
Cuff 307–308
Cultural 224
Cunningham 17
CUNY 202
Cure 299
Curler 280
Curling 186

Curran 72
Curren 6, 164
Current 99
Cynthia 174

D
D'Orio 188
Dad 338
DAI 179
Dale 218
Dame 203
DANILO 164
Danish 5, 137
Dansick 284
DAR 331
Darious 306
Dartmouth 7, 141, 146, 148, 150, 236
Darts 86
David 31–32, 38, 79, 189, 203, 255, 257
Davis 165, 279
Day 41, 60, 105, 138
DBA 77-78
Dean 317
Debbie 163
Dec 12, 245, 249
December 42, 89, 128–129, 144, 187, 208–209, 236, 293, 302, 310, 312
Declaration 284–285
Dedicated III
Dedication III, V
Defect 165
Defense 191
Degree 230
Del 177
Delaware 280, 283, 291
Deliveries 278
Delivery I, 12–106, 155–156, 168–169, 193, 220, 277–333, 336–338, 341

Delphine 165
Democrat 328
Democratic 261
Demonstrated 40
Dempsey 312
Denmark 226
Dental 178
Dentistry 170
Denver 191
Depart 310
Department 82, 87, 97, 99, 145, 152, 154–155, 160–161, 166, 171, 174, 177–178, 180, 213, 222, 274, 279, 311
Depot 51
Depression 14
Dept 16, 38, 163, 171, 193, 200
Der 135, 307
Derby 41
Dermatology 193
Dermatopathologist 166
DeRocher 165
Detroit 224
Dettbarn 57–58, 86
Developed 212
Development 224
Dey 244, 246–249
Dey's 245
Diagnostic 200
Diagnostics 181
Diana 3, 141, 221–222
Diane 196, 218–219
Dick 52
Dietician 335
Dijck 293
Diploma 272
Diplomat 274
Dircsz 287
Director 3, 48, 58, 71, 87, 135, 154, 157–158, 160–162, 164–165, 172, 174, 176, 179, 182, 189, 191, 197, 212, 229, 290, 342

Directors 7, 152, 173, 182, 224, 273
Dirk 307
Discharge 340
Discussion 94
Disease 14, 50, 58, 210, 323
Dispensary 278
Dispensing 315, 317–318
Dissection 303
Distinction 272
Distinguished 269
District 2-3, 46, 77, 82, 106, 157, 169, 183, 188, 208, 226, 231, 270, 280, 282, 287, 335
Division 13, 42, 128, 144, 151, 199, 204, 231
Doc VI, 235
Dock 250, 253
Doctor 11, 82, 126, 136, 143–144, 268, 273, 302, 304, 336
Doctors 87, 150, 198, 268, 297, 336
Dog 300
Dohme 316
Dolly 154
Dominick 1, 83, 187
Don I–V, V, 1–2
Donald 51, 82
Donck 305
Dongan 292
Donhowe 158, 165–166, 220
Donohowe 335
Dora 71, 73, 198, 222
Dorance 204
Doreen 225
Doris 1, 136, 147, 149–150, 273
Dorothy 157, 257
Dose 317
Double 255
Doucet 166, 189
Douglass 297, 302
Dowling 98

Drama 223
Draper 185
Dropsy 299
Drug 321
Druggist 316
Duane 307
Dubois 302
Dudley 129
Dun 218
Dunbton 318
DuPress 166
Dupuy 302
Durban 181
Dutch 90, 280–281, 283, 286–287, 291–293, 298, 302, 307
Dutchmen's 285
Dyck 289
Dykeman 167

E
East 190, 279, 306
Eastern 136
Easton 231
Eaton 191
Economic 75
Economical 315, 317
Economics 7, 151
Edinburgh 301
Edison 30, 39
Edition II
Edmond 165
Edmund 172
Education 136, 162, 175, 272, 274
Educational 171, 224
Educators 161
Edward 164, 204, 218, 225, 298
Edwin 25
Eencluis 293–294
Effect 299
Effective 322
Eighteen 91
Eighteenth 82, 277, 300

Einstein 193, 199
Either 226
Electric 11, 13, 25, 37, 46, 151, 262, 320, 329, 335
Elena VI, 205–206
Eligible 87
Elis 224
Elisabet 289
Elizabeth 11, 127–128, 162, 180, 205, 231, 245, 249, 289, 326–327
Elks 145
Ellen 198, 245
Ellis 68, 74, 80, 90, 102–103, 105–106, 127, 131–132, 135–136, 145, 149, 166, 170, 186, 192, 197, 224, 274, 321, 335
Elma 188
Elmer II, 5, 13–14, 17–18, 22, 39–41, 61, 104, 226, 228–230, 339
Elmer's 208, 226
Elmhurst 180
Elnora 70, 72
Elson 167
Elyas 294
Embryologist 220
Emergency 68, 209, 237
Emeritus 85, 146
Emily 249–250
Emma 161, 329
Emmett 307
Empire 93, 145, 162, 319
Employee 162
EMS 209, 237
Endometrial 163
Energy 213
Engaged 143
Engineering 37, 179, 230
Engineers 37
England 136–137, 167–168, 246, 249, 280, 297, 319, 331
England's 82

English 63, 66, 137–138, 169, 196, 223, 280–281, 292–293, 302, 323
Enos 168–169
Enterprising 270–271
Environment 137
Epidemics 295
Episcopal 127
Equitable 255
Era V, 102
Ernest 125, 226
Ernst 11
Esopus 292
ESP 75
Essendelft 283
Esther 248
Ethan 160
Eunice 223
Europe 82, 137, 153, 319, 327
European 145, 277–278, 280
Evangelical 203
Evans 330
Eventfully 304
Eventually 277
Evidence 96
Examination 171, 183
Examiners 148–149, 274
Examples 49, 300
Excellence 136, 169, 268, 270–271
Exchange 180
Executive 7, 157, 168, 191
Exeter 186
Exhibition 252
Expeditionary 127
Extension 167
Exterior 34
Extract 288
Eyck's 301
Ezekiel 254–255

F
Faber 25

FACCE 161
Facilities 7, 89
Factory 247
Faculty 155, 317
Faggi 129
FAH 7
Fairfield 304
Faith 203
Falls 144, 165, 211
Families 209, 259
Family V, 5, 11, 142, 197, 237, 288
Fan 66, 156, 169, 196, 198, 341
Fan's 185
Fancher 298
Fantastic 230
Farley 175, 271
Farm 13, 240
Farmville 204
Father 11, 316
Fathers 65
Fatima 192
Feb 130, 248–249, 288–289
February 37, 42, 55, 105, 230, 287–289, 294, 309, 315, 317, 327, 333
Federal 14, 171, 218
Federation 7
Fellow 139, 148, 171, 180, 182
Female 154, 342
Ferdinand 125
Ferry 301, 305, 317–318
Fertility 274
Fetal 200, 337
Fever 326
Field 144, 309
Fielding 37
FIGHTER 323
Finally 4, 106
Finance 151, 200, 213
Financial 3, 91, 96, 158, 197, 200, 218
Fine 239
Fink 64, 67, 76, 169–170

Finland 152
Fire 194
First II, 2, 19–20, 60, 304, 335
Fiscal 289
Fischer 160
Fisher 302
Fitkin 203
Flah's 136
Flegauf 323–324
Floral 254
Florida 64, 230
Fluids 299
Food 321
Foods 166
For-profit 97, 99, 100-101
Force 160
Ford 223
Fords 312
Foreign 171, 191
Form 315, 318
Forster 87
Fort 1, 83, 170–171, 203, 280–282, 284–287, 289, 291
Fortunately 25, 75, 78
Forty 324
Foundation 8, 70, 136, 157, 199, 224, 268–269
Founder 23, 28, 208
Founder's 105
Fountain 55
Fraley 171
France 66, 302
Frances 11, 78, 160, 213, 215
Francis 145, 149, 178
Francisco 86, 173, 199
Frank 186, 249
Franklin 152, 154, 252, 296
Frasier 318
Fraternity 145
Fred 163,197
Freda 226
Frede 82, 84–85, 172, 342

Free 127
Frele 211
French 18, 82, 291, 323
Frito-Lay 191
Front II
Frost 249
Frostbite 215
FTEs 92
Fulford 319–320
Fuller 11, 309–314, 316–318, 320
Fuller's 315
Fulton-Montgomery 213
Fund 224
Funeral 53
Funyuns 191

G
Gaffigan 172
Galactosemia 180
Gallo 172
Gallup 87
Galway 57, 59–60, 105
Gamma 186
Gandhi 25, 131–132
Garden 52, 134
Gardner 310
Garrett 257, 261
Gaston 170
Gazette 25, 297, 302
Gebhardt 31
Geerlyn 286
Geganbagh 72
Gemma 212
Genealogy 243
Geneseo 193
Genetic 205, 335
Geneva 326–327
George VI, 8, 31, 37, 49, 79, 87–88, 1127, 152–154, 223, 267, 319–320, 327–328
Georgia 50, 150
Georgian 32

Gerald 223
Gerard 211
GERARD 182
Gerardus 302
German 13, 69, 283, 323
Germany 42, 63–64, 125, 128, 137, 196, 211
Geronimo 47, 323
Gerrit 283, 286-287, 289
Gerry 175
Gertrude III, 13–14, 134, 268, 276
Gibson 252
Gift 36, 56
Gillette 11, 326–328, 330–331
Gillette's 327–329, 331
GILLIES 225
Girl 136, 179
Gladys 132
Glamour 52
Glasgow 172, 204, 244, 248
Glavin V, 1, 3, 7, 76, 78, 107
Glen 127, 197
Glendale 90
Glenn 173
Glens 165, 211
Glenville 225
Global 137, 320
Gloucestershire 248
God 292
Going 270
Gold 59, 62, 71–72, 137, 173, 270
Golden 136, 270, 301
Goldie 59, 62
Goldman 329
Golf 47, 127, 148, 186, 217
Golub 102
Gonorrhea 49
Goody 230
Gouverneur 144
Government 143
Governor 8, 88, 223, 297, 327

Grace I–V, V–2, 5–6, 53, 11–106, 128, 134–135, 137–138, 142–143, 146, 154, 156, 175, 187, 191, 196–197, 200, 207–209, 215, 221–222, 226–227, 229, 231–234, 236, 240–241, 243, 252, 267–333, 342
Graduate 167, 171
Graduation 231
Granby 326
Grand 105
Grandfather's 226
Grandma 233–234
Granville 160–161
Grattidge 1, 3
Graveside 134
Greene 281–282
Greg 153
Gregg 145
Gregoris 285
Gregory 285
Gretz 85, 173
Groote 181
Group 86, 162, 174, 193, 199, 220, 222–223, 236, 269
Grover 174, 342
Growing 3, 228, 231
Guadalcanal 133
Guarneri 198
Guilderland 161, 167, 178, 192, 222
Guischard 302
Gutsche 174
GYN 47, 146, 148, 161, 167, 174, 176–177, 183, 199–200, 203, 211–212, 221–222
Gynecological 87, 149
Gynecologist 207
Gynecologists 149
Gynecology 8, 149, 153, 163, 166, 192
Gysbert 304

Gysbertsen 287

H
Hagaman 304
Hall 261
Hamilton 67, 174, 307
Hammond 1, 19, 93, 101
HANK 192
Hanns 283
Hans 282–287, 290, 293–294
Hanson 318, 320–323
Hanson's 321, 323
Harman 285, 308
Harmen 282, 285
Harper's 53
Harriet 37, 79
Harris 312
Harrisburg 167
Harry 66–67, 85, 146–147, 173, 236, 244, 246–255
Hartford 146, 149, 156, 178, 180, 223
Hartley 308
Harvard 132, 174, 176
Hayday 252
Head 159, 163, 167–168, 187
Headquarters 213
Health 8, 77–78, 87–89, 97–99, 106, 161–162, 175–177, 181, 193, 199, 204–205, 213, 215, 222, 272, 325
Healthcare 81, 106, 136, 154–155, 174, 268–269, 271, 275, 342
HealthCarePlus 147
Heart 269, 337
Heath 16
Heights 162
Helen 85, 233
Helga 226
Hellegond 292
Hematology 49
Hemphill 250, 255

Henderycksz 289
Hendrick 307
Hendrickson 290
Hennessey 175
Henriett 45
HENRIETTA 192
Henry 230–231, 234
Herbert 85, 173, 250, 255
Heritage 333
Herkimer 304
Herman 257
Herry 289
Hershey 168
Hetherington 299
Heuval 307
Hiatella 175
Hickory 28
High 63, 81, 105, 170, 178–179, 193, 213, 218, 223, 230–231, 269
Hill 153, 307
Hispanic 101
Historians 277
Historic V, 26, 107
Historical 331
Historisch 304
History V–XLIII, 37, 139, 277, 312
HIV 8
HMO's 88, 200
Home 11, 19–20, 23–24, 90, 143, 191, 229, 300, 333
HONG 163
Honor 186, 224, 275
Honorary 136
Honoree 269
Honors 127, 161
Hooghbergh 289
Hoosick 144
Hopkins 158, 205, 211
Horatio 318
Horst 51

Hospice 205
Hospital I, V–3, 5, 13–14, 17–19, 26, 35, 41, 53-54, 58, 61, 64–65, 68, 70, 77–80, 82, 84–86, 90–91, 93, 96, 102–103, 106, 125, 127, 131–132, 134–137, 144, 149–152, 154, 157–158, 160–173, 176–183, 185–187, 189–190, 192–193, 195, 197–199, 203, 205–206, 208–215, 218, 222–224, 267, 269–274, 279, 291, 312, 314, 321, 327, 335
Hospital-based 210
Hospital's 7, 102, 174-175
Hospitals 8, 15, 67, 77, 87, 94, 144–145, 186
Hostesses 80
Hotel 76, 261, 272
House 52, 303, 305
Housekeeping 193
Housewives 223
Houston 163
Houttuyn 288
Howard VI, 2, 6, 43, 138, 146, 189, 206, 209, 222, 235–241, 243, 249–250, 252, 268, 342
HSBC 7, 137
Huber 226, 233
Hudson 58, 179, 201, 261, 287
Hugh 175, 271
Hughes 290, 330
Hull 37
Human 160
Humane 331
Humility 36, 56
Hunter 301
Huych 282

I
Ian 82
Iceland 137
ICSI 81

ILG 86
Illinois 174
Imaging 172, 174, 342
Immaculate 18, 24
Imogene 193
Impure 299
Inadvertent 180
Inaugural 137
Inc 77, 102, 105, 199, 268, 275
Independence 327
Index VI, 16
INDEX 349
India 203, 283, 286–287, 292
Indian 86, 286, 299, 307, 3323-24
Indiana-DR 19
Indians 305, 323
Industries 191
Infant 14–16
Infantry 125, 323
Infirmary 90, 326
Information 7
Ingen 306–307
Injection 81
Innovation 175, 219
Innsbruck 84–85
Inoculation 297
Inquirer 242
Insitu 163
Institute 82, 163, 201, 218, 252, 270
Instructor 171
Integrity 36
Interim 179
Interior 29–30, 34
Intermittent 66
Intern 131
International 136, 161, 176, 230, 272, 275
Intracytoplasmic 81
Introduction V
Investigate 328
Investigations 329

Invited 154
IPR 275
Ira 64, 67, 76, 169, 312
Irish 182
Ironic 329
IRS 321
Irwin 309
Isaac 302
Isabella 244–246, 249, 331
ISBN II
Island 98, 153, 193, 197, 224, 280, 289
Israel 177
Italian 36, 56, 323
Italy 137, 187
Ithaca 126
IVF 81, 220

J
J's VI–1, 6, 139, 141, 207, 231–232
Jack 52, 237
Jackson 319
Jacob 284, 289–290
JACQUELINE 187
James 3, 46, 76, 78, 107, 145, 191, 244–245, 248–249, 267, 301, 307–308, 312
Jameson 25, 67, 129–134, 150, 173
Jameson's 130-131
Jan 172, 245, 249, 282–283, 287, 289–290, 294
Jane 158–159, 195
Janeke 283
Janet 11, 331, 333
Jansen 282, 286–287, 292
January 42, 46, 51, 80, 85, 137, 145, 176, 178, 272, 292, 302, 306, 316, 323, 326
Japan 218
Jay 36, 235, 249–250, 301, 307, 332
JCAH 168
JDs 143

Jean 7
Jeanne 102
Jefferson 150, 199
Jenner 298
Jennifer 168
Jens 230
Jersey 170–171, 280
Jeurlaen 285
Jeurlaensen 284
Jeurlansen 284
Jewett 327
Jim 7, 238, 308
Jinnah 192
Joan 50–51, 160, 184
Jochem 284, 289
Jochims 288
Joe 36, 86, 196, 200
Johannes 290, 302
John 1, 3, 7, 30, 37, 42, 77, 132, 141, 145, 158, 165, 170, 174, 201, 205, 212, 222, 242, 244–247, 249–250, 253, 263, 299, 301–303, 309, 312
John's 141, 146
Johnny 228
Johns 158, 211
Johnson 178, 191, 261
Johnstown 125, 127
Joint 67, 175, 328
Jon 327
Jonas 282, 292
Jonathan 327
Jones 31, 79, 301
Jorgensen II–V, V–2, 5–6, 11, 13, 17, 19–20, 22–23, 25, 27–28, 36–37, 39–41, 43–44, 49, 52–57, 59, 62, 64, 72, 76–78, 83, 86, 102, 104–106, 134, 138, 142–143, 146, 154, 156, 175, 187, 194–197, 200–201, 203, 206, 208, 215, 221–222, 226–227, 229, 233–234, 236, 243, 267–276, 279, 342
Jorgensen-Westney 159
Jorgensen's 18, 25, 39, 55, 60, 63, 105, 226, 233, 252
Jorgensens 22, 25, 103, 106, 226
Joris 292
Joseph 41, 52, 145, 306, 323, 330
Joseph's 146, 307
Josephine 13, 75, 191
Josephs 76
Journal 37, 100, 215, 317, 327
Journey 286
Joy 156
Joyce 187
Jude 203
Judith 132, 230
Judy 161, 210, 278
Julie 230
July 18, 70, 85, 87, 132, 164, 244–245, 249, 274, 282, 292, 325
June 62, 105, 169, 245, 248–249, 297, 305, 312, 326, 331, 335
Junior 160, 195, 246–247, 250
Juriaensen 284
Juris 143
Just 140, 208

K
Kaleigh 54
Kappa 136, 145, 275
Karen 70
Katherine 59, 62, 71, 173, 245
Katie 59, 62, 72, 137
Katrina 231
Kay 45, 136
Keller 233
Kennedy 54
Kentucky 169
Keough 176–177
KEOUGH-AMYOT 176
Kerfbyle 302

Kerr 331
Kettering 275
Khanar 203
Kiel 212
Kierstede 282–283, 287, 290
Kierstedt 284
Kiliaen 281, 287–288
Kill 312
Kimball 145
King's 239, 301–302
Kingston 166, 292
Kinsey 342
Kissel 333
Kitchen 34, 193
Kiwanis 191, 218, 230
Klaus 125
Kleitz 127
Klerstede 286
Klerstedt 285
Knapp 86
Knolls 68, 320, 335
Kodalkanal 132
Korea 179, 189, 215
Korean 218
Krafts 166
Krikor 75
Kris 335
KRISTINA 176
Krol 282
Kulbida 177–178
Kurt 128
Kyngpook 189
KYU 163
Kyunggi 179

L
Lab 58, 71
Labor 155–156, 168–169, 193, 220, 336–337, 341
Laboratory 37, 48, 58, 157-158, 165, 187, 212–213, 316, 335, 337, 342

Labs 68, 177
Lactation 205
Ladies 333
Lady 18, 170
Lafayette 295
Lahore 192
Laid 32
Laing 161
Lake 86
Lamaze 66, 161
Lancaster 152
LAND 26
Landen 285
Landscaping 35
Lane 1, 31–32, 38, 79, 149–150
Languages 7
Lanka 130, 132
Laparoendoscopic 178
Latch 132
Latham 3, 209, 225, 236–237
Latimer 178–179
Laura 231
Lauren 85
Law 77, 86, 173
Lawrence 144, 166
Laws 93
Lawson 70
Lawyer 143
Lay 306
Layout 340
Leader 272
Leaders 268
Leadership 136, 270, 275
League 217, 329
Leanne 4
Lecture 174
Lee 90
Leeches 298
Left II, 45, 104
Legacy 269
Legal V, 107
Legion 145

Legislative 328
Legislature 88, 267, 328
Lehigh 86, 173
Leipzig 125
Leland 326
Lena 43
Lending 218
Leombruno 52
Leon 249
Leonard 185, 192
Leubert 257
Level 73, 81, 168
Levine 4, 342
Lewis 13
Leyden 290, 302
Liberal 179, 189
Liberty 301
Librarian 317
Library 44, 146
License 171, 274
Licensing 171
Life 136, 153, 323
Lifetime 225
Like 185, 198
Lily 207
Lim 179–180, 185, 342
Lima 179
Lina 71
Linanne 201
Lincoln 312
Linde 283, 285
Line V, 107, 223
Lineage 226
Linton 185
Lisa 142
Lishakill 28
Litoff's 278
Little 12, 46
LLC 220
Local 8, 191
Lockheed 153
Locomotive 335

Lodge 127, 145
Logios 71, 180
London 132, 181, 301–302
Long 98, 153, 197, 267
Long-time 223
Lord 293, 302
Loreto 170
Los 153
Loudon 245
Loudonville 132
Louis 261, 329
Louisa 248, 250, 310
Louise 45, 71, 160
Louisville 64, 169–170
Love 36, 56
LPN 184
LPN's 184
LPNs 184
LTD 136
Lucas 1, 236–237, 263
Lucia 203
Lucy 231
Lugaya 164
Luke's 86, 173
Lunn 328–329
Lupolt 286
Lusk 328
Lutheran 174
Luxembourg 42, 128
Lydia 178
Lying-In 279
Lyndon 261
Lynn 46, 199
Lysabet 289

M
Mabee 72
Mabel 66, 156, 169, 185, 196, 341
MABLE 169
MacDonald 57, 60
Mack 333
MacPherson 180–182, 342

Madame 261
Mae 167, 198
Magazine 87
Magdeburg 283
Magee 181
Mahatma 25, 131
Maintenance 88
Majesty's 301
Malloy 184–185
Mama-watch 209
Mammography 175
Man 253
Management VI, 7, 213, 227
Manager 58, 151, 156, 161–162, 164, 191, 212, 218, 220, 225
Managers 152, 321
Manchester 228
Manepay 130
Mangini 185
Manhates 286
Manhattan 93, 183, 282
Manipay 132
Manners 142
Manor 287
Mansion 25, 28–30, 34–35, 41, 43, 57, 61, 74, 80–81, 193, 227, 229–230, 337
Manzini 203
Maple 241
Mar 13
Marcel 85
March II, 136, 235, 248, 252, 268, 270, 289, 297, 304, 309, 315–316, 328, 333
Margaret 244–245, 249
Marguerite 162, 237
Maria 1, 83, 168, 170
Marie 71, 161
Marin 166
Marine 7, 136, 236
Mark 270
Market 102, 211

Marketing 163
Marking 74
Marriage 142
Marriott 272
MARSA 166
Marshall 105, 152, 154
MART 199
Martha 125, 160
Marting 186–187, 189
Mary II–VI, VI–1, 4–6, 11, 13–14, 17–20, 22–25, 28, 40, 43, 49, 53, 55, 57, 62, 104–106, 172, 187, 193–195, 198, 205–206, 219–220, 226, 229, 231, 235, 244–250, 252, 254, 279
Mary's 17, 185, 212-213
Maryland 166, 211, 280
Maryn 285
Masonry 270
Masons 127
Massachusetts 151, 166
Master 283, 286
Master's 146
Mateo 257
Mater 154, 311
Maternal 16, 176, 200, 204, 220
Maternity I, V–1, 11, 14–15, 18–20, 23, 33, 77, 125, 135, 143, 152, 163, 167, 169, 178, 189, 197, 218, 222, 229, 241, 273
Maternity-HospitaL 149
Mather 297
Matilda 248
Mauro 187
May 51, 53, 62, 65, 75, 93, 125, 127, 138, 202, 229, 235, 237, 242, 245, 248–249, 255, 284–286, 292–293, 310, 328
Mayflower 327
Mayo 153
Mayor 295
McBride 42

McCarthy 187
McCook 149
McCord 181
McGaffin 51
McGinnis 187
McGrinder 182–184, 202, 211
Meadow 190
Meanwhile 96, 312
Measles 69
Med 75, 192
MED 161
Medal 212
Medicae 302
Medicaid 8, 61, 67, 88, 96, 101
Medicaid-covered 91
Medical 2–3, 7–8, 15, 18, 50, 53, 58, 70, 73, 78, 82, 92, 100, 102, 105, 126–127, 132–133, 135–137, 144–146, 148–150, 154, 163, 165–166, 168, 170–172, 174, 176–183, 186, 188–190, 197, 200, 203, 209, 211, 214, 220–221, 229, 236–237, 268–269, 273–276, 303, 305–306, 310–312, 315–317, 322, 326–327, 331–332, 342
Medical-related 212
Medicare 67, 100
Medicine V, 11, 82, 86, 103, 105–106, 126, 144, 152–153, 169–170, 173, 177, 179–181, 189–190, 193, 197, 199–200, 205, 273, 280, 299, 302, 308, 315, 318–320, 323, 325
Mee 155
Meeting 163
Megapolensis 292
Mei 198
Mele 1, 83, 185, 187–189
Member 155, 225, 273
Members 268, 270
Membership 225, 275

Memberships 274
Memorial 64–65, 146, 149–150, 163, 178, 197, 203, 211–212, 275
Memories VI, 206
Memory 134
Memphis 64, 170
Mercury 306
Mercy 190
Merit 267
Meritorious 268
Met 294
Metropolitan 146, 150
Mexico 177
Meydertsz 282
Meyndersen 285
Michael 98, 185, 220
Michigan 162, 224, 230
Middleton 303
Midland 7, 136
Midwifery 278–279
Midwives 278
Mignon 249
Mihm 166
Mike 220
Mildred 213
Military 190
Mills 330
Milton 168
Mims 80
Minuit 282
Mirswa 235, 252
Missiles 153
Misthal 189
Mitchell 231
Mobile 127, 175
Model 50
MOHASCO 213
Mohawk 6, 28, 47, 87, 127, 148, 186, 286, 306–308, 325–326
Moll 85
Mom 338

370

Moms VI, 231, 338
Mona 142
Mondragon 102, 189
Monitor 191
Monopoly 235, 253
Montagne 289–290
Montcalm 244
Montefiore 179
Montreal 244, 246
Moorefield 174
Moreau 161
Morgan 32, 38, 79
Morgantown 167
Morrissey 46
Morrow 1
Mortality 15
Mortar 301
Moscow 137
Moses 7
Mother 226
Mother's 215, 231
Mount 180, 217
MSS 287
Muhammad 163
Multiple 222
Mundelein 162
Murdoch 300
Murray 11, 331
Museum 219, 261
MUSSARAT 162
MVP 88
Mynderse 32, 38, 332
Myskania 224

N
NAACOG 169, 204
Nadherny 190–191
Namkoong 189–190
Narrative 286
Nassau 190, 280
Natal 181

National 136, 151, 160–161, 179, 191, 224, 261, 268, 272, 274, 321
Native 282, 286, 304, 307
Natives 282
Nava 75
Navin 148
Navy 132–133, 151–153, 174, 186, 236
Nealon 18, 22, 75, 143–145, 191
Nealon's 144–145
Neff 102
Neil 102
Nelson 36, 191, 223, 230
Neonatal 81, 205, 222
Neonatology 171, 342
Nerves 322
Netherland I, 280–281, 283–290, 292, 304–305
Netherlands 281, 292, 305
Network 205, 268
Neural 165
Newborn 172, 204
News 178
Next-Step 201
NIAZ 192
Nicholas 177
Nicknames 219
Nicolaes 304
NICOLAS 177
Nicoll 301
Night 168
Nineteenth-century 278
Ninth 323
Niskayuna 25, 26, 28, 31, 33, 38, 64, 88, 103, 132, 136, 150, 154, 166, 192–193, 208, 218, 222, 268
Nixon 7, 75, 223
Nolan 71
Nominee 267
Noon 60

Nordlund V, 11–12, 56, 231–232, 271
Nordlund's 12
Noreste 177
Norlands 226
Norlund 53, 231
Normal 337
North 225, 280, 287, 317–319
Northeastern 61, 74, 86, 148
Northern 90
Northwell 98
Northwestern 167
Norton 160
Not-for-profit 100
Notre 203
Nott 63, 213, 218, 230
Nov 248–249, 253, 289
Novel 174
November 51, 64, 78, 83, 129, 145, 292
NSG 55
Number 296
Nurnberg 63
Nurse 45, 87, 158–159, 161–162, 167–168, 175, 184–185, 204, 217–220, 222, 279, 337, 339–341
Nurse-epidemiologist 210
Nursery 73, 156, 222, 336, 338–341
Nurses 128, 163, 169, 204, 216–217, 340–341
Nursing 53-54, 70, 158, 161, 176, 179, 191, 204, 214–215, 228, 341
Nutrition 339
NY's 101
NYC 284
NYNEX 202
NYS 78, 175, 237

O

O-R 163, 193
OB-GYN 147–148, 166, 177–178, 181–182, 197, 204, 214
OB-GYNN 148
Oberlin 165
OBGYN 154
OBST 192
Obstetrical 87, 149
Obstetrician 207, 211
OBSTETRICIAN 149, 209
Obstetrics 8, 65, 149, 153, 163, 166, 192
Obstetrics-Clinical 269
Obstetrics-Gynecology 163
OBYGYN 335
October 59, 77–78, 87, 268, 291, 293–294, 312, 314
Office 213
Officer 3, 158, 168, 172, 181–182, 191, 197, 200–201, 222
Officer-Surgery 181
Ogden 330
Ohio 171, 186
Old 132, 298, 333
Olympics 241
Oncology 183
Oneida 286
Onions 191
Ontario 166, 319–320, 323, 331
Operating 172, 209, 216–217, 341
Operations 201, 213, 222
Operative 87
Orange 280–282, 287
Order 7, 145
Organization 224, 237
Organizations 88
Orient 129
Orientation 170
Orisean 309
Orissa 203
Orr 329
Ortho 47

Oscar 226
Ostrander 45, 192
Ott 43, 71
Outdoor 279
Outstanding 272
Ownership 26, 93, 101
Owoo 54

P
Pacific 132, 197, 235
Pacing 42
Page 15, 238
Pageant 254
Pages 37
Paik 87
Pain 87, 155
Pakistan 192
Pakistani-born 163
Palatable 315, 318
Pale 319–320, 322, 324
Palliative 205
Palmyra 249
Palumbo 53, 180
Pamela II, 104
Paneling 38
Parade 105, 254
Pardanani 148
Pare 300
Parenthood 148, 197
Parents 338
Parillo's 198
Paris 301–302
Parish 162
Park 163, 172, 174, 225
Parker 159
Parkside 225
Participation 66
Partners 106
Partum 338
Party 223–224, 329–330
Pat 208
Pataki 8, 88

Patents 12
Pathology 58, 165–166, 176–177, 181
Patient 71, 136, 168, 219, 272
Patients 45, 135, 218, 336–337, 340
Patrick's 127
Patroonships 281
Pattison 192–193
Pau 289
Pauitf 290
Paul II, 3, 5, 18, 20, 23, 36, 53, 72, 104, 135, 143, 194–195, 211, 229–230, 272
Pawlet 240
Payment 306
PCC 168–169, 219
Peace 18, 329
Pediatric 171, 176, 180, 183
Pediatrician 189, 340
Pediatrics 171–172, 180, 186
Peebles 331
Pelviscopy 272
Penitentiary 167
Penn 168, 199
Pennsylvania 86, 145, 171, 173–174, 181, 225, 235, 244, 280
Perinatal 176–177
Perioperative 70
Personnel VI, 125, 151, 160, 162, 191, 212, 225
Peter 226, 282–283, 302–303
Peter's 92
Peters 82, 106, 200
Petersburg 64, 170
Pettibone 327
PFC 42
Pharmaceutical 320
Pharmaceuticals 47
Pharmacopoeia 315
Pharmacy 318
Phi 136, 145, 186, 275

Philadelphia 3, 150, 225, 235, 242–244, 250, 252–253, 297, 318, 323–324
Philly 245, 248–250
Photo 44, 216, 219
Physic 297
Physical 205
Physician 3, 206, 336–337
Physicians 44, 179, 236, 268, 297, 340
Physics 183
Physiology 150
Piannenstiel 212
Pictures 37
Pieter 285
Pieters 294
Pietersen 283, 285
Pilar 170
Piles 299
Pill 325
Pills 319–320, 322, 324
Pink 319–320, 322, 324–325
Pint 299
Pinterest 50
Pioneer 37
Piper 230
Pirs 289
Pittsburgh 171, 181
Pius 137
Place 320
Placenta 228
Planned 148, 197
Planning 77, 97, 213
Plunge 300
Point 312–314
Poker 86
Police 145
Policy 93
Politically 127, 145
Politics 225
Polyclinic 167
Pools 230
Poor 16, 303
Pope 137
Populating 280
Port 180, 280, 284
Porter 231
Porteus 300
Portrait 57
Post 87, 145, 338, 342
Post-Boy 302
Post-partum 338
Potential 93
Potters 309
PPO's 200
PPU 338, 341
Practical 214
Practice 3, 8, 197, 204
Practiced 192
Practitioner 162
Praxcos 302
Prectioners 297
PREE 166
Preface V, 5
Premature 15, 336
Prenatal 335
Presbyterian 135, 199, 221
Present 278
Presented 273
Presideercnde 289
President 7, 75, 102, 137, 163, 166, 182, 189, 191, 197, 200–201, 213–214, 223–224, 230, 261, 270, 312, 317, 320–321, 332, 342
President's 312
Presidential 224
Press I, 323
Prevention 58
Price 102, 143, 322
Prices 265
Prince 204
Printsky 1, 4, 40, 158–159, 193, 195–196

Prior 16
Priority 62
Proactive 191
Proclamation 267
Producing 299
Professional 160, 162, 164, 175, 197, 201, 268
Professionally 216
Professor 165, 177, 200, 204
Professorship 190
Profit 93
Prognosis 163
Program 70, 75, 179, 202, 210, 225, 272-273
Project 201
Promotion 162, 272
PROPERTY 26
Proskauer 330
Protective 145
Protestant 127
Province 293, 297
Provincial 181
Psychology 146
PTA 191
Public 77–78, 93, 97, 125, 143–144, 162–163, 205, 225, 295
Publishing 204
Pucci 86, 197
Pulmonology 171
Pulver 163, 197
Punjab 192
Purchasing 151–152
Purdue 167
Pure 321

Q
Quaker 235, 240
Quartet 198
Queen 18, 248, 331
Queens 166, 332
Quest 181

R
Rachel 57, 60
Radio 230
Radiological 191
Radiology 82, 162–163, 198
Raetspersoon 289
Raider 133
Raleigh 203
Ralph 331
Randolph 11
Rasenberg 291
Rathbone 312
Rather 97, 99
Ravensteyn 294
Raymond 37
RCA 30, 39
Reade 66
Reagan 137, 223
Real 195
Reale's 216
Rec 299
Reception 336
Recognition 267, 271
Recollections VI
Record 315–316
Recorder 323
Records 26, 174
Recover 219
Recruiting 342
Red 162, 179, 328
Reed 190, 254–255, 256–258
Reeducation 273
Reformed 304, 307
Regents 183
Regiment 125
Region 87, 145, 178, 239, 269, 271
Regional 136, 217, 237
Registered 216
Registrar 181
Registrar-Resident 181
Registry 200
Rehabilitation 205

Reimbursement 102
Relations 162–163, 225
Relief 87, 155
Religious 162
Remedies 315
Rensselaer 281-282, 287–288, 326
Rensselaerswijck 281, 287, 290
Rensselaerswyck 288
Rensselaerwyck 282
Renzi 198
Rep 225
Report 102, 106, 289
Reporter 225
Reports 297
Representation 304
Reproductive 199
Republic 153
Republican 127, 145, 223–224, 330
Research 8, 69, 157, 175, 199, 320, 335
Reserved II
Residency 8, 180, 205
Resident 171, 180–181
Resolved 299
Resources 160
Restrictive 93
Resume VI
Reuss 199
Rev 292
Revenge 312
Reverend 297
Review 15, 77, 268
Revisiting 93
Revolution 277, 295, 302
Revolutionary 240, 306
RH-factor 70
Rheims 301
Rheumatoid 208
Rhode 193
Rhogam 47
Richard 79, 87, 301
Richmond 203

Ridge 27, 127, 174
Rights II
Ripley's 261
Risk 81, 269
Rita V, 1, 3, 7, 45, 72, 76, 78, 107, 164
Rittner I–V, V, 1
River 28, 287, 291, 325–326
Road 28, 30–32, 36, 132, 150, 229
Roasted 158
Robert 11, 41, 67, 87, 151, 215, 309–310, 317–318
Roberta 71
Robertson 254
Robinson 37
Rochester 153
Rockefeller 223
Rockville 190
Rogers 327
Roland 166, 189
Role V
Rolf 249
Roll 300
Rolling 222, 235, 241, 251–259, 262
Rollo 235, 237
Romano 50–51
Romper 196, 218–219
Ronald 137, 223
Room 42, 68, 196, 209, 216–219, 336–337
Rosenberg 87
Rosendale 150
Ross 36, 86, 196, 200
Roswell 163
Rotary 186
Rotating 179
Roth 1, 3, 83, 86–87, 103, 158, 200–201
Rotterdam 46, 72, 287
Route 230
Rowe 41

Rowley 7
RSC 54
Rub 300
Runner 41
Rupert 240
Russell 53–54, 58, 135–136, 161, 176, 179, 200, 271, 273, 275
Rutgers 170
Ruth 237, 249
Rutledge 52

S
Sackett 4, 201
Safety 340
Sage 53–54, 58, 102, 135–136, 161, 179, 200, 271, 273, 275
Sager 68
Saile 102
SAKE 323
Sales 160
Sally 172
Sam 328
Samuel 292, 301–302, 329
San 86, 199, 203, 257
Sandforth 1
Sandra 75
Sandy 83
Sanford 3, 83, 86, 158, 200-201
Sanforth 103
Sanitarium 127
Santa 206
Saratoga 13, 78, 231
Sate 148
Saturday 310
Savings 85
SAVOX 82
Scandinavian 208
Scare 328
Schafer 231
Schaible 36
Schenectadian 318

Schenectady I, V, 11, 14–18, 25, 30, 35, 40, 43, 51, 53, 64, 68, 79, 90, 92, 102, 127, 129, 132, 134–135, 143–146, 148, 150, 154, 170, 186–187, 192, 197–198, 213, 215–216, 218, 223, 230, 234, 236, 267–268, 270–271, 273–274, 279–280, 294–296, 298–301, 303, 305–310, 312, 317–318, 320, 322–323, 325–328, 330–333, 335
Schenectady's 2, 125, 137, 280, 307, 313, 326, 329
Scholars 224
School 86, 105, 132, 144, 150, 152, 158, 162, 165, 167, 169–170, 173–174, 176–179, 183, 186, 188–190, 193, 197, 205, 211, 213–214, 218, 223, 230–231, 235–236, 310, 312
Schroyer 257
Schutt 283, 286–287
Schuur 181
SCHWAB 202
SchwenkJr 131
Science 7, 136, 199, 219
Sciences 142, 179
Scientific 224
Scientist 199
Sclerosis 222
SCN 336
Score 44
Scotia 38, 299
Scotian 32
Scotland 244, 331
Scott 36
Scout 133, 136, 179, 191
Scrub 164, 217
Seal 133
Sean 209
Search 169
Sebastian 282

Second 2, 250, 272
Secretary 290
Section 90
Seditious 328
Selected VI, 151, 268
Semper 312
Senator 175, 267, 271, 319, 326
Senior 181–182, 191, 199, 249–250, 267, 342
Seoul 179, 189–190
Sept 162, 289
September 16, 68, 86–87, 125, 127, 138, 164, 283, 285–286, 292–293
Service 151, 164, 172, 268, 271
Services 152, 158, 164–165, 169, 172, 204, 209, 225, 267
Seventeenth 280, 284, 304
Seward 333
Seward's 333
Sex 342
Sexually 210
Sharpe 316
Shield 162
Shift 193
Shill 222, 235, 241, 244, 246–259, 261, 263–265
Shill's 243, 247, 253, 256, 260
Shills 257, 264
Sic 312
Sice 299, 304
Sigma 127, 145, 161, 186
Signs 336
Silver 273
Simple 342
Simplicia 305
Simplified 317
Sinai 149, 177, 180
Sinatra's 148
Sir 301
Siska 41
Sisson 231

Six 90
Sixty 271
Skory 204
Slecht 292
Sloan 275
Smallpox 293, 296–297
Smile 142
Smiling 264
Smith 72, 241
Snowmass 155, 269
Social 277
Socialist 328–330
Society 18, 37, 53, 127, 136, 145, 148–149, 161, 170, 176, 178–179, 186, 197, 214, 268, 274–276, 279, 303, 305, 317, 331–332
Solomon 304, 329
Son 7, 30, 204
SONI 202
Sonography 200
Sons 136
Sony 202
Sophia 71
Sophie 72, 196, 198, 218
Soroptimist 272
Source 50
Sources VI
South 180–181, 250, 280, 307, 312
Soviet 137
Space 153
Spain 170, 193
Spanish 183, 304–305, 321, 323
Speakers 154
Specializing 125
Speech 223
Speedy 299
Spencer 191
Sperm 81
SPINK 202
Spotlighted 268
Spring-time 210

Springfield 178
Squad 341
Sri 130, 132
Staas 287–289
STAAS 288
Staats 289, 302
Stabilization 75
Staes 288–289
Staet 288
Stafford 178
Stanford 152, 199, 326
State VI, 8, 11, 58, 61, 67–68, 72, 77–78, 88, 91, 125, 127, 136, 145, 154, 160, 162, 168, 170, 176–177, 179, 182, 184, 199, 203, 206, 209, 211, 215, 218, 223–224, 226, 230, 267, 269, 271–274, 276–277, 280, 286, 301, 303–309, 320, 328, 330, 332, 337, 342
States 13–15, 25, 61, 82, 144, 226, 269, 279–280, 312, 315, 323, 327, 329
Station 38, 205, 340–341
STD's 8, 210
Steinmetz 12, 37, 329
Stephanus 292
Stephen 60, 89, 342
Stephentown 144
Sterling 274
Steuben 307, 309
Steve 86
Stevens 161
Stockade 325
Stone 25, 27–32, 34–35, 37–39, 79–81, 193
Stone's 37
Stoneridge 28, 30–31, 36
Store 247
Stork 39–41
Story 203
Stracher 204

Strader 74
Stuart 191, 249, 263
Students 65
Stuyvesant 292
Style VI, 227
Styles 172, 204
Submarine 151
Success 125
Suffragette 78
Suite 337, 340
Summing 229
Summit 137
Sunnyview 186, 215
SUNY 176, 178, 193, 202, 224, 230
SUNY-Albany 225
SUNY-Stony-Brook 165
Supervisor 58
Support 153
Surge 156
Surgeon 284–285, 291
Surgeons 44, 290, 297
Surgery 178
Surgical 155, 164, 169, 179, 272, 312, 327
Susan 171, 202
Suzanne 178
Swartout 290
Swaziland 203
Swede 11
Swedish 11, 283
SWIATEK 205
Swits 307–308, 313
Switzerland 85, 137, 226
Sylvius 302
Symphony 198
Syracuse 158, 197, 201
Syrup 241, 308
Systems 7

T
Table V
Tablet 11, 316, 318

Taiwan 224
Tampico 177
Tang 87
Taprobane 132
Tar 309
Tau 161
Tax 94
Taylor 320
Tea 142
Teachers 218, 223
Technician 58
Technological 37
Tedesco 267
Teen 225
Teeth 301
Telephone 214
Television 37
Tempel 294
Temple 152, 205, 225, 294
Temporary 180
Ten 61, 72, 84, 293, 301
Tennent 302–303
Tennessee 170
TERESA 187
Term 267
Terrace 63, 213, 218
Testimonials 319
Testimony 285–286
Testing 187
Teunis 294
Texas 203, 205
Theater 132, 145, 312
Theresa 13, 71, 180, 231–233
Theta 161, 192
Thinking 227
Thomas 30, 39, 82, 136–137, 172, 199, 285–286, 309, 327
Thompson 132
Thousand 311
Thresher 37
Threshing 37
Thuringia 13

Thursday 285
Thus 286–287, 335
Tie 223
Tienhoven 284–286, 290
Time V, 107
Times 318
Tom 53
Tomas 285
Toms VI, 205–206
Tonic 322
Tonko 272
Top II, 104
Tornado 35
Tortilla 191
Tostitos 191
Total V, 5
Town 79, 103, 181, 238
TRACE 26
Trade 321, 329
Trading 247
Tragedy 42
Trainer 162
Training 190
Transfusion 180
Transmitted 210
Trask 231
Treasurer 317
Treatment 180
Trenton 235, 249
TREVOR 180
Tribute 136
Trijntje 288
Trinity 49, 106
Triturates 11, 316
Troy 7, 32, 51, 58, 135, 192, 229, 325, 328
Trumbull 327
Trustee 321
Trustees 204
Tryn 282
Tryntgen 292
Tryntje 292

Tube 165
Tumor 163, 299
Tussaud's 261
Twentieth 11, 253, 318
Twenty 265
Twenty-first 89
Twiller's 291
Twitty 172, 204
Typhoid 326
Tyrannis 312

U
Ulrich 286
Ultrasonography 199
Ultrasound 81–82, 342
UMDNJ 170–171
Uncle 235, 237, 328
Union 5, 24–25, 31, 131–133, 135, 138–142, 148–151, 188, 190, 204, 211, 218, 220, 227, 229, 269, 305, 307, 310, 312, 316–317, 320–321, 326, 329–330
Unit 81, 191, 338, 341
United 13–15, 25, 61, 82, 144, 224, 226, 269, 274, 279–280, 312, 315, 323, 327, 329
Universidad 177
Universitaet 211–212
University 44, 84, 86, 105, 126–127, 150, 152, 161–162, 165–171, 173–174, 176–177, 179–181, 189, 191–193, 197, 199, 201–203, 205, 213, 223–225, 228, 269, 274, 301, 331–332
Update 269
Upstate 231, 269
Urban 60, 85
USA 187, 190, 211–212
Useful 322
Utica 333

V

Vaccinations 298
Vaginosonography 272
Vale 309, 313, 323
Valencia 170
Valley 58, 179, 201
Van 135, 280–281, 286–287, 290–291, 299, 302, 304, 306–307, 326
Vande 288
Varrevanger 290
Vassar 213
Vatican 137
Vaughn 210
Veda 74
Velde 288
Ven 288
Venice 230
Venier 45
Venus 304
Verhael 304
Verizon 201
Vermont 160–161, 240–241
Veterans 82, 176, 191, 224
Vice 102, 182, 189, 197, 200–201, 213, 223–224, 317, 332, 342
Vice-Director 291
Vice-President 230
Vicky 1, 4
Victoria 248
Victorian 247–248
Vietnam 190
Vietz 211–212
Vieux 203
Vigliotti 212–213
Vincent's 180
Virgil 68
Virginia 11–13, 17, 44, 64, 167, 203–204, 248, 250, 253, 280
Virginianum 305
Virginias 203
Vlackte 289
Vogue 51–53

Vol 145
Volume 15, 310
Volunteers 80, 223
Vonnegut 128
Voorheesville 213
Voort 135
Vosburgh 11, 78, 213–215
Vote 331
Vrooman 36

W
Wage 143
Wagner 218
Wakeman 231
Waldman 329
Wall 224
Wallace 309
Walnut 37
Walt 86
Walter 1, 3, 190, 226
War 42, 125, 127, 144, 197, 218, 240, 306, 312, 319, 321, 327–329, 335
Ward 167, 215, 217, 231
Wars 191
Washington 7, 190, 231, 312, 327
Wasmer 13, 231–232
Wassenaer 304
Waterford 78
Waterman 25, 37
Watervliet 178, 325
Wax 261
Wayne 72
Weber 71–72, 196, 198, 218–219
WEDRYCHOWICZ 219
Weekly 16
Weisgerber 250, 255
Welch 70, 167, 185
Welfare 188
Well 207, 272
Well-Being 272
Wes 229

Wesley 150
West 11–13, 17, 146, 167, 211, 231, 283, 286–287, 291–292, 306, 324–325, 333
Westinghouse 30–31, 37, 79
Westminster 211
Westney VI–1, 6, 43, 77, 86, 146, 162, 201, 206, 220–222, 235–237, 240–244, 247–250, 252–253, 263, 268, 275, 337, 342
WESTNEY 220, 222
Westport 129, 146, 150
Westtown 235–236
WGY 148
Wharton 190, 213
Whitesboro 223
Whitney 160
Whittelsey 223
Whittlesey 223–225
WIC 287
Wide 309
Wife 263
William 18, 22, 25, 32, 38, 42, 67, 127–133, 143–145, 150, 173, 175, 245, 249–250, 252, 257, 291, 297, 302, 319–320, 330, 333
William's 319, 323
Williams 319–320, 322, 324–325
Willie 244, 248–250
Willis 318
Willsie's 185
Wilson 328
Wiltse 71, 73, 198
Wiltsie 222
Winchester 151
Winter 81
Wisconsin 165, 181
Witt 329
Wizard 12
Woman 78, 136, 268, 270
Woman's 175, 193

Woman's 78, 81, 87, 90–91, 103, 105, 176, 182, 199, 223, 269, 271, 273
Women 106, 134, 136, 192, 211, 225, 268, 270–272, 301, 326–329, 333
Women's 329
Women's 8, 78, 81, 102, 106, 132, 147–148, 155, 161–162, 167, 174, 176–177, 181, 199, 214, 220, 222, 267, 269–270, 272, 275, 332
WON 189
Wood 1, 66–67, 85, 146–149, 173, 195, 230, 342
Woodlawn 188
World 42, 127, 144, 197, 225, 272, 329, 335
WRGB 218
Wright 225
WTEN 219
WWI 213
WWII 186

X
X-ray 49, 67
Xerox 82
XII 137

Y
Yacht 148
Yale 146, 150, 186
Year 78, 106, 267–268
YMCA 225
Yonset 179
Yorkwhere 96
Youth 225
YWCA 136, 270

Z
Zimbabwe 181
34

www.ingramcontent.com/pod-product-compliance
Lightning Source LLC
Chambersburg PA
CBHW051625230426
43669CB00013B/2188